voices of connemara

Raymonde Standún & Bill Long

NEW
ISLAND

*To my husband, Donal, and children, Cliona and
Laragh, and to all the children and grandchildren of
those who contributed their stories to this book*

VOICES OF CONNEMARA

First published 2010 by
New Island Books, 2 Brookside,
Dundrum Road, Dublin 14, Ireland

Published by New Island as
Singing Stones Whispering Wind – Voices of Connemara in 2001

Concept, Interviews, Research and Photography copyright © Raymonde Standún, 2001, 2010
Editing, Introduction and Notes copyright © Bill Long, 2001, 2010

ISBN 978-1-84840-040-5

**New Island Books gratefully acknowledges the generous financial support
of Meitheal Forbartha na Gaeltachta Teo, An Clár LEADER II, An Roinn Talmhaíochta & Bidh,
An Aontas Eorpach in transcribing the oral interviews herein.**

**New Island Books gratefully acknowledges the generous financial support of
the EBS Educational Building Society towards the publication of this volume.**

British Library Cataloguing in Publication Data
A catalogue record for this book is available from the British Library

Design and Typesetting by Artmark
Printed in China through Asia Pacific Offset

Table of Contents

Contents (continued)

Foreword

I cannot remember whether it was a common creative interest, or just friendship, which led me to regularly visit Jesus Modia, in his Stone Art Gallery in Spiddal. He was a well-known sculptor. Like his famous namesake, children called in and were always rewarded for their visit. It was Jesus who suggested that I should take photographs of local people and have an exhibition in the Gallery. Talking later to my father-in-law, Máirtín Standún, who himself always had a story to relate, I decided to combine story-telling with photography, while interviewing over fifty people in 1992. Some of these interviews were in Irish, and have since been translated here. Sadly many of the participants have since passed way.

I had been attending festivals and fairs for many years, taking photographs of events which usually combined religion, festivities, sports, music, dancing and some buying and selling. I also had the good fortune to meet Bill Long, a well-known writer, who expressed a great interest in the project. I visited Japan around that time and received a gift of a Japanese book of stories, by people from different walks of life, which we decided would be a suitable model for the format of this book.

While the stories in this book tell of very different lives, they all share the same home, that of the South Connemara Gaeltacht, from Barna to Carna, the same stretch of passing time, and the same quest for peace and happiness. Their stories are their gift to all our children, stories of a way of life closely associated with nature. They tell of a time when people shared with their neighbours their successes and also their sufferings. They were content with little in the material sense, but had a wealth of resources within themselves which have made this area what it is today, a nucleus of Irish culture – language, music and dance. Behind the new prosperity is the strength and determination of those who lived through an occupation, wars and the building of a new Ireland. Sadly, many of them have passed away, including my friend, Jesus Modia; however his wish will shortly be fulfilled. My thanks to all who made this book possible.

Raymonde Standún

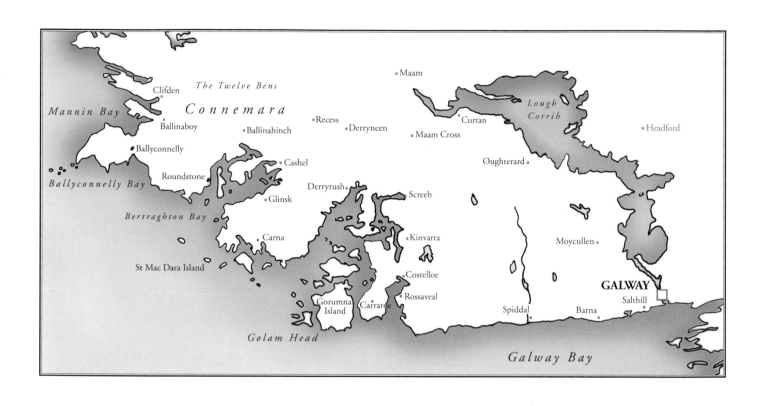

Introduction

Sailing westward from Connemara, out beyond the Aran Islands, into the roiling, grey-green Atlantic, the next landfall is the rocky, saw-toothed coast of North America. After thousands of miles of capricious, inhospitable ocean, the equally inhospitable coast – from Boston north to Newfoundland and Nova Scotia – has, for generations, 'welcomed' Irish immigrants. Though 'welcome' is probably too cheery, too optimistic a word to use in describing the arrival of the thousands of Irish – men, women and children – who survived the nightmare voyage to wash up on the lonely littoral of this 'New World' of their dreams and hopes.

Most of them washed up, metaphorically speaking, dishevelled, ill from the long voyage; others, not so fortunate, were literally washed up, dead by drowning when their often overcrowded ships foundered on the rock-shoals that, like killer sentinels, ringed this foreign shore. One such boat was the *Brig St John*, built by Tony Conneely of Leitir Meallán. On a Sunday morning in the 1840s, just one hour out from her scheduled Boston landfall, she ran aground on some rocks and split in two. Most of the emigrants were from south Connemara. There were very few survivors. Of the dead, forty-five had no relatives in the USA, and were buried in a mass grave. The remaining dead had relations in Boston and were buried in family graves.

Imagine then, the culture shock to those Connemara people who survived such voyages, when they arrived in a large, cosmopolitan city like Boston. Most of them – from Cois Fharraige, Rossaveal, and out to the islands – had never even travelled to Galway city. Fortunately for them, Boston and the smaller settlements along the coasts of Massachusetts and Maine, had one great common denominator with the Connemara they had just left – the sea.

The one great omnipresence in their lives, from their first moments in this world, had been the sound of the sea. They had been born to the sound of the sea, and from the cradle the sound of the sea had permeated their lives. In Connemara they woke to the sound of the sea; indeed, often in bad weather, they were wakened by it. They fell asleep to the sound of the sea; or, again, in bad weather, were kept from sleep by the sound of the sea. More than sun, moon, stars, or any mechanical timepiece, the sea, like some hypnotic metronome, dictated the rhythm of their days and nights.

So, many of them chose to settle near the sea. In Boston itself, they began to make their own currachs, and celebrate Connemara, and the craft, with an annual festival of currach racing. Some even drifted as far south as New York and New Jersey. Here they were met and helped by a generation of Irish who had emigrated before them, and who had established themselves in however modest a way. Many of the people whose stories are told in this book had gone early in their lives to work in the USA and in England. And it was, very often, only possible for those who stayed in Connemara to do so with the help of those who had gone away. The steady trickle of American dollars, and 'American parcels', helped those who remained in their struggle to survive. The American dollar made it possible for those who wanted higher education at home to pursue it. The money was also often used to book a passage for those ambitious young people who had their own dream of the New World.

Many of those who prospered returned, after long years, to settle again in Connemara. Old family homes, long neglected, were refurbished, and in many instances rebuilt. The landscape had not changed. Lone, stunted trees were silhouetted, like gallows, on outcrops of rock. The only vegetation standing proud of the rock were little coppices of twisted whins or gorse, all leaning, like obeisant pilgrims to the east. After storms had passed, the sun and the silence worked their miracle in the flat, open spaces. Light drowned in the eyes of the grey, stone walls, where, expediently, stone was laid loosely on stone, in perfect equilibrium, without mortar or pointing.

The prevailing winds here were westerly, blowing in off the open Atlantic: bending, twisting, flattening everything in their demented path. The pigmy whins crouched, like the remnants of some defeated, tattered army, in the lee of the deserted farmsteads and ancient ruins, dotting this antediluvian landscape. The low stone walls, divided the fields, giving scant shelter to the ragged root crops that, somehow, year after year, managed to survive the searing sea-wind and the scudding salt spray. Of the cabbages, potatoes and other vegetables grown here, the locals said, with self-deprecating wit, that it was never necessary to add salt in their cooking or eating; they were salted enough in their growing by the sea.

Here and there, the silver streams that vein the land, straggled out in sandy deltas to the sea. At such places, small stone piers accommodated a few currachs or púcans, and little knots of thatched, white-washed houses huddled in the lee of the low stone walls, on the edges of the flat, alluvial estuaries. Even now, all day and all night long, the voices of Connemara – the voices of the living and of the dead – sing in the rough stone, and whisper in the soughing seas that inexorably pound this immemorial coast.

Bill Long
Connemara
August 18th, 2001

Martin Flaherty

Born 1900. Native of Spiddal. Emigrated to California
where he worked in transport before returning home.

Everyone spoke Irish when I was growing up. And back in my parents' time it was all Irish that they spoke. The funny part was that I spoke Irish to my mother and to my sisters I spoke English. And the question as to why I did that we'd often discuss out in California, or when I'd stop in Boston to spend a couple of days with my nieces and nephews. They've got the same background as we have. They're from Páirc Thiar – (Park West) – my sisters, Mary Walsh, Mary Costelloe and Delia Hall.

I didn't know much about my father. I was only six years old when he died. But I do remember him. I was twenty-eight when my mother died. When we went to school it was all Irish we spoke to the other boys and girls. But we had the English text books, English conversation and English transcription. We also had Irish conversation and an Irish book. This happened in pretty much all of the classes. And after I left they had the maths and geometry in Irish. I did it in English. There was a namesake of mine, Martin Flaherty, who had a brother, Georgie, who taught in the school. There was a James Flaherty who died, and a John Flaherty, who went to England and is still there. But Martin Flaherty was a brilliant student. He was good at everything. He was like myself. After seventh grade we took on problems of our own, doing maths, geography,

and problems in algebra and geometry and trigonometry. My own kids now wouldn't have been taught as well as us. We had Grogan in Third Class. Greaney was the Principal. In America, depending on where you are, some high schools won't teach algebra. It depends on the place and what they expect of the teachers. The standard of schooling here was very high at that time, although we didn't think it was.

The changes travelling from California to Ireland are incredible. You get the train in San Francisco and then you get a plane there. You cross to New York and then another plane from New York to Shannon. And then you're around here for a while wondering, 'Where in the blazes am I?' I guess my age has a lot to do with it. I've got a few months to go before I'm ninety-two. Was born on the 28th of January, 1900. I take it from day to day. I'm relaxed, to a certain extent. As long as the family are well and everyone all right, I don't get too keyed up.

In school, I was one or two grades ahead of Máirtín Ó Cadhain. I remember the day when they used to call the roll. I was in the schoolroom on the north side, next to the priests' house, across from the Library. I started there in the low infants, in the Library. But what I remember of Máirtín Ó Cadhain was the roll call. Himself and Grogan were all excited and there were some rumours that something was going on. And it was a composition that he wrote that got their attention. Then he went to some other school in Ireland. I tried to track him down one time. I came to check him out in Dublin, but he was

*Two generations: Martin Flaherty visiting his home
in Baile an tSléibhe, holding a photograph of his mother*

doing a course in Russia. He was in the same grade as Peaitín an *Gabha* and a very bright student called Máirtín Lydon. And then there was Máirtín William from Baile Liam. They were poor, dear souls, all of them. All very clever. But there was no one to promote them. If they were there today, I can tell you, I'd set about seeing what could be done for them. Because you'd think the teachers – Greaney and Grogan – would have taken an interest in them. And they could afford it. They could have advertised it and got the money from the Bishop's people in Galway to put them through their schooling. They missed a lot of chances.

Like all of us, Máirtín Ó Cadhain's family were living from day to day, self-sustaining, like we were, with the potatoes out there in the stacks, and cows to milk, and butter to make and maybe a hundred chickens set for the eggs. And there was a lot of turf. I remember we had turf from one end to the other around the haggard, ten or twelve feet high and at least the same in width. And we sold two or three times a week in Galway. That was my big chore, on Saturday morning, with my donkey. I wouldn't have been more than nine years of age and I used to walk into Galway with my donkey to sell the turf. I'd leave very early, but the horse carts would overtake me and we'd arrive at the turf market at about the same time. And maybe you'd be there for ten minutes, or you could be there for two or three or four hours.

Before World War One turf was around two and sixpence a load. Then it went to two and nine pence and then to three shillings. During the war itself it went up to three and sixpence and four shillings. That was for a donkey cart. A horse-cart used to sell for between five and sixpence and six shillings. And it eventually went up to ten and fifteen shilling in the end. The donkey-cart was six or seven shillings, and that was a lot of money in those days. There was a great demand for buttermilk too in certain places in Galway. People used to buy it by the pint and half-pint. They used to drink it and also mix it with the flour to make bread. And I remember, it used to sell for two and sixpence and then it went up to two and ninepence and then to three shillings for the tankard. During World War One it went up to five shillings. And my mother used to walk to Galway, with several pounds of butter and some eggs, to sell. And she walked up the steps of the big houses in Salthill – and in some cases they were very high steps – and knocked on the door and asked – 'Any eggs today? Any butter today?' And she was one of the greatest!

My father died on the 1st of April in 1909. I remember very well. He used to do weeding when we grew the turnips, or whatever. And whether it was a bog towards the mountains or the hills, or in the other direction, down towards the bay where our house was, he'd go. He'd sit on the shaft of the donkey-cart or the horse-cart and put his elbow on the rump, until we got to where they'd help him in to do the weeding. And they might have to break down a wall to where the weeding was. I'd always bring him a hot lunch. I remember, I used to do that for years since I was about seven years old. And then, when he died my mother carried on running the house. And she lived until

1928. She had twelve children and I'm the youngest. She married five of them with a dowry. And I remember Kate too, who got married before Julia in 1907. There was a big chest in the back room. And she saved all the sovereigns and guineas in that. The guinea was worth twenty-one shillings; the sovereign was worth twenty shillings. They were all gold coins. And I remember the last one that got married, especially, and they taking away the containers in which they'd put the money. I gave the chest a rattle and she smiled and said, 'Remember those days!' My mother married Margaret, Mary, Kate and Julia. She was gone when Brigid got married. She was the youngest of the girls and she was in America for a while.

Gaeilgeoirí outside Coláiste Chonnacht in Spiddal

When they married with a dowry it was customary to give the girls some bedding – tick. It was very durable and lasted forever. That was passed down from mother to daughter afterwards. And then, before my time, it was the custom, for those who could afford it, to give a heifer and a calf. I don't know if any of my sisters' marriages were match-made. The match-makers used to go around on a horse and saddle with a bottle of *poitín* at their hip. Sometimes it was maybe a couple of people who made the proposition for you. People would know, directly or indirectly and then it would materialise. Kate met Mike, because Mam's sister was married up near where Mike lived, near Moycullen. And they knew these people. And that's how that materialised. And another of them was in America for a while, and she met Stiofán there, but I still don't know how that happened.

I spent a couple of years in Galway, in St Ignatius's. And I left school when I got the first flu in 1918. And I was two years there. The prefect of studies was a wonderful man – Dr Boyle Barrett. He was a Jesuit. After getting his PhD., he had spent some years teaching in America. We became great friends. I remember he said to me, 'Martin, you can have my English if you give me your Irish.' He left the Jesuits eventually and wrote several books. The first was *The Magnificent Illusion*, and another was *While Peter Sleeps*. He bought a beautiful place down near San José – several hundred acres. He was just across the Bay from me. I lived in Oakland, San Francisco. He was there for a while and he said Mass before he died.

After my schooling with the Jesuits I worked on the farm. Then I went to the Irish College here at home and got my Diploma to teach Irish. But there were no vacancies so I went to America on the Cunard line. I worked as a conductor on the trains, and in 1932 got six months leave of absence to attend the Eucharistic Congress. While I was home I was offered a job teaching Irish, but didn't take it. I went to do a private Irish course in Galway University. One of the teachers on the course was Siobhan McKenna's father. We became good friends. We had a lot of *seanchas* together.

When I was finished that course I went back to California again to work again in transportation. I liked working in transportation. We had passengers from the East Bay, because we used to connect with the ferry boats, and I met a lot of very wonderful people. After that I worked at a lot of different things. I worked in the PGE – and electricity departments for almost two years. But I always loved the trains. In my time off I used to go to the various stations just to watch the trains. My wife is third-generation German. She had a stroke about four years ago, but she's doing fairly well. I called the other day to see how she's doing. And she's being watched closely by the daughters and sons and grandchildren. We have five daughters and three sons, and seventeen grandchildren.

My mother used to speak about the landlords now and then. It was mostly about who they were and where they lived and who their relatives were. The Lynchs lived where Coláiste Chonnacht is now. And there were quite a few in Furbo. The people living in the area were very apprehensive about this subject. The old-timers remembered the Famine and the evictions. There were people evicted in Loughrea and Gort and around that area. I don't think there were many evictions around here, along Cois Fharraige. My mother was from Furbo, a place called Straidhp. It was up the road that comes right into the schoolhouse, on the south- side of the street.

My aunt was married up in the mountains, in Leitir Gungaid (Lettergunnet). She was a Concheanainn. My mother was a Concheanainn from Furbo. They were tenants of the Blakes. An old-timer showed me where she lived. He showed me where the walls and floors were. That's about all that's left. I always wanted to pay that visit, but only got round to it last week. They're all Concheannainns there, and they're all related. *Tá siad fite fuaite.* There are still a few Choincheanainns left in Furbo. My mother's mother was a Lydon from that area. The landlords were very strict in Furbo. There was a big house there and it could have been the Blakes who lived in it. My mother had a lot of history. She was a great, great person. They even knew her out in America. They still talk about her.

I remember the Black and Tans very well. Lloyd George thought the Black and Tans would take care of us here in Ireland, that they'd put us in our place. They were ex-soldiers and down-and-outs out of the English jails. And they did take care of us. You didn't know, going out in the morning on your bicycle, if you'd be alive that night. It was very frightening. They had a terrible reputation. They used to come out at night putting petroleum on places. But the IRA and Sinn Féin were in action before the Tans came. I remember the IRA marching in Galway to where I was lodging, when I was at school there. There was a lot of friction all over. It was pretty rough in some places. I never took any orders, right or left, from any officer, English or Irish. I never shot a gun in my life. I would never shoot a gun to kill a person. That's the way I feel.

Julia Greaney

A talented craftswoman from Spiddal.
Worked for the Killanin family.

In those days things were very hard. There was no children's allowance. There was no dole. The Old Age Pension was five shillings. And you had to be seventy to get that. Spiddal, Bearna and Furbo weren't too badly off. Their way of living was the turf. The education was very good because there weren't that many pupils in the school. The population wasn't in it.

But the mighty day was the day of the fair. We used to sneak off school and go around to the relations to see if they sold anything. And you might get a penny. A penny was a big thing. You'd sell a bundle of carrots in the market for twopence. And it was the same with parsnips and onions. And you'd sell twenty eggs for one and sixpence or one and threepence. And you'd sell a big roll of butter, about a pound and a half, for tenpence. If you made a pound in the market you were a millionaire. I used to sell in the market in Galway on a Saturday. I sometimes walked in there. You hadn't the price of the bus, even though the bus was only tenpence. You'd sell two huge pigs at the time for five pounds. You fed them for three months and minded them like babies. The only living here was if you had a horse and cart and sold turf. And you got from three and sixpence to five shillings for a big creel. And you had your own milk, butter, eggs, fowl and vegetables. All you wanted was tea and sugar and flour, and a bit of meat if you could afford it.

The people were very domesticated. They were able to knit their own jumpers and mend their own stockings. And if one was able to do something they co-operated. If you couldn't cut out the shirts, which were made at that time, you asked your neighbours and they helped. In that time it was all white shirts. You could sell turf. And with that you were kept from school. You had to go. Once you did your Confirmation you were okay. It became compulsory to go to school when I was thirteen or fourteen. But before that they didn't mind, not even the guards, if you missed school for the bog. We used also stay at home the day of the tide to cut the seaweed. That was the big day. Even if you were on crutches you had to go to the sea. In those days the shore was divided; each one had his own piece. And you had to be careful that you only cut your own. They had a hole drilled and they painted it. St Patrick's Day tide was the big tide. You used the seaweed as fertiliser. And there was an island out there and you had a currach or a donkey and a straddle, and you went out as far as you could cutting the weed. The children used to stay on the beach. The big tide came every month. And the seaweed was cut then.

In our area we weren't badly off. If you needed something you could fill up a creel of turf and go into town and sell it. The people were full of kindness and charity. They shared. The Irish-speaking people of Connemara managed with the English language in Galway City. They used sign language. You had to keep potatoes for seed. And

Julia and Walter Greaney

that time you sowed fields of cabbage and potatoes. People aren't growing anything anymore. The land was good enough to grow things and it was tilled every year. And the land was so precious that none of it went to waste. You had some potatoes and oats and turnips. The turnips were for the horse and the oats were threshed. The neighbours always helped you. You banged the oats down on the stone.

The straw part was kept for thatching. And everyone was able to make their own baskets. And they made small ones for the children to pick potatoes. I was able to make baskets and thatch. It's very tricky to make a basket. You had to have a scraw, and you started with the foundation. There are three bows on the corner to keep the corner straight and two of

these go around. And the first weaving holds the basket together. Four rods had to go into the start of it. And its the way you bond the first row that holds it together. The bottom was always very tricky. You had to fold them over. They had their own sally. It grows tall and straight. The baskets were used a lot going to town with the butter.

If young people here had an aunt or an uncle in America they'd send them the passports and tickets to go to America. It was only twenty pounds then to go to America on the boat. The eldest went to America and sent back money and parcels. They were so kind in America. The aunts and uncles would never forget the relations at home. They used to send money to buy coats and that in the spring. I had seven children. Two of them went to America. They used to help out. Secondary education had just started to come. The kids needed an education. There were five of us. I'm the youngest. My sister went to America first. And she sent the passage to my brother. And then, between them, they sent the passage to the other brother. So there were three of them in America. They used to come back to visit. The houses were very small for a big family. There were seven of us and an uncle. There wasn't time then to do anything with the house, or to add to it. You had to work with the land. You were kept going with the outdoor work. You had to sow the potatoes and oats and do the threshing and dig the turf. We had a loft. Most of us slept there. We used to fight to go to the loft. The older children, in America, would always send clothes home for the younger ones for their Communion and that.

The thatcher would be up on the ladder and we'd be waiting on him. We'd bring him the straw and the scallops. They could all thatch. There's a lot to thatching. If it's too dry you have to wet it because it's too stiff then. We used to help one another. You sewed your own shoes. We used to put soles and heels on our shoes. You'd buy the leather to make the shoes. You cut them out yourself. There was wax, as well, to go on them. That coloured them because the leather was white. We had to do them all ourselves. It was great *craic*. The best of material was in them and they lasted and were handed down. And then you rubbed soap into them when they were made. Your foot slid in better. They weren't like the ones made in the Aran Islands. Those were called clogs and were very hard to walk on. Ours had softer leather. You had special shoes for Sunday. If you had a clutch of chickens and you looked after them you had those for town, to sell. And with that money you could buy a pair of shoes. They were your Sunday shoes. After Mass you took off those and put on your home-made boots. It was great going to Mass because it was all so grand. Everyone walked to Mass.

The Fair Day was once a month in Spiddal. It was the

Making Hay in Spiddal: Matt and Morgan Mhaitisín Keady

first Monday of every month. There's one in October now and that's it. They stopped them about ten years ago. It was a great day out even for the old people. The women spent a lot of time sewing and making things. But then the clothes lasted so long. And you probably had only three sets of clothes. And everyone wore shawls. You wore the crocheted shawl until you were fifteen or sixteen. And then, when you got married, you got a big shawl. That was bought. It was bought from Moons in Galway. It was wool, with designs of branches and tassels. They came in different colours. There was a light grey and a deeper grey. They cost two to three pounds. On your wedding day you wore a navy dress and a shawl. The men wore a pair of navy trousers that were dyed. And they had the white, home-made shirt and a jacket which was bought. During the week the elderly people wore *báinín* and waistcoats. They were all home-made.

My husband remembers the landlords well. The Blakes were living in Furbo in my time. Conor Daly was a big man and he left the place to his only daughter. And she drank every penny of it. They had to sell it in the end because there were bills from every hotel in Dublin and round the world.

Potato ridges overlooking Galway Bay

She was a lovely blonde girl and she used to come out from the hotel with a mattress to sleep in the house. My husband's father was caretaker there and there was a lot of staff there at the time. They had nurses and maids and everything. They had fowl and everything. It was knocked down and had to be sold. She was the last of the Blakes. She was married to a Winterbottom, and then married again to someone else. Four of them were buried in the tomb beside the church. One night the tinkers came and when my father-in-law went up next day they had taken everything except the corpses. He had to gather them up and he put concrete over the door of the tomb, so you couldn't open it after that. But they took everything, all the copper and such. The Blakes left the money for the church in Furbo. It was built in 1933.

During the time of the Famine they came from Mayo, Sligo and Leitrim. And they came here to be near the beach. At the back-side of my house there are still walls left where they lived. They had no bedroom. They had moss and straw and an old blanket and they used to sleep huddled together. They cooked the fish and the periwinkles there. They were, literally, starving. The blight was the cause of the Famine. So what they used to do was take the eye out of the potato and use those for growing potatoes again. We weren't too bad around here because we had the sea. Families used to come here in turns, but nobody stopped anyone, because you were glad to see people staying alive.

My aunt went to America. That was way back, in the last century. They used to go from Queenstown, Cobh, to America. They hadn't the money to pay for first or even second class. They went third class. They used to have to bring their own food, tea and sugar and their own mattress for the long voyage. The food had to last them for the month the voyage took. They had nothing else to bring but the suits on their back. Now they couldn't afford suits in those days, but you got what was called 'tick' or 'ling' (credit). You could go to Standúns and you could get the clothes there. And they paid them back as soon as they could. They were always sending money home as soon as they got work in America. They were fantastic.

The 'potters' were the people who divided the sea and the land. It was a good thing that they did. Everybody then had to have their own entrance. Otherwise people wouldn't care, for land had no value in those days. The land you got depended on keeping in with the 'potters'. So you kept in with them. You might give them a bottle of *poitín* or something. If they got a bottle of *poitín* you were away with it, because that was a novelty to the 'potter'. These people

Currach Festival Parade, Spiddal: (front) Pádraig Ó Neachtain and Magdalen Conlon Mc Cana; (back) Máirtín Ó Coincheannainn and May Standún

were strangers sent down from Dublin. Whoever talked the nicest to them got the best deal. If you got a bit of land you were all right, you could grow your own food – swedes, cabbage, onions, turnips, potatoes – and you could have hens and butter and eggs.

I worked for Rose Morris, Lord Killanin's sister. She was deaf and dumb and blind. And the miraculous thing was she could pick out the right medicines on the medicine table. I was very young at the time, about fourteen or fifteen. I was taught how to say good morning to her. She developed with the touch and braille. She had a maid and the maid left and she sent for me and asked if I would work for her.

The place was huge at that time and the gate lodge was beautiful. The Dillons lived in that. Rose Morris had a little house to the side. And I used to stay there and sleep there at night. She had a nurse as well. She always wore black. And she had a hundred pairs of shoes – tiny, buttoned shoes. She could crochet the most beautiful crochet. And she played cards – patience – with a special pack of cards. She suffered from lupus, a terrible disease that marked her face. I never got to see her face, though I tried to peek. But the bonnet was so tied down that you couldn't see. And she wore the bonnet to bed. She used to go for a walk every day, with her nurse. When we were young we were afraid of her. We used to run away. You see we rarely saw any handicapped people in those days. They were always kept to the house. People had children in those days when they were old. And you couldn't marry relations.

In my time teachers were treated like God. Teaching was a very hard job. You needed a lot of patience. When we were going to school we were scared of the teachers. But the discipline has gone now. Nowadays children don't even know the 'Ár nAthair' (the Lord's Prayer), or ' 'Sé Do Bheatha a Mhuire'. They don't teach the religion as they used to. I was about twelve when I made my Confirmation. Then, when you made your Confirmation, you could leave school and go to work. There wasn't that much pressure on girls to marry. If your brother married a girl some of them lived with their parents-in-law, and their sisters and brothers-in-law. They all knew one another. They were all brought up together. You didn't go looking for the loan of a shovel or a spade. You just went in and took it. And then you put it back when you were finished with it. That's all gone now. And people don't visit each other's houses anymore. Sure there are no marriages anymore. They're just living together.

John William Seoighe (Joyce)

Islandman from Inse Ghainimh.
Champion currach racer, sailor, fisherman.

There were just two houses on Inse Ghainimh when I was born there. My father was born in Inis Barra in 1915. At that time Inse Ghainimh belonged to the Clohertys. But the Clohertys couldn't keep paying rates and everything for the whole island, like they used to, so the landlord came down on them and took half the island from them. My father got the first preference to go over there. The landlords were the O'Tooles in Leitir Móir (Lettermore). Now the two islands were roughly three-quarters of a mile from each other, so it was easy to get from one to another. I was on Inse Ghainimh until 1944, when I was in my twenties, and then I moved to Inis Bearcháin (Inish Barra). I was the only one of the family to move. I got married to a girl from Inis Bearcháin. She was a Connolly. There are still people on the island. My brother also married and lived on the island. He died a few years ago, but his wife and other members of his family still live there.

My wife was the only daughter in her family so when we married, we settled down to live with her family for a while. We had eight children. There was no school on the island when I was growing up, so we went to school in Leitir Calaidh (Lettercallow). You could walk there when the tide was out. It was a long walk but it wasn't dangerous.

Sometimes, the tide might come in when we were walking through, but we always made it. We had marks, such as rocks, to let us know if it was safe. And when the tide was in we used to go by boat.

The land was fairly good on the island, but we weren't depending on the land. We used to collect seaweed and save it and dry it. And when it was dry we used to put it in heaps and burn it to make kelp. That was during my father's time. They used to bring it to Cill Chiaráin (Kilkerrin) to sell it. And it used to go from there to Scotland. I was just a kid when they did this, but I remember it all right. I remember cutting the weed from the rocks with a hook. The seaweed was a brownish black. You had to go for it when the tide

Currach races in Spiddal

was out and cut it. It wasn't washed up on the beach. The seaweed used for potatoes was no good for kelp. In Cill Chiaráin there were people selling seaweed at the top price, and they used to bribe people to get the top price. They used to test it and maybe your kelp would be sent home. If your kelp wasn't sold you just had to bring it back home again. Now if you were friendly with someone who sold their kelp, they would take it back and sell it for you at the top price, because they were doing favours for the men who took the kelp. And you lost out in the end. It was harsh having to go over. You had to move three or four tons of weed onto the boat. The boat was a currach. And you often might have the finest kelp, but if you didn't pass the test you had to bring it home. People are collecting seaweed, but not that kind, now. They're collecting the weed near the shore and taking it to the factories. They're doing all right. But they have to cut it with a knife from the rocks. There's an art to doing it.

We didn't build boats on Inse Ghainimh. They built them on Inis Bearcháin. *The American Mór* was built on Inis Bearcháin. We had a boat from there as well. Pádraig Seoighe was building boats there and Joe Waters was building as well. They worked separately. *The American Mór* was built there for the O'Donnells. They mostly built for the people of the island. My grandfather, Seán Mac Seoighe, had a boat built there. There was another man, Joe Joyce, building boats on Inis Bearcháin, but he died young. He never built a hooker. He built *púcáns* and rowing boats. Pádraig Seoighe built hookers. *The American Mór* was a hooker. There were a lot of tradesmen on Inis Bearcháin – very handy people. Almost everyone there could do something handy. Máirtín Joyce is a handy fellow and very brainy. He has a great mind – always knows what he's talking about. I was sailing myself when I was fourteen. I used to sail to the Aran Islands, bringing turf over. There was very little turf on the Aran Islands.

During and after the Famine a lot of people emigrated from here, mostly to the States. The St John boat used to take them from Galway to America. That boat, called *Brig St John*, was built by a Conneely from Leitir Mealláin (Lettermullen). They had made two or three runs with her to the States. Then this time they went over, and before they reached Boston a gale of wind hit them. It tore their sails and everything. So she had to run head-on then. She was a big boat, loaded with people. They were about an hour from Boston. And she sank there. They still have some of the boat left in a museum. The Captain's gold box is still there. If he had let her down further to Hyannis Port or Cape Cod she might have survived. But he let down the anchor at this place and the next thing she hit a rock and split in two halves. I saw the picture when they were leaving her. A lot of them had relatives in Boston so they took the bodies and buried them there in family graves. But there were some – about forty-five – who had no relatives in America. They're buried in a mass grave. There were people from Clare, Mayo, Clifden, East Galway and all round. There weren't that many from around here. There were some survivors.

John William Seoighe near his home in Ros a' Mhíl

It happened on a Sunday morning in the 1840s. I often heard about the story. Years later I visited my son in Boston and we went to the museum to find out exactly what happened. They had parts there of several Irish boats that were lost. Part of the *St Clarence* was there as well. There were a lot of boats that sailed from Galway. And a lot of them were lost because their gear wasn't that good and they ran into a lot of storms.

I lived in America for eight or nine years and I knew the Mulveys there. I came back from New York on a boat. It was a bad morning when we came into Cobh. Cobh is a beautiful place. The boat was anchored way out. There was a turning there and you had to follow the deep channel into Cobh. You then had to get into the ferry to come into the quay. We moved to Galway City when we came back. That was from 1970 to 1976. Then, I got sick of cities and built this house here. My wife wasn't happy in America either. She wanted to come home.

Three or four households from Inis Bearcháin went to the new Gaeltacht in County Meath. I wasn't there at the time to take that option, but I would never have taken the opportunity to go living in the middle of the country. I had to live by the sea. Boston was different. It had boats and yachts and the sea. They even have currachs there now and currach races. I was there when the Quinns and McDonaghs were there. The race was in September. They've continued the tradition over there ever since. There was currach racing around here all the time when I was growing up. They had the wooden currachs. In 1964 the Tostal started in Galway. But there were plenty of races before that – in Cill Chiaráin, Leitir Mealláin, Roundstone and Máinis (Mweenish). There were all kinds of races there. I had a share in it – sailing. We used to sail, here in Connemara, in our younger days, and we won competitions sailing and rowing in the wooden currachs. Some currachs now are thirty-five feet long. In those days they were twenty-one-and-a-half feet long. Mostly we had the same racing partners. There was John, Máirtín and myself – all Joyces. I started rowing when I was about thirteen or fourteen. We loved rowing and used to row in something every Sunday. Rowing to us was like walking up and down the road.

Drying seaweed in Ceantar na nOileán

The weddings on the islands were great *craic* when I was growing up. They used to celebrate for a week. They used to drink and there was plenty of *poitín*. They made plenty of it on Inse Ghainimh. We grew barley on the island specially for that. It had to be of very good quality. Some of the barley was brought in from Galway. People used to report the people making the *poitín* and the police used to come over and catch the makers on the island. Usually the people who told the police were jealous that we could get away with making it on the island. We used to sell it on the mainland. We might sell it to people who were getting married. They might take five or eight gallons of *poitín*. Or, if there was a wake or a funeral we would sell the same amounts. That's the way it was.

I would never agree with a lot of the stuff that was going on. There was a lot of matchmaking, for instance, which wasn't right. It had a lot to do with land and the place to go; he had to have plenty of land and cattle. I wasn't match-made. We met on the island, in one of the houses. And we had known one another growing up. Though most people would have known each other growing up. But in a lot of places they match-made people who didn't know one another at all. They travelled to another village, to other places. They might have been ten miles apart. The guy would have to go to see the girl beforehand. Usually they went themselves with someone else. If he was a good man, and had plenty of cattle and land, she would have to go to live there because her parents would press her. And that, I think, was completely wrong. And sometimes a young girl would have to marry an old fellow. He could be fifty and she might be only nineteen. But sometimes, the fellow was young and good looking. The parents at that time would do anything to get the daughters out of their hands. A lot of that stuff was there in my time.

There were tradesmen on the islands. There was a tailor on our island. There wasn't a weaver. The tailor would make clothes for you if you asked him. It was all *báiníns* and flannels at that time. And there were shirts with black stripes and velvet and big buttons. They were very warm. The tailor would have to come to the house and measure you. He would, if you wanted it that way, cut it out and you could stitch it yourself. We didn't have a shoemaker on the island. You had to make your own shoes, and it wasn't easy. You had bits of leather and a needle and what they called 'the tay'.

The celebrations for Christmas were great then. Things have changed so much now. They don't take down the Christmas trees now until nearly Easter. We didn't have Christmas trees on the island. We didn't have much of what's going on today. We had plenty of raisins. They were a big treat because you wouldn't see much of them for the rest of the year. You didn't have to pay cash for things then like you do today. When you bought something that went down 'on the book'. And then at the end of the year, after the Christmas shopping, you paid for everything. That was your groceries for the year and you'd have to pay for all that before you started another new year.

But the shopkeepers were good and decent people. There was Mrs O'Toole in Leitir Móir. She was good. And Mrs O'Connor in Tír an Fhia was very good. And there was Patrick Conroy of Ros Muc. He had a fine shop there and he'd never refuse anyone even if you couldn't pay on the spot. For instance, something happened to a man from Trá Bháin once. He got caught with a sale of *poitín* and wasn't paid. And he was depending on it to pay for his groceries. He didn't have a penny piece to pay. But the shopkeeper didn't let him down. She sent the usual delivery of stuff to his house. They were very decent that way and never let their customers down.

The majority of people in those days had boats. Some

had hookers for going to the Aran Islands. If you had a boat – whatever kind of boat – you wouldn't go hungry. Trading with the Aran Islands you would exchange a load of turf for a load of fish. 'Twas the barter system and it worked well. They would give you so many pounds weight of dried mackerel against the load of turf you'd brought over. And you would sell that to one of the shops when you came back and you'd make a few shillings on the deal. Some of the people on the Aran Islands were better off than they were here.

The birth of a baby was a big celebration. They had a big party. They would take the baby over to be christened in the church. The mother didn't go to the church. There was this child being christened Pádraig, and his father was very funny. After they had 'wet' the baby, this woman asked the father what he was going to call him. The father answered, 'I'm calling him Pádraig, and I love the name so much that if I had sixty more children they would all be called Pádraig.' He said this because he knew that she was nosy. They had a big party and the *poitín* came out again. It was hard on people who had to leave the island, especially if they moved far. One man who had moved to the new Meath Gaeltacht was so lonely he returned here.

At Easter we had the goose again. And you had plenty of eggs as well. Every house saved them up for Easter Sunday. They had holy wells and they really believed in them. There was no holy well on our island but there was one on Leitir Calaidh, outside our island. We had the

stations on the island. The priest used to come over twice a year. That was a big day, the day of the stations. You whitewashed beforehand. You hoped that you got good weather the week before. And you had special food for the priest. They were treated with great respect and they expected it too. They expected that special food as well. They weren't like they are now, not expecting anything. The priests were very stylish. It was a lot of pressure on the family. But they were good cooks. You had to give them a full meal. They sat on their own in the room. And you had the table ready for them. Nobody sat with them. Three priests used to come together – the parish priest and the two Curates. You made rashers and eggs and sausages, and tea and your own brown bread.

Then, when the priests had left, the neighbours would stay and they'd have tea and rashers, eggs and sausages as well. They'd also have a drop of good *poitín*. And that night there was a dance. They had set-dancing. We used to dance the Connemara Set. People sang the real old songs. They were great singers. They sang of love, or some lady who broke up a marriage. They made up the verses themselves. In half an hour you could have the lot. There were eighteen verses in some of them. Songs about emigration and boats – everything. A lot of the songs have been forgotten now. Micheál Perkins from Trá Bháin composed a song when he was passing through one Sunday morning and the sun sparking down – *Ag Dul Tríd An Ailléideach.* He made up a lot of songs. I'd say that Anthony Perkins is a relation. He composed another song

John Beag's hooker ready to sail at Leitir Mealláin

about Pádraig Seoighe and Cearnaigh. There was another great storyteller, Colm de Bhailís, who came from Ceantar na nOileán. It's too bad Radio na Gaeltachta wasn't there at that time. It's a real disaster to have lost all those stories. I heard a lot of them when I was a kid, growing up, but it's all gone now and more's the shame. There's a different pronouncing now and a different Irish. I wouldn't even call it Irish. I was able to read the Irish that I learnt in school. But I can't read any of the Irish that they publish now, because I can't understand it. Cóilín Kelly has the old Irish. And he has problems getting his books published because of the *ráiméis* Irish they have now. He's related to me. They seem to be changing it from English to Irish. They're doing a direct translation. The stories and language they had years ago was a gift. It was a real pleasure to be able to pronounce the words. They'd be better off nowadays speaking English. I wouldn't think anything of their Irish nowadays, though there are some that can speak it properly.

I still go out to the islands. It's very sad and lonesome to see all the empty houses of the people who have gone away over the years. I find it sadder going to my own island. You see the places where you had great *craic* with your cousins and friends and that. And most of them are dead and gone and buried.

25

Anonymous

A woman who grew up in The Manor, Baile an tSagairt.

My father was from Baile an tSagairt and he worked in the Manor House with Mrs Palmer from when he was fourteen years of age. My mother was from Cnocán Glas. And she worked in the Manor as a cook. We lived in the manor all our life. We grew up here and we went to the Convent School. The Manor was a huge house. And it had several bedrooms and a big kitchen and dairy. There were seven children in the family. Mrs Palmer was alone. She was a Protestant. She inherited the place from her parents – the Bunberrys. And her husband was one of the Palmers of Galway – the Palmer's Flour Mills. He died and we were there with her all these years. And her sister lived in Bruach na Mara, which was called Paterangi at the time. The man who owned it then was Bunberry, an uncle of Mrs Palmer. And he left her the place.

Mrs Palmer had a sister called Mrs Smith who lived in a cottage near Hughes' field. She had another sister, Mrs Brody, who lived in Bruach na Mara. Her husband was a doctor and he shot and killed her. There aren't any of that family left. The Brody's didn't have any children. Mrs Smith had one daughter, Flo, who lived in the Manor for a short time and then went to live in Galway City. She was in poor health and her doctor, Dr Sands, brought her into Galway.

Mrs Palmer was ninety-two when she died. She was Susan Katherine Bunberry and she married Jack Palmer and they originally lived in Salthill in a big house called 'Brinkwater'. He died of a heart attack, leaving her alone. And we lived with her. It was lovely there because it was so different from the rest of the place around. She was Protestant. She wasn't very wealthy. My mother was her cook and her housekeeper. And she gave us a lot of space in the house. I don't know why she did it. She might have been lonely. But she was the lady of the house and we kept out of her way. However, as she got older we used to go for walks with her. But we didn't eat with her. My mother waited on her, hand and foot. She died in 1931. She used to have a governess growing up, but never went to finishing school. The Bunberrys came to Spiddal in the early 1800s or the late 1700s. Before that the Manor was owned by another family. Actually, I think it was during the Famine that Mrs Bunberry bought the place. She had tenants. They probably didn't think she was very nice at the time because they had to pay her rent. But for as long as I can remember, she never interfered. They tried to get more land from her but she wouldn't give it. She was tough enough. A Mr Lockeade collected her rents.

'Twas in 1917 or 1918 the trouble started when people started looking for more land. They sort of boycotted us, because we worked for her and lived with her and she was a Protestant. And that was the most awful thing you could be in those days. Mrs Palmer attended the Protestant Church regularly. The minister lived in the house where the Secondary School is now. Nuns live there now. My brother used to bring her to that church in a pony and trap. When she was younger she walked there. For the last ten years of her life she didn't go out much at all.

There weren't any other Protestants in the area only herself. When the 'Bird's Nest' was here it was a Home for Protestant children. But that was gone before I was born. I was told that Mrs Palmer used to visit a Mrs McNamara in Dublin. She ran the place. The priest at that time, Fr Conroy, and several others with him, were against having the Protestant children there. They were afraid that the Protestants would eventually take over. So the children had to leave because they were being boycotted. The children in the Home were often nearly starving. And Paddy Francis' grand-father, or great-grandfather was the

Old Manor House of the Bunberrys and Palmers in Baile an tSagairt

baker at the time, and he used throw bread in over the wall at night to feed the starving children. Mrs Palmer often told us about that time. As she got older we used to sit with her for company in her bedroom or drawing room. The Minister used to come to the Manor to visit her. The church

was closed down then. There was a Pensions Officer, Mr Merson, who lived in the house where the nuns live now. And a Mr Nash, the Minister from Galway, used to visit Mrs Palmer for years.

Mrs Palmer never tried to influence us. She always insisted on everyone doing what was right for them. I remember Canon McAlinney being over when she signed the Will. She left the place to my brother. He was her favourite. He was very musical, like Festy Conlon. It was a lovely old house. We have very happy memories of her. She was a lovely woman. And she left the other place – Bruach na Mara – to my father.

There was every-thing you could want at the Manor and I growing up there. They had a coach house and they had a lot of horses before my time. They used to go away as far as Tipperary, and my father used to bring them in the coach. Sir Robert Staples owned the Manor before the Bunberrys owned it. Legend has it that he shot himself and his two dogs and that they are buried in the grounds. But when they dug it up, years later, to build the factory, they never found anything. In the back of the Manor there was a big pantry. When Mr Palmer died and my mother first came there they still had a few servants. Kate Faherty was there before my mother. There weren't any horses there in my day. There were lovely trees and gardens in the Manor. They're all gone now. There was a pump in the lawn to pump up the fresh water. They had a proper sort of toilet with water that used to come from the shoots. There was a bit of a river there but I don't think they were bothered with fishing rights. They were as wealthy as the Killanins. Lord Killanin's sister, Rose Morris, used to visit Mrs Palmer. Rose had been a nurse in the Boer War and she had lupus. She was the lady with the veil. She lived in Dublin and came here during the summer. She always had a companion with her. She used to have afternoon tea with Mrs Palmer in the parlour. They had very elegant china cups. They dressed well. Mrs Palmer always had frills and fancies. She wore the long skirts. She got her clothes from McBirney's of Dublin. They used to send down clothes and she picked out what she wanted. My mother didn't make our clothes. There were people around who made clothes.

In the Manor there was a big fireplace with an oven at the side. And next to that was a side plate and there was a tap with water in it. These were found in the old mansions. They used to eat fowl. If visitors came they had legs of lamb and chicken for them, all reared around here.

Then there was grouse shooting and people used to come for that in August. The twelfth of August was the beginning of the grouse shooting season and the relatives from Tipperary always came up for that. We grew the usual things in the garden. We had celery, parsnips, carrots and turnips. They went grouse shooting on foot and they had beaters as well. And when they got the grouse my mother had to cook it. It was trial and error, preparing and cooking it. My mother's mother died when she was very young and she was reared by an aunt or cousin who was Lord Killanin's laundress. She grew up in the cottage across the road from the entrance. She came from Cnocán Glas. She had an eye for what they cooked at Killanins. When I was growing up I was expected to sew and cook.

When I was about sixteen years old I don't think Mrs Palmer had much money left, so she started taking in guests from the Irish College. We took them into the Manor. It was quite contradictory to her life before that. I'm sure she didn't like it. The bedrooms were very big and the ballroom was huge and that made a fine big dormitory for the *Gaeilgeoirí*. We had about twelve staying. We started taking them in 1923. My mother cooked for them all. Richard Mulcahy's wife and children used to come in the summertime. Sean T O'Kelly's wife and sister came and later Sean T came and stayed with us too. And Gavin Duffy's wife and daughter used to come. It was a hard life, but seemingly we did it without any great effort. Mrs Palmer didn't speak any Irish at all, but she was very old at that time. It was my mother and myself who hosted the guests. My mother never ate with the *Gaeilgeoirí*. They were treated like real guests. The *Gaeilgeoirí* came in the summer and the inspectors came in September.

I got married in 1927 and moved to Achill. My husband was a Sergeant in Spiddal when I met him, and was transferred to Achill later. He was from Mitchelstown in County Cork. We had our wedding breakfast in the Manor. The only thing we couldn't have at the wedding was *poitín*, because he was the Sergeant. I went to school until I was fifteen. Unless you had money you couldn't go on further in your education. The bus to Galway didn't start running until 1927, too late for my schooling. Everyone went to America then. I helped at home. You stayed with your parents until you got married. My older sister went nursing in 1919. And my older brother went to America. I had six children of my own. Two are in America and two are in Dublin. One is in Ennis – a retired guard. And I have a daughter in Kerry. My youngest is fifty.

We used to go to *céilís* in the College in the summer. It was the highlight of the year, going to the *céilís*. And sometimes, we had plays in the College. Pat Sheain Tom used to do them with me. I used also do plays with Peadar Duignean. I enjoyed doing the plays. Oh, I remember so many things. I remember the Black and Tans setting fire to Sean Costelloe's house. I remember when Lord Killanin had the only car in the area. I remember bartering a pound of sugar and two pounds of tea for one dozen eggs. I remember how much my mother loved Mrs Palmer for her great gentleness and kindness. I remember the lovely collection of parasols she had. All satin-lined and a different one for every outfit.

The poverty in the city was worse than in the country because it was harder to go hungry in the country. And we had the sea here. I can remember the Gabha's house and the Stiofán's house were kept as clean. And there was no poverty here, no apparent poverty. When my daughter, Nuala, went up to work in the Civil Service in 1945 or 1946, the wages were two pounds fifteen shillings a week. And you could live on that. Rashers were one and a penny a pound. And butter was a shilling a pound. I remember in 1933 my sister was home from America, and she bought a lovely tweed suit for two pounds ten shillings. So you see, that has all gone. Standúns was lovely when they had the food shop, but they don't have it anymore.

Fr Tomás Ó Cadhain

Parish priest in Spiddal since 1976.
Much respected local historian.

I started out as a curate in Carna. Then I spent twenty-one years in Galway, fifteen of them as Chaplain in Galway University. Then I was a year or two as parish priest in County Clare. And I'm here in Spiddal since 1976.

In 1989 the Institute of Architects in Ireland was a hundred-and-fifty-years-old and Roadstone decided to bring out a calendar to commemorate it. They picked six of the most architecturally significant buildings in Ireland. And they picked this church; no cathedrals – just this church. The church was designed by William Scott, Professor of Architecture at Trinity at the time. The reason he was here was that he was building the first house that belonged to the Killanins. That house was burned in 1922. Scott didn't build many churches. The church here was based on Cork's Chapel of Cashel. It's Hiberno-Romanesque architecture. William Scott mainly designed 'big houses' for the Anglo-Irish gentry. The Killanin's Spiddal house was rebuilt in 1927, and enlarged. But I'd say that they kept the old design a bit.

The church here is what's called a 'low' church. They call it a saddle roof. And it was built for six thousand pounds. The windows and the stations of the cross were put in later. The first window is St Michael the Archangel and that was for the first Lord Killanin – Michael Morris.

Fr Tomás Ó Cadhain (left) and Fr Colm Sweeney saying Mass at the Mass Rock, Spiddal

Then there is the Killanin coat of arms. That inscription says – 'If God is with us, who's against us?' The second window is St Martin. That was the second Lord Killanin, uncle of the present Lord. Martin never married. When the house burned down in 1922 he went to England and never came back. We have the picture of St Martin on horseback meeting the beggar. So he cuts his cloak and gives half to the beggar. And then you have the Morris coat of Arms again, and you have St Enda coming ashore in Spiddal, bringing his faith. That was the tradition. There is the torch of faith and the bible. And that man has a mighty face. That was in the memory of George Henry Morris, who was the father of the present Lord Morris. He was killed in the First World War in 1914. He was a cavalry officer in the British Army fighting in France. He was killed in the forest of Compiègne. Depicted in the window you can see a horse riding without a rider and he wishing for his heaven, which could have been Spiddal or heaven. There's a tremendous lot in these old stories.

The stations of the cross were put in around 1919 at a cost of twenty-two pounds each. Two of them were damaged over the years and they cost two thousand five hundred pounds each to repair. Ethel Rhind designed them. She was born in Scotland. Her father was an officer in the Indian army. Canon McAlinney was the parish priest at the time. And when the Morrisses were presenting the window they wanted an English inscription on it. He told them to keep it unless they put it in Irish. So, gentlemen to the cause, they compromised and had it put in Latin. Catherine O'Brien designed the windows. Her two daughters came here to look at them and they told me the story. The Clancys donated the plaque. There's a cross over all the stations, but they start on the wrong side of the church. Ethel Rhind wasn't a Catholic so she didn't know that. This is the only church in Ireland like that. We still do the stations of the cross during Lent and that.

A pot beside Tully Church, used by the 'Soupers' or 'Jumpers' to feed the people during the Famine

It's from the phrase *d'iompaigh sé* that the term 'the soupers' came. *D'iompaigh sé* means he changed, or converted to. There's a big pot by Tully's modern church and that was the soupers' pot – or the jumpers' pot. In Clare there were a lot of jumpers. And you could sign on in the Jumpers' Office and get food for the winter. And when they passed the church they used to say, '*Slán agat anois a Dhia, go bhfasfaidh na fataí*', which is 'Goodbye now, God, until the potatoes grow.'

Ruins of the old Abbey in the churchyard of St Enda's Church, Spiddal

Down in the valley is the *Mainistir*, or the Abbey. And that is mentioned in Rory O'Flaherty's book *Iar-Chonnacht*. Rory died in 1719. They put an inscription into the foundation stone. And the people of Spiddal said that they were building the church two hundred yards from St Enda's monastery. They thought that that was where Enda was. That would have failed when the Penal Laws started and they had to go to the Mass Rock. That was up in Baile Éamainn.

I'm almost certain I've traced the name of one priest who said Mass at that Mass Rock. His name was Edmund French and he was ordained by Bishop Taidhg Keogh, who was consecrated Bishop of Clonfert by Oliver Plunkett, in 1680. And St Oliver was beheaded a few years later. The Penal Laws of 1696 stated that all bishops had to leave the country. And priests and monks who lived in groups also had to leave. They allowed one priest to stay in each Parish. But they had to register with the Government and get two people to guarantee their good behaviour. In 1704, Fr Edmund French was registered in the parish of Spiddal and Seaside – *An Spidéal agus Cois Fharraige*. That was the whole coast. But there weren't many people living on the coast at that time. In 1798 there were only eighty houses between Spiddal Bridge and Furbo Bridge. The people came here after the Famine and as a result of the Famine. The real bad year here was 1881. It was a real bad winter and the Famine was at its worst, and there was an outbreak of typhoid. The priest here at that time was Fr William Wilson. He's buried here. His people came from Wexford. His father was an excise man. He used to watch the coast for smugglers, with the coastguard. Poor Fr Wilson died at the age of twenty-nine. He was the one who wrote the letters which started the Spiddal Relief Committee, of which he was chairman. And Dr Brody, who was the local doctor, and who killed his wife, was the secretary. Willie Aran, who was the court clerk and lived where the convent is now, was the treasurer. And Paddy Francis of the Post Office – his grandfather was member of that committee. Josie Folan's grandfather was a member, and John O'Connor, a road contractor, and James Madden were also members. Their sources of funding were the Mansion House Fund, the Lady Marlborough Fund and the New York Fund. And the sums they got ranged from twenty to fifty pounds a month. They managed to keep people alive. It lasted only one year. It was a bad winter and very wet and the crops didn't grow. They weren't able to save the turf and cattle prices fell to nothing. That was when they gave out the meal. By June or July of 1881 it was over.

The priest who came in place of Fr Wilson was Fr Newell. And they had a totally different style. Fr Wilson used to plead and make humble requests for funds, whereas Fr Newell was more demanding. He was tough and rough. This little church, in the middle of the cemetery, was built in 1776, the year of American Independence. In between the old one being knocked down and the new church being built Mass was said out at the Mass Rock. Fr Edmund French was ordained in the

The convent (once a summerhouse for Lord Westmeath) and St Enda's Church, Spiddal, designed by architect William Scott and finished in 1908

open-air in Clonfert. He had no problems with saying Mass in the open-air. He was in no danger as long as he kept his mouth shut. Fr French died about 1719. The thing about the Mass Rock is that you can say Mass there without using a microphone. And it was a perfect spot. In 1876 Fr Tómas Curran became P.P. of Spiddal and was there for twenty years. A marvellous Gaelic speaker. He refused a post

as Gaelic lecturer in Maynooth. He would have been a grand-uncle of Timín Joe Tim, Bairbre's husband. There were no roads at that time. A lot of the roads were built as a result of the relief schemes. Giving out anything for nothing was totally contrary to the social sociology of the time. They always gave money for work. When the old church was found to be unsuitable, and when they built the new one, this one was converted into a national school. In 1922 they got permission to teach through the medium of Gaelic. Since 1910 they'd had a concession for the Gaelic language. If the teacher wished to teach Gaelic in the school he was permitted to do so, provided he only did it for half an hour and after school hours. And some of them did it that way.

This corner was probably God's acre for more than a thousand years. The nuns came here in 1909 and they just had a small house. When the present church was being built the parish priest was Fr Marcus D Conroy. And he was the uncle of the writer, Sean Pádraic Ó Conaire, who died in 1928. Marcus D was a very prim and proper man and had no time for Pádraic, who was a bit of a drinker. Pádraic had left his wife and he enjoyed life. I think Marcus D went to the funeral when Pádraic died. Marcus D moved out of Spiddal in 1909. Pádraic is buried in the new cemetery in Galway. His father was from Gairfean and he owned two pubs in Galway at one stage, but he fell into bad health and fell on bad times.

The road to Ros Muc didn't have any status at that time. There was no tar on it and the main way of carrying the goods was by waterway. And they used the hookers for that. And the Conroys had two hookers. When they were coming to and from Galway they used to stop here at Spiddal Quay and call up to the Convent to Kate Conroy. She was the boss woman at the convent – the Reverend Mother – and she had a great heart in her. The men from the hookers always came up for the tea. And she always gave tea to Seán Pádraic, her nephew, when he was going through Spiddal. Now, there was a good-looking young nun in the convent and didn't Pádraic write a love poem to her, in Irish. Kate got a hold of the letter and Pádraic lost his tea there forever.

There was another church before the 1854 church. It was a thatched church and it's mentioned in Lucas' *Topographical Guide to Ireland*, written around 1845. The thatched church was situated where Óstan an Droichid is now – The Bridge House Hotel. There was only one priest here at the time and his name was Lannin. He's actually buried, with a tombstone, in the monastery. The date on the tombstone is 1829, the year he died. The church lasted until they opened the one that was here before the present one. That one didn't last very long. It didn't have a concrete floor and it had no seats. It was a school until the next one was built. And afterwards it was used as a hostel to take the overflow of boarders from the boarding school.

Cáit Bean Uí Chiardha

Retired schoolteacher. Native of Spiddal.

My family are local, for years and generations, back to Cromwell's time. They came from Athlone. Neachtain was my father's name. My mother came from Park, in Spiddal. My mother had been in America on some kind of scheme – the Vera Foster Scheme it was, I think. When she came back she married my father. They met at a funeral and eloped to Galway. My mother's generation was better off than what came after that. In the Thirties every good-looking girl had to go off to America.

But when it came to my time education had improved a lot. The nuns were very good, although they were very cross. In my school classes were small. There would have been around twenty-three students in each class. And out of those about six would expect to get a scholarship to secondary school. And after that they did the Post Office Exam and they got on very well. One or two would go to Agricultural College. And some would go to work in shops. These would have been boys and girls. The girls would go to Agricultural College to do Cookery and Poultry and all that. All the girls and women at home did the heavy work in the houses. No boy or man was ever allowed to distemper, paint or whitewash in the West. All the girls did that work – inside or out. They did every domestic chore in the house. It was never expected of the boys to do it. But that attitude is gone now, thank God. In

Nicky Anthony (Curran) on St John's Night, 23rd June, Cnocán Glás, Spiddal

my own case it was gone the day I married. The men did everything in the house.

From very early on you had visitors coming to Spiddal. The Irish College was there. And then, like many other houses, every summer, Christmas and Easter we had visitors staying in our house. Spiddal was so near town – Galway – that it was further ahead than other more remote places. The people all worked to bring things to the market in town. The women were occupied with the *Gaeilgeoirí*. My father never believed in women going to work at the strand or in the sea. He'd say, 'Stay at home and mind the house and you'll find something to do.'

There was always something happening in Spiddal. The college boys from Belvedere came down at Easter. The cadets used to come down as well. And *Clann na hÉireann* came as well. So there was always something going on, even though we didn't mix much with them socially. We might go to a 'campfire'. You were allowed to go out, but there were so many instructions. We were always asked, 'Where were you and who was with you?' But we did go out. And you could go for days without hearing a bad word. You weren't afraid. There weren't any bad men or boys. And then we went in groups, fishing, down by the rocks. There used to be gangs of us with the lines. And sometimes we had a wee net. And the bonfire nights were great nights altogether. They were on the 23rd of June, St John's night. I think it was a pagan rite. That was a very big night. And there was terrible competition between the villages. There were festivities during the day – music and dancing. It was lovely. You could stay out 'til twelve or one o'clock in the morning and no one thought anything of it.

I used to spend my whole life up in Conlons. The family home was opposite where the Standúns live, up where Amelia is. That was more my home. There was always music there. The granny was a noted singer of Connemara. We suspect that it was Bríd na n'Amhráin who was in Patrick Pearse's book. It was about a one who went to Dublin to the Feis. She was a beautiful singer and so was Festy's mother. And you can see that it has passed on to Mómó. The granny used to sing the *caoineadh* at the funerals. It sounded desperate, like the banshees. It used to sound like cats crying in the night. But that's gone out now. Well, you might hear it an odd time now. The coffin was left out on a special chair outside the door. And they banged on it just as the corpse was leaving the house. It was a special lady in three villages, or further afield as it was in Festy's granny's case, that did the *caoineadh*. After the funeral the chairs would have to be brought in and washed. Nobody was allowed to sit in them until they were washed. It was a tradition. Neighbours would all join in the *caoineadh*. The last *caoineadh* I heard was my grandmother. That would have been around 1930. I think she was over a hundred when she died. And this cousin came from the next village. She was *ag caoineadh* as well as Festy's granny. I always remember what she was saying; 'And all the times you came back to visit us ....' And it

Shaped like the prow of a boat, this large rock was said to have been used by St Colmcille to come from Aran to An Bhánrach. A Mass is celebrated every year there on 9th June

went on and on. They used words, phrases, in praise of the dead person, woven into the *caoineadh*, about how good they were and how they would be missed.

There were so many of us going to secondary school that we had our own bus going up to Tourmakeady. We were one of the last groups to go because they were going to close the college. It was during the War years. Then I went to Dublin to the Training College in Carysfort. I was well used to Dublin because my sister was living there. Carysfort was strict but I loved it. I didn't find life in Dublin much different. But most of the people around us were from Spiddal and all of them were Irish speakers. A lot of the teachers, and even Professors in the colleges, at that time, came out of this area and from Carna too. There was a special concession for people from the Gaeltacht. But you had to work hard for it too.

If you wanted to go to university you could, but I wouldn't have been encouraged to go. An awful lot went to university. Some had scholarships, but a lot went without scholarships. People were very good about wanting an education. There was a great spirit of education here, and you felt you had to keep up with that. They believed in it. Some of them, like the Neachtains, even wrote books. The culture, theatre-wise, was very good at that time. It isn't what it's like now. I think it was much nicer. Maybe after Mass on Sunday there would be a session in our house. People you knew would come in and maybe bring a friend from Carna. Carna was full of music, and still is. Then they might come to the Guards' Céilí, or some big 'do' like that. The Local Defence Force

and the guards used to have a big night on St Stephen's night. That would go on 'til four in the morning. There was nobody in the area teaching music, but some went into town to get music lessons, piano mostly. But there were good accordion players. They had to make their own music at the time. It was beautiful. We used to go into Galway to the Taibhdhearc. A good few used to go. There was a local theatre group as well. They put on plays in the College. I was with them. A lot of the plays were translations into Irish. They were very good.

I remember one night coming home from College. It was Easter time. And we thought we were marvellous, with our new suits for Easter. It was Holy Thursday night. And this lady looked down at us and said, 'Oh, the natives are home!' That was the night I made up my mind never to speak English to my children. She was trying to let us know we weren't 'cultural' enough because we spoke Irish.

A lot of people had TB in the early days. They were sent to Merlin Park at the time. And if they didn't have it going in, they had it coming out. People didn't go into hospital then unless they were really on their way out. They felt it was an end to their lives. There was a great fear of hospitals. In the olden days there was a 'handy woman' if you were pregnant. In my days there was a nurse – a midwife. I went to hospital to have the children, but my mother had the 'handy woman', who delivered all the babies around here in those days. My mother's life was tough. It was desperate. It was terrible. They had very large families then. And my parents seemed old to me when I was growing up. My mother was in the States, like others at that time, with other Irish women. Most of them were housekeeping for some rich lady. And they stayed together. They never went out of that circle. And then they came home and they threw off the glamour. They never kept it up. It was strange. They never improved themselves. I suppose America was backward at that time, as well. They didn't have much freedom over there either. And when they came back they returned to their old ways.

The shawls were very much in fashion when I was young – the ones with the Claddagh pattern. And then they changed to black. It was very important that you were dressed on Sunday. You had a black satin apron, a black skirt and a blouse. They were very keen on bright cotton coloured blouses. But they worked very hard. We had an old oil stove in the cottage when we had guests, and we had the pot hole. And Mam used to make the most beautiful bread and pot roasts. The ranges came in after that. I was in Spiddal when the electricity came.

They had sidecars to go into Galway. If you didn't have one then someone else had and they gave you a lift. That was in my mother's time. The cars were around in my time and so was the bus. The bus is here since 1930. There were private buses. One was called, I remember, 'The Queen of Connemara'; and one was called 'Fag an Bealach'.

On Sunday morning someone always knocked on your door to get you up in time for Mass. And on Christmas morning they were in and out of our house. Our house was the last house before the village. They came in before and after Mass. It was like a halfway house. They played cards there at night, the blacksmith and the tailor. They all gathered in and the tailor used to get the paper. It was the only paper in the village. Everyone would get a read of it. The tailor could only read it at night when all his work was done, so we would read it during the day. It was passed from house to house. And there was a lady who, when she heard a story, used to say, 'Well, it wasn't in the tailor's paper!'

I went to the Pattern once. Noël Browne was a TD at the time. That was a very big day and all the relations used to come back. They used to bake currant cakes and bread in the village for days beforehand. You went around the well saying prayers. And there was a boat there. That was to represent the boat St Colmcille came on. There's a lovely beach there. And on a fine day they said Mass on the beach. It's on the 9th of June. There were beautiful cottages there as well. We used to have the ceremony in the evening. You had to go down one road and up the other, where Noël Browne used to live. A lot of people used to go to the ceremony – Maumean. I didn't. And then there's Croagh Patrick and Oileán Mhic Dara. They're very famous.

I never went back to Carna as a child. But before I got married, we used to go back there to the shows. We used to cycle. Carna is the place for the boats. There were never any big boats here, like the *púcán*. They used travel from Carna to Galway by boat, but we were so near town we could go by road. The fishing was just a pastime here. My father had a phobia about people who collected periwinkles and such because he said the people got enough of them during the Famine. They came down from

Oughterard and the mountains to this area, by the sea, during the Famine. It's a tradition here to go and collect periwinkles on Good Friday, because you can't eat meat.

The landlords, the Smiths, had a house across from us. I remember, when Lord Killanin was twenty-one, he gave a birthday party to all the tenants. And we were at it. It was down by the big pier, in a field. There was a big boathouse there, with a flat, carved roof. And he had tents and buffets. There were hundreds of people at it – all our village and going back. My family were tenants of his. Baile Liam and Baile an tSagairt were also tenants. Lord Killanin was a gentleman and a Catholic. I remember when my father was building our old cottage, Lord Killanin came down and offered to pay for a slated roof. But my father didn't want a slated roof. He wanted a thatched cottage. But it was very kind of Lord Killanin to offer. He thought it would be too much work for my father to thatch it himself. And it was the modern thing to have it slated. When they got a grant to build a new house they had to guarantee to knock the old one. This was to get rid of the thatched cottages. They had to knock the chimney off the old house and that's why you see so many stone houses with no roofs around the area.

My father did the thatching. It was mostly straw, and they had their own straw. They had everything they wanted. They were always looking ahead. They'd cut the straw themselves and bind it in the big kitchen in November. The bundles were then put aside until they were needed. They kept the sally rods in a special place. They were grown specially for this. You had a big basket that was outside if the weather was fine. There

might be only one or two in the parish handy at the thatching, so they obliged the neighbours by doing it for them. They cut straw and put pegs down and worked from that.

The old songs were about sadness and death. And some of them were about lovely looking girls. A lot of songs were about tragedies. They were lovely. And they sang every single verse. There could be anything up to twenty-seven verses, or so. They were passed on from one generation to another. And there were certain

Jam pots

families who kept them up. The weddings and the wakes were parties. They danced at them and everything. The coffin was often still there, but I never saw this. The songs were very important. There were certain songs that certain people had, like the Conlons, and they sang them. The songs went back to four or more generations. I can't sing and neither can my family. The gift skipped generations in some families. The Irish songs were peculiar to Connemara. But then you had 'The Rocks of Bawn'. There were a lot of English ballads. There were a lot also about 1916. They were very fashionable. During my own time there were some beautiful ballad singers who sang in perfect English. And they were Irish speakers. People think that if you speak Irish you can't speak English. If you have Irish you can learn French, or anything. We learned Latin at school.

Máirtín Chóilín Choilmín Seoighe (Joyce)

The last inhabitant of Inish Barra Island. Farmer, fisherman, currach maker and champion currach racer.

The first man who came to this island was my great grandfather – Patrick Joyce. Isn't it funny that I'm the last and from the same family. Patrick Joyce came here originally with some sheep, from Maam Tuirc. Everyone was moving to live by the sea at that time. It was a lot easier to live with the whitefish and shellfish. Shellfish was so plentiful it was for nothing at that time. They were living on it here on the island. You could load a lorry with the old shells around the island. There's some fish still there. I love fish. It's not as good as it used to be. I eat all sorts of fish and would eat it three times a day if I got it.

Well, anyway, Patrick Joyce came over here with his flock of sheep. He had a small cabin there, down by the pier. I heard that they found the first quarry over here when they were cutting the turf. After that they were able to build stone houses. They were cutting the turf a lot. Turf was a gold-mine at that time. They didn't have any turf on the Aran Islands, so there was always a great demand. There used to be fourteen families on that island over there – Oileán Iarthach.

I'm Joyce on both sides. My mother was Joyce too. There were a lot of inter-marriages here. A lot of island people married other island people. We used to go

Máirtín Seoighe on his island of Inis Bearcháin (Inis Barra)

around to one another's houses for entertainment. And we had parties and dancing over in the old school. We used to visit houses and play cards. The cards were for men only. There were four schools on the island, but there was only one teacher and there was no secondary school. So you spent longer in primary school. They kept the older children at home to work. I was the eldest son, but I was the third one in the family. You had to be able to help the people at home. If you were a good worker you were kept at home every second day. So you were better off to be a bad worker, because then you got to go to school every day. I was a good worker. You had to dig and sew and cut turf. You had to survive that way. We didn't get a chance to go anywhere, even though we were just as brainy as kids on the mainland. It would cost too much to go to boarding school. Some went to America and did well for themselves. And they would have had no English at all. It was only towards the end of my schooling that they started to teach English on the islands. But they taught Catechism everywhere. There was no priest on our island, so you had to go across to the mainland by boat, every Sunday, to go to Mass. The priests stopped a lot of entertainment on the mainland.

A Famine house on Inis Bearcháin

Although they couldn't do anything about it on our island, they did grumble a lot, especially when they heard there was *poitín* being made on our island. My father spent all his life making it, but never drank a drop of it. Though the people on the island could drink a fair amount of the stuff, they never lost control. They used to make it with barley and malt. They had their own barley and oats. They had all their own stuff except for the yeast. I think they used porter to make the yeast. But it was just as good as real yeast. I didn't ever make it myself, but I saw my father making it. Sometimes two families would come together to make it. They were making it at that time with turf. They use gas now, which is much quicker. The thing with the turf was that the Guards could see the smoke. There weren't any Guards stationed on the island, but they used to come in a lot and we had someone on the look-out all the time. We would all protect each other and warn each other when it was being made here. They used to make *poitín* down by the shore too. They used to make it behind the rock and then cover it up with sand. They had the fire there. They used the *scrathach* to cover the *poitín* and for the drying. It was a nice dry place with shelter and nobody could see you. And you could see if there were boats coming.

I went to England when I was eighteen. After that I was going back and forth for about fourteen years. I never found it hard to settle down back at home. Maybe if I'd stayed away for a long time it would have been hard. In the old time, back in the early 1880s, when my grandfather came to the island there were forty-two families. When I was going to school that was down to fifteen families. And then, in 1966, it was down to three families. And there were only three children going to school. So they had to close the school. The teacher at that time was Stiofán Ó Cualáin. He's retired now. When I was going to school I had nine different teachers. They only stayed maybe a year or a year and a half. There was one teacher who only stayed six months. There were a lot of female teachers. The first teacher that I had is still alive. Her name is Mrs Molloy and she's in her nineties now and lives out in Cornamona. I was only two and a half when I went to school. The teacher took me to get me out of my father and mother's way, because they had to work. I used to count periwinkle shells in school. And I didn't know the difference between the *naoineáin* and the first class. My aunt from Killarney wrote to me and asked me what class I was in and I said – 'the winkles class'.

I learnt to speak English in England. I spoke very little when I went to England first. It was a terrible disadvantage. They made a big mistake in the schools here that they didn't even have half-an-hour of English every day. They spent a lot of time teaching Catechism . They drove it into your head like you'd drive a nail into a piece of timber. They should have had more English and less Catechism. We didn't learn much history or geography. It was out of order. They didn't teach it right. The children were brainy and should have had better opportunities. If they'd got the real thing from the teachers it would have stayed in their minds and they wouldn't have forgotten it. The boys and girls went to the same school. They weren't going to *céilís*, so they didn't forget what they were learning at school. They were great. All they worried about was their lessons. They did their lessons at night when the adults were playing cards. And if you didn't have your lessons done you got a slap. I got plenty of the belt myself. It didn't even matter if the teacher was lodging in your house. You still got it.

I remember, there was a long belt left on the mantelpiece in the school, and one Friday evening a girl went up and cut a piece off it. She used to get a lot of slaps. So on Monday morning the teacher saw it and he asked us who had done it. We wouldn't tell him and the girl didn't own up to it. So two of us got seven slaps on each side. She didn't get any because we didn't tell. We wouldn't tell for anything.

There are eight families who still own land here, but they never stay on the island. They come to the island every day – sometimes twice a day – because they have cattle still here. I own a lot of the land here now because I bought it from people who left. And the houses they left are still in good condition. They were built very well from stone. In them days they had their own stone from the quarry and they built their own houses. They were very talented, the people on this island. They used to burn their own limestone too. They got the limestone from the

Máirtín Seoighe's home on the island

Aran Islands in exchange for the turf they took out there by boat. And they burned the lime for mortar for the house-building. They had their own sand as well. They sold sand also to the mainland.

They made their own clothes. They had their own flannel. You went to the weavers. They were in Carraroe. They had their own wool, well, most of it. Most people wore *báiníns* and woollen jackets. There were shops around here, on the mainland, selling all sorts. There was a little shop here once, on the island – Tigh Hiudaí. It was just a small shop that sold tea, sugar and sweets. It didn't sell any clothes. But there were a few good shops on Tír an

Fhia side. You had to go to the mainland if you wanted anything like that. The island was never really isolated, because you had to go the mainland such a lot. They grew their own vegetables on the island. They had everything. The best thing they had was fish. The shoreline was divided up between the families. The seaweed was also divided. They used the seaweed and the carrigeen moss as manure. And they sold the carrigeen and the periwinkles. They used natural cures when people were sick, although I don't know exactly what they were. I do know that they used carrigeen for colds. The best cure, at that time, was *poitín*. They used that for flu. And it's good to this day for cattle. If your cow goes down in a dyke, give her half a bottle when you get her out. I can't remember what else they used as cures. There were so many cures. For dyeing clothes we used the moss on the rocks. It's very easy to use – they used to boil it with the clothes. We called it *scrathach*. It's a yellow-green colour. And if they wanted to change the colour, they put something else that they bought in the shops through it. They were old habits. They had no *piseogs* here.

There were a lot of tradesmen on this island. Everyone was able to make their own house. And if they weren't able to make their own boat they were well-able to repair them. And they were brainy as well. The trades were passed on from father to son. My uncle was a boat-maker. I was too late to be taught, because everyone was gone by the time I was growing up. My father was at the boat-trade but he was dead. I would have been good at it if I had gotten the

Currachs at Spiddal

chance. My mother died when she was fifty-two. And she wanted to send me somewhere to learn the trade of boat-making. My uncle moved to live in Galway, so that was the end of it. I had to go on with what I'd picked up from my father. If he had been here it would have been easy to pick up a lot more. I'm too busy with the cattle and the hay to be thinking of making boats now. In the fine weather I have to fill the tanks with water for the cattle. There are plenty of wells on the island.

I used to build currachs. I didn't build hookers. They're very expensive to build and run. Those who build for the races build hookers and they can win a lot. I race in the currach. It costs a lot of money to bring the boat to places like Oileán Mhic Dara. And then you waste a lot of time. It's an expensive hobby. But it's a main social outlet and only for that we wouldn't have it at all. I built around six currachs a year at one stage. I built the currachs for Spiddal in 1972. They had two sets of currachs for racing. I made two to start with and they ordered six more next time. Spiddal is a lovely place for racing. You have to use oak to make a currach. You have to boil it to bend it. I had a big tub in which to boil the oak. You bend the ribs. You got the wood cut in the yard. Each piece was about five or six feet in length. The width was about an inch and a half. You had to make a piece to put around it to keep it together. That was the same for each separate piece of wood. You had to put white canvas on it then and three coats of tar, so that it would be thick enough. They use fibreglass nowadays. You would have to buy everything. It would cost you five hundred pounds to make one now. If you made a special one you could sell it for a thousand pounds. When you were making standard currachs they all had to be the same. I made the oars as well. You shaped it out – three inches by two inches. I made more oars than anyone else did. I still make oars. I was making them last night. I spend almost every evening at it. There's a very special technique to it. You put sails on the currachs then. The small sail goes on the front of the boat.

Making the oars has affected my sight. I use gas lamps instead of electricity. I have a cylinder of gas. I do this work at night because I have too much else to do in the daytime. They put stones in the boat to keep it balanced. There were particular stones and particular sizes. The weight of the stones depended on the cargo you were taking. Every family on the island had two or three boats. They had a boat for seaweed – a three-ton boat. They had a boat for fishing and a small boat for going to the mainland.

Oak is very important in the making of the currach. You use oak for the ribs inside, and you use white teak for the other parts of it. Oak is a better material. It lasts longer. They use oak inside every boat, it doesn't matter what kind it is. If you put a nail through oak you can never move it. The white teak is softer. If you put a nail from the soft wood through the oak it will never come out. It's a real craft. The oars have to be four-and-a-half-inches apart for rowing. I don't think that I'll make the currachs again. The oak is better than the teak. The start of making it is the hardest part. If you have the pattern you're okay. I've made about twenty, or maybe twenty-two miniature currachs and I give these away as presents. They're the same type. They make some in Aran, but they're only plywood. They're not real. I use oak.

I don't know how I escaped getting married. A lot of people that lived on islands never got married. In the past a lot of women wouldn't come out to live on the island because they didn't think much of the island. Transport has made all the difference now. Half of the islanders never got married. It was easier for the women on the islands to get married. The men who went to England got married. The women were good at everything in the house because they didn't learn anything else. And they were able to row a boat. So they had a better chance of getting married. I suppose they had to be good at everything. They made their own clothes and blankets. They made their own socks and dresses.

There were eleven in my family. A lot of them went to America. One was in America for years but came back. A lot of people emigrated, but some had to stay with the old people. I stayed with my father until he died. It was different on an island, because you couldn't leave them on their own. My own father was still able to row at eighty. He died when he was eighty-five. And his own father died at eighty-five as well. And they were healthy until they died. They always wanted to be outside. My father was here with me until he died. And the last family here moved out about ten years ago. There were big families here on the island. The average was about ten in each family. There were more in my family.

Emigration was sad at the time, but they had to go. Although there were those who didn't have to go, but just wanted to see the world. And then there were those who wanted to come back but never did. They got caught. I know that some people on the mainland didn't have to go, but they didn't think much of their own place and they went away. But most of those came back and settled down. They were glad to have it when they came back. They thought they would do better in America. I had to come back because everyone else was gone and I had to look after my father. I felt that I lost out, in a way, because I thought if I had stayed away I might have done better. If I had gone to America I think I would now be a rich man. My brother is in Boston for years and he's a rich man.

There's a lot of fish farms around here nowadays. They're farming salmon. Before ever the farms came there was a lot of fish around here. They sold the fish directly to the shops. They used to sell scallops and lobster. They didn't weigh the lobster at the time because there were so many of them. They used to sell them by the dozen. And you got thirteen to the dozen. They sold a hundred and twenty fish at a time – six scores. You'd get five scores now and they sell the lobster by the pound. You sell all shellfish by their weight now. They sold them by the hands first. They weigh everything now. When they sold the periwinkles they had ten-stone buckets. This place was good for periwinkles, scallops and cockles. The season for shellfish was from April to September. Everybody was able to fish, but I'm afraid it's going to change with the co-ops. And you have to get licences now. It's not here yet, but I'm afraid it will happen. There's a lot of scallops still here. We had the open fire to cook. That's the best way to cook a scallop. You can eat them raw. I don't like raw shellfish.

When the first people moved into the islands all they wanted was to build a house in a day. All they needed was shelter for the night. Then, after a while they moved and built a house further in. This was in the late 1700s. They might look around for a week before they came to see the easiest way to build a house. Most people started between two big rocks, and usually had three or four others to help them.

People were offered land in Meath from the Land Commission. So they divided this land between the people who were left on the island. The Land Commission swapped the land in Meath for the land here. There was a landlord here who owned the island. His name was McThomas and the people had to pay him rent. He was drowned. There's a place back there called Léim Thomáis and that's how it got its name. He was trying to escape from the people and he tried to jump across a wide channel and he was drowned. He was here before the 1870s. He owned three islands – Inis Oirc, Oileán Iarthach and this island. People paid him so much a year – around ten shillings. And that was a lot then. Two hundred years ago ten shilling would have easily been a thousand pounds. I don't know who was there before him, but a woman called Sinéad Ní Sheachnasaigh, in Leitir Móir, came after him. She lived where the barracks is now. She was the landlady. She married a Flaherty and had three sons. Cahal Flaherty was a Spaniard. He wasn't a Flaherty by right, but he changed his name to Flaherty. They're the same Flahertys that are in Carraroe now. His name was Cathal, or Carlo. He went out shooting. That was his habit – shooting rabbits, or whatever. Whatever happened he met a girl on the bog and he got her in trouble. He left soon after that. His name was Cathal Óg. There's a branch of the Flahertys all over the country. And that's how Cnoc Chathail Óig got its name. She was the last landlady of the islands. She wasn't that nice. She wasn't paying her people right. She was like Maggie Thatcher.

There's an island across from the church there, called Inis Ghainimh. She had that island there on her own. The O'Tooles had the island then because they were very friendly with her. And Kruger O'Toole used to collect the rent for her. And then, they got most of the land. That's how the O'Tooles got all their land. They used to change their name because they always wanted to be on the strongest side. And you used to pay fourpence. The McDonaghs were the O'Briens from County Clare. There were two sets of McDonaghs. The real ones and the O'Briens from Clare.

You have to go with the current. I have to go out early in the morning to go to the mainland, because the tide is with me. But you can walk out cattle at low tide. It's not an island for three hours during the day. But in wintertime, if the weather is bad, it won't dry at all. The boat is still the best form of transport.

Cáit Nic an Iomaire

A native of Sheanadh Phéistin. Gifted craftswoman and dressmaker. Lived at Costelloe where she ran a B & B.

My maiden name was Keady and my mother's maiden name was Joyce. And I was born and reared up in Knockadoagh. That's just up between here and Sheanadh Phéistin – up in the mountains, you could say. There was a little village there. There were seven houses there at that time, and there were a lot of young people growing up there. We were very near Glenicmurrin. There was a lot of youth there as well. There are only three or four families living in those two villages now. People nowadays want to live nearer to town. The majority of the young people went to America in my day and they stayed there. That would have been around 1937. The eldest usually went first to America and then used to send for the next one and the next. A few came back on visits and one came back and died at home. They went on boats from Cobh. None of my family went. We were quite happy at home.

I got married in 1934, when I was nineteen. There was a woman from our village who was married at sixteen and a half. It was a match-made marriage. A man would come with a bottle of *poitín* and make the match. And if he had plenty of land and a nice house and cattle the parents would be delighted to see their daughter settled down. And they may not have met him until the night before. They got married young at that time, because that was the rule if you

wanted to stay in Ireland and settle down. And marriages never broke up. My own marriage wasn't a match.

Any girl who got pregnant was sent to the Magdalen Institute, never to be seen again. It was cruel. If she had brothers and sisters they would 'get' the man and he would abscond to England. But in many cases, they didn't tell who it was. It was never discussed. Certainly the men got away with it. The choices were very limited. If you didn't have a boyfriend with land or a house to bring you to, the parents didn't like that, because there were no job prospects. I don't think parents ever went to the Magdalen House to visit their daughters. It was just a place you didn't go to. But I think after many years the Home changed and they were let out. They could keep their babies for the first year and then, when the babies were strong enough they were fostered, or maybe adopted. The men who courted the young girls were from seventeen upwards. But, at that time, even the men were afraid.

My parents lived on a farm. My father had a horse and cart and he worked on the roads as well. He used to cart turf down to the pier to send to the Aran Islands. That went out from Ros a' Mhíl (Rossaveal) and over at the Lodge. There's a quay there too. He didn't go himself on the boat. Sometimes they sent back dried mackerel if they liked the turf. They also paid in money. Everyone needed money at that time. Sometimes they gave limestone as payment. We used to put that into a kiln and burn it to make lime out of it.

I remember hearing how cruel the landlords were when

I was very small. They took everything away, even the potatoes, and the people starved. People used to hide things from them, like food, so they wouldn't find them. And if you couldn't pay your rent they burned down your house. The rent was paid in money. And if you didn't have the money they took cattle from you. I remember hearing that a woman over near Tully church had a baby. And the next youngest had pneumonia, and she was trying to look after the baby and the sick child and the other five children and her husband. Well, they came for the rent, which they didn't have. So they threw the mother and children out into the street and burned the house. And they were all dead in the morning. The poor father was devastated. They never even got a chance. The landlords were the Blakes. They were Protestant and they were dreadful. I remember hearing how bad the Blakes were. If there was a girl getting married in Tully church the Blakes used to take her and 'have' her on her wedding night before letting her go to her husband in the morning. As a way round this the priest

Cáit Nic an Iomaire

would often marry people at two or three in the morning so nobody would know. That was actually happening when I was a child.

But the Blakes of Tully never bothered us. We always had our rent paid so they never came near us. They called the place where they lived 'Caisleán' – or 'Castle' after the castle that was there. People were so frightened they didn't even want to talk about the Blakes. They were so cruel, especially to Catholics. There was a Protestant couple from the North that used to come and stay with me when I had boarders. And the woman was very nice. She used to say that the Catholics were lovely in the North but they were very badly treated. And around here, as well, there were other Protestant landlords who, like the Blakes, treated the Catholics very badly. There was a Protestant minister in Peacocks, and over in Oughterard and also in Spiddal.

The priests were very strict when I was growing up. They had to be strict. If they saw a boy and girl walking together along the road they used to give out to them. But they had to be like that because they were afraid the girls would get into trouble and have to be sent away. And parents were very strict with their daughters. If you went to a dance you had to come home with your own brother. It didn't matter if you had a boyfriend and your brother had a girlfriend. But if anything happened to a girl in my time it was because of love. They really respected each other and usually they would be going out together for ten or eleven years if anything happened. And they used to get married. The priest never had to call to any of the houses in our village, or the next village, or the next one after that. No girl that I knew around here got pregnant before getting married. The parish priest in Spiddal used to ask the girls getting married to produce a doctor's certificate, stating that they weren't pregnant. He wouldn't marry a couple where the girl was pregnant until after the baby had been born, so that the baby could be born to the couple. He was the only priest I ever heard of doing that. We were very conscious of religion at the time. You had to be on time for Mass. It isn't half so hard now and yet nobody wants to go to Mass. At Mass the men used to sit on one side and the women on the other. They weren't allowed to mix. And the 'aristocrats' had the front seats. They claimed them. There were people around here who thought they were better than the ordinary labourer. They weren't really 'aristocrats'. They might own a pub, or be a teacher. There was a lot of class-distinction at that time. That used to madden me more than anything else. So-called professionals were put on a pedestal. And you had to put them on the pedestal, because they put themselves on the pedestal.

I did dressmaking, but I was never trained to dressmake. I just did it. I took the knitting and the crochet from my mother. I was knitting when I was eight years old. I made my first dress, for a small girl, when I was twelve years old. I used to make dresses for little children. I got the gift from my mother. The way that I started was that my friends would ask me to make a dress for them and they would thank me. Then I decided that, because I was bombarded with this, that I would charge for it. And then I got lots of work and did it full-time for years and years. I enjoyed it. I used to design my own clothes and also my knitting and my crochet. Because of my eyesight now, I only do it for my grandchildren. My mother did it for just the family. I was knitting jumpers for all of Carraroe at one stage and I never took a penny for it. I'd be sitting up late at night, finishing jobs, when they'd all be in their beds asleep. But then I got wise.

We didn't go to Galway to shop, because there were no buses at the time. So you had to be self-sufficient. And it was important to make the children's clothes. I used to make everything for them, even pants for their Confirmation. It was, as I said before, a gift. My sister didn't have it at all. She could knit, but only simple stitches. It was a great pastime, especially during the long winter nights. We used to listen to radio before the television came. And the children used to sit around the table, studying. And they had no distractions, nothing to bother them. I made my own wedding dress.

My husband was working in Costelloe Lodge for years. So there was money coming in, every week, to the Bridge House. He worked for the man who built the *Titanic*, Bruce Ismay. His sons and two daughters used to come here. They were very nice to work for. And every Christmas they used to send a cheque to everyone who worked here. My husband used to fish with them and he'd mind the river in the wintertime. He was like a bailiff. It was like being on holidays all the time. He loved the life even though he had great responsibility. Mr Ismay came here around 1935. I don't think he came ever again. But Mrs Ismay came once again. She was a nice lady. She used to go down to the school with sweets for the children. It was a nice place to bring up children. But the river was on both sides and that was dangerous when the children were young. The Ismays were nice to us and to everyone around. They were well-liked. They owned all the fishing rights around here for salmon and sea-trout. There's a crowd of them now who own it. The Tooheys are living in the Lodge – Costelloe Lodge. They own that, but they don't own the fishery. That was sold separately. They bought the Lodge about ten years ago. They had an auction in the house. I wasn't at the auction. Before the Tooheys a syndicate from the North of England bought the Lodge. My husband didn't stop when the Ismays sold it. His job went on for a few years after that. Then the new owners wanted to move us out. It went to the High Court in Dublin in the early Fifties. And they built a wall between the river and myself so I couldn't get water. We

had to be out of Bridge House by the 21st of January, 1954, so we started digging the foundations for this house on September 23rd 1953. I was only about three years married then.

But I have happy memories of the Lodge and Bridge House. We could take all the fish we liked from the sea, but we couldn't fish the river. That belonged to the Lodge. The fishery was one of the best in the land. They were on constant watch for poachers. The salmon used to go up the river in November to spawn. If they were poached before they spawned the fish would be ruined. They caught lots of salmon. They used to pack them quickly. They packed them with rushes, which was supposed to be like ice to preserve them. They used to send them off to their friends in England, and all over.

I used to keep boarders at the Bridge House, where we lived, when they came here to fish. Major Carment and his son stayed with me for a week at a time. We had three bedrooms upstairs and a sitting-cum-diningroom-kitchen downstairs. We had three bedrooms downstairs too. I got to know a lot of genuine aristocrats at that time. Major Carment was lovely. He used to come up to the kitchen and talk to me. I used to clean and cook the fish they caught. You could poach it or fry it. We had a range. The Major would always thank you for what you gave him and would always praise the meal.

The Ismays are dead now. The son's name was George and he had two daughters. One was married to a Scotsman, who used to be out in the early morning, playing the bagpipes around the Lodge. They had bailiffs there during the summer, watching for poachers. My husband's name was Máirtín. He's dead four years. I remember being there at a party, when I was sixteen, before I got married. It was a great party. Like a local wedding. My father was the bailiff at the time. That's how I was there. My father's name was Bill Keady. My father and my husband knew one another really well. I saw him going down in the side-car and he was bridling the horse. He was with his mother and his sister and they were going to the Holy Well. And ever since that day I had a soft spot for him. I was longing to see him again.

After that a new priest came to Ros a' Mhíl, and he got the men together to act out Colmcille coming to Ireland. I don't think there was a Mass, but it was a great drama. I don't have the whole story on Colmcille. They say he came from Aran, in a stone boat. I don't know what year it was. They stopped it then because there was a lot of fighting. We used to have to go to the Well and say the Rosary at night. But all that is gone. Nobody ever went to a *céilí* in those days without saying the Rosary

Sean Thornton shearing sheep in Leitir Péic

before they went out. There would be five or six side-cars at the Pattern and they would leave them in Sean Ann's field. They used to let horses into the garden. Everybody was so nice then. And the summers used to be so hot. You'd be parched with the thirst and there was no water apart from the water from the lake in the mountain. And the householders would have to draw water in the day before for the people going to the Well. There could be a hundred people down there. And the night before they used to come from Carna and they used to stay listening to the music in Tigh Pheadair Mhóir. Very few went to Féile Mhic Dara in Carna at that time. The people with the bikes used to go. There are more that go there now.

I went though a lot of both happiness and sadness in my life, losing three babies and the last of them was stillborn. My husband went to England when he lost his job, and then he came home and he had a stroke. He recovered but then he had another stroke and fell and broke his leg, and a clot went to his heart. It was tough on him going over to England, but I had a brother there and

51

he was working for him. He'd come home after two or three months working there, and spend six months at home. While he was away I had the dressmaking to keep me busy. There was no social life at that time, nowhere to go.

Then I started Bed & Breakfast. Before long I had bishops and doctors and priests staying with me. And I had the Irish Ambassador to Australia. I hadn't time to think. I was busy making lunches and teas all the time. And in the wintertime I knitted and crocheted and made sheepskins. I cured the sheepskins myself. I used to get them from the butcher. When I was growing up I carded wool, I spun wool and I dyed wool. And I used to hang it on a tree to have it ready for the weaver. I dyed wool with the top of the heather. And I dyed it with the moss on the stones. I used to gather a good bit of it, out it into a net, boil it well, lift it up and squeeze it. Then I used to put it in with a good pinch of coarse salt, so that it wouldn't fade until all the dye was soaked into the wool. Then it would be yellow. The heather made it purple and *cosáinín* (carrageen moss) made it green. I would try anything to see what it was like. I'd try it and if it failed there was nothing lost. But it never failed.

I had plenty of sheep at the time. But then, when the children were all going to college, I got rid of the sheep. The skins cost me ten shillings from the butcher. There was a sergeant in Carraroe by the name of Lally. He used to bring them in to a shop in Galway and sell them for me.

When I got the skins I would take the meat off them. Then I would salt it. And I rubbed it well into the skin. Then I would leave it for two days, get it out and shake it off. And then I would put another dose on it. After another two days you'd wash it and the wool would come out lovely. But you'd have to put it out to dry on the line and you'd have to make sure the sun didn't get to any of the raw skin. And you let the wool dry. When that was done, and the wool was dry, you brought it in and pumiced it. And you kept pumicing it. There was a lot of work put into it. Everything was done before I dyed it. The way that I did it was – I got a lot of pegs and put it down in a tub and left it there for two days. And then I would turn it around and leave it for another two days. And I would put lots of weight on it so that it would be soaked up. Then I would rinse it and hang it out on the line. There was lot of work in it, but the winter was long.

Tom Lee

Born in Leitir Mealláin. For thirty years of his working life he spent six months each year in England.

I was born in 1910. I didn't hear much about the Famine, only that there are a lot of graves around here, where people from the Famine died. On the Western seaboard all the people fled to the shore because there was more food there – fish and periwinkles. But in the end there wasn't enough for everyone. Still anyone who managed to come to the seaside managed to survive.

There aren't any descendants around here from the Spanish Armada. As far as I know they didn't come out further west than the coast of Mayo. But a lot of Spanish traders came into the city of Galway, because Galway was well-known as a place of trade. There were several trades in Galway and you had people from Spain and Denmark coming there. There were boats coming in every day with cargoes of wine and gold and silver. That was long before my time, at the time of the Armada. The McDonaghs were pirates at that time and that is how they made all their money. They owned all the land around the port and they had a big, strong, heavy boat on the sea. And in calm weather the small sailing boats couldn't move so the McDonaghs would take what they liked from them. The story is well-known. There were a lot of pirates around here then. The McDonaghs used to keep watch for the boats at Slyne Head. And when the weather was calm and

Currach races in Ceantar na nOileán

they saw the boats coming, they were armed with guns, and the smaller boats could do nothing.

That was before they moved to Crappagh and set up a big business. Crappagh is an island of about one hundred acres. They owned all that. There was a man called Ó Direáin, from Aran, on the island when the McDonaghs came along, but he had to leave because he wasn't able for them. The McDonaghs were too strong, too powerful. They had money and boats and everything they needed to set up there. Thomas McDonagh descended from them. Monica McDonagh, Thomas' sister started a business as well on Merchant's Road. They owned Merchant's Road. They had the big store in Crappagh, but they also moved down to the bridge and they had that store there as well. Another McDonagh moved out to Geoghegans in Tír an Fhia. They had a bakery shop there and a store selling all kinds of ironmongery. They had a blacksmith and a baker working there in that shop. Tommy McDonagh was born in Crappagh, and he went over to Poll Uí Mhuirinn to start a shop there. But that shop caught fire, so he went off to Galway city and started another shop there. And he never saw a poor day after that.

My own family came from this area. My mother came from the Comerfords. They were landlords here from the early eighteenth century. You might say that my mother was descended from the gentry. My grandfather was aboard the *Brig St John*. He went across to America on it. The Lees were from Indreabhán (Inverin). They were Irish gentry. Then the Martins of Galway came in and got after them and they had to run for their lives. They separated everywhere. Some went back to Máinis. One of them landed in Carranthuathail, and that's where my grandfather came from. He was a Lee and he married a Connolly. Then, my father was Bartley Lee and he married Ellen Flaherty. Lee is a very common name around here, and so is O'Flaherty and McDonagh.

The bridge was built way before my time. It was certainly built before 1914. The Congested Districts Board was formed around that time to build roads and bridges as a form of earning around here. And so they built bridges and cleared passages because there are a lot of islands around here. And there was no way in or out except you waited for the tide to drop. So the bridges were very important. The towers were markers for the sailing boats.

Around here the fishing was very important. People were very poor at the time. They had nothing. They made a bit of money with the fish around here. They had buyers coming in buying lobsters and periwinkles. They never ate the lobsters around here. They had to sell them. The McDonaghs bought a lot of them, and sent them to Galway by boat. And there was a man from Clare, called Scuffil, who used to sail in here once a week to buy fish. They had a storage farm in Clare and used sell from there to England.

There weren't that many big hotels around here then, or indeed in the whole of Ireland. I'm talking about the years 1914 to 1936. They gave thirteen lobsters to the dozen and they cost five shillings. It was fairly hard work to catch lobsters. They had to put out the lobster pots and sometimes spend a long time just watching them. They also caught mackerel, pollack and another fish called *gurnard*. They saved that fish for themselves and salted it so it would last the year. Fish, fresh or dried, and a mug of milk, was their main meal for the day. They ate very little meat then, in my young days, but later they took to eating a lot more meat. When they got on a bit they had their own hens, geese, ducks and sheep. They used to kill them and eat them. And they made their own butter and stored it, and they had as much of it in wintertime as they did in summertime. They stored it for use. They had big 'butter jars' made from delph to keep it in. The bog was a great place for storing, but they didn't use it at all. They didn't sell much of the butter. And they didn't kill many pigs to eat. They reared the pigs to sell, because they got a lot of money for them. Potatoes, *gurnard* and a mug of milk was the main diet at that time. That was the main meal when I was growing up. My mother, and others, all made their own bread. It was a long while before any bakery started selling bread out here. The first one was Francis' in Spiddal.

I left school at thirteen or fourteen years of age. The school in Leitir Mealláin was a fairly good school. There were one hundred and twenty pupils there when I was going. It was a two-roomed school and Mrs Healy was the Principal. She was a native of Donegal. There were two teachers. And a few good scholars came out of that school. There were teachers, and priests and garda sergeants among them. One of them was my uncle, Anthony Lee. He was in the old RIC. And another was Patrick Connolly. They were both sergeants. And there was Fr McDonagh. And there was Mrs Connolly, a teacher and several other teachers. You couldn't go to secondary school around here unless you had the money to send your children to Galway. My father

Island fishermen from Ceantar na nOileán

was farming all the time. He had a few cattle and a bull, and he had sheep, geese, ducks and hens. So we didn't go hungry. I sent money home to help repay him for raising me. I was the eldest in the family.

I went to England first in 1936, and I worked there for a year. And then, in 1940, I went back to England during the War, and spent five years, working out in the wilderness, building aerodromes. I got married in 1939, just before I went out. And for nearly thirty years after that, I went across every year for six months. That's how I reared my family. I couldn't get work here. The only work you might get at home was five or six week on some 'relief' job coming up to Christmas. I went every year until I had a car crash and then had to stay at home. It was a hard life. I broke my two legs and an arm. It happened and I coming from Mass one evening. That happened in the 1960s. I spent six months in hospital. It was a lonely life going to England, but you had to do it. I had eleven children, a big family to raise. It was difficult for the family too. Nearly all the men around here had to go to England. Some of them stayed to fish, but you made much better money by going away. When I first went to England I rented a room in a house in Kingston. I paid five bob for that. And I was working for one shilling an hour which was fifty bob a week. For a pound I could pay for my digs and feed myself. That left me with thirty bob a week to put in my pocket. I sent that to my father, as I wasn't married at the time. In my family there were three girls and three boys. And one of the boys, Mike, died. He was fourteen at the time. I sent money home to help them. Most people sent money home. That was their motto. But then, unfortunately, there were people who never sent anything home.

It was tough going and leaving your family behind. I knew a lot of people over there, because there were a lot of Irish, and a lot from here were over there then. They were all like myself. They had to do something to raise their families. When you got a day off, you went out walking. But there weren't many days off. There were no social clubs in those days. But the beauty of 1936 and '37 was that beer was only four pence a pint. The pub was the only outlet. We used to go there at weekends – Saturday and Sunday evenings. We used to work fifty hours a week. It was long enough.

When I came home for good from England we moved in to my wife's father's house, and then I paid a man to build this house. The tradition at that time was to move in with parents, but we had started on our own, before I started going to England. We lived in a small house for a long time. There was no way to go to Galway until the buses started. We used to make our own clothes. The women made a lot of clothes, but the men's clothes were mostly made by tailors. We wore flannels in the summer. It was hot in the summer, but you had nothing else to wear. We bought shoes in the local shops.

We had no social life at all, only dances at the crossroads. There used to be dances in the neighbours' houses too. The parents were very strict on the girls. They might get out at the weekend for a dance, but during the week they were under strict control. They were kept prisoners. They had nowhere to go anyhow. We used to play football games. And we played cards in the wintertime. The women didn't play cards. We used to play twenty-fives and forties. We used to play for a pig's head or for a few pence. We had a goose at Christmas-time. There weren't turkeys in my time. The weddings were big events around here. They married locals, mostly. They were near-related.

Sean Mannion

A native of Ros Muc (Rosmuck). Remembers Pádraig Pearse.

The first time I saw Pádraig Pearse I was collecting hay at the side of the road with my father, and he came along and stopped and said '*Bail ó Dhia oraibh*' – 'God's blessing on ye'. You would think that he was a Connemara man the way he said it. And my father and himself had a chat about farming and fishing. Pearse used to fish at that lake there near the cottage. He wouldn't speak much, but he was a great listener. He used to speak to the shopkeeper. The shopkeeper, Michael McDonagh, was in politics as well. He had a shop in Ros Muc. Pádraig Pearse also visited the schoolmaster, Pádraig Connolly. He was a great Irish-speaker. My father was a carpenter, so Pearse used to visit our house whenever he wanted a job done at the cottage. When my father found out what sort of man he was he wouldn't charge him anything.

Pearse used to drill about forty to sixty men near the cottage. Young and old. School-age and pension-age. They didn't have any guns. They used to march up and down. I used to watch them from the side of the road. We were crazy about the piper who came along to play the music. I was only six years of age at that time. Everybody was in favour of Pearse. There was just one person against him. And that person would prefer to think of Pearse as a dangerous man rather than a good man. Then there was his brother Willie, who used to come down to the cottage

often with him. They used to stay for a month during the summer. They got on very well with the locals.

Lord Dudley lived in Inver Lodge. I remember him. He went to England and he didn't come back. Before that he used to come fishing for a month or two. He never stayed in the winter at all. He didn't mind the fact that the locals were in favour of Pearse. I think Pearse and himself knew one another. Pearse used to stay for a month or two. He used to leave often during that time to visit Dublin and other places. He visited Kerry as well. People here were certain something big was going to happen. It was as though they were training to capture the whole world. I remember the 1916 Rising, though I was very young then, between six and seven. Pearse was in the IRA. They had started before he started. During the War of Independence there was only one ambush around here. One Black and Tan was wounded. Most of the people here were afraid of the war. They were afraid of too much trouble in the country. They were afraid of fighting, because nobody wanted murders.

We were living in a very quiet place in a rural area and we got a big shock when Pearse came and spoke the way he did. I don't know if it was good or bad. Mentally Pearse gave the people a great image of themselves. He made them feel good about themselves, good that they could do things. The Land League Union was always in their minds and they wanted more freedom. The stories that people told at night were about what good you could make to the country. That was the mood that the nation was feeling.

They used to talk a lot about that. They used to talk about a miracle. A miracle coming and getting rid of the English from Ireland. They had ghost stories as well. There was a ghost in every corner. I could tell you one story about the place where I was living. There were only small sheep. And they used have to go fourteen miles into the mountain district to get wool. They spun it themselves to make flannel of it, to make clothes. This woman started out one morning, going fourteen miles across the mountain. She was coming back and this lad of ten years was behind her. And she looked again and there was no sight of him. And so she started calling him, 'Pádraig! Pádraig!' And then she saw him about twenty yards ahead of her at the edge of a cliff. And she went up and grabbed him down and brought him home. And the next day he was paralysed. And the

Pearse's cottage in Turlach Mór, Ros Muc

woman told the boy's mother that Pádraig had been taken by the fairies and an old man left in his place. But he was that way for six months. He had to be fed by a spoon. He wasn't able to walk or talk. One day there was a traveller going around and he asked for Pádraig. The mother told him what had happened. And the traveller said that that wasn't Pádraig she had with her at all. So he told her to go to any lake and get some bulrushes and put them under him in the bed. And the following

morning he was dead. He wasn't a fairy, but he was dead. And they buried him in the garden.

I remember Colm Ó Gaora. He was a courageous man. He was in the drill with Pearse, but he was only a young lad at the time. He followed Pearse's thinking. There was no other thinking. There are a lot of short stories from that time. A lot of the short stories were Colm's, on account of his being the leader then, locally. People used to gather in the houses and tell stories. Pádraig Pearse didn't go around much to the houses. He trained people and got on very well with them as well. He only wanted to have a chat with people along the side of the road, or that. He dressed normal. He wore a hat.

We were hardworking, growing up. We were happy. We used to look forward to coming home at the end of the day, to the fire and a hot cup of tea. I never got married. My nephew has the place now. And he's a great worker on the land. A lot of people have left. About fifty years ago a lot of the young people went away to America. There was only one glasshouse round here from the Government scheme for growing tomatoes. And it didn't work. They had no market for them. That's why all those glasshouses failed. They didn't make much *poitín* in my area. They were afraid of the police.

Piaras Ó Conaire

Retired Science teacher. Native of Ros Muc.

My father and mother were both schoolteachers. They met in Mayo, where my father went to teach in 1911. My mother was from Mayo. In addition to his teaching my father was a writer and wrote several novels and short stories. You can find them in the Public Library. It was embarrassing, at times, to have my father as a writer. I never tried to get away from it. I never wrote myself. None of the family did.

Now, my father worked, in those early years, under Conradh na Gaeilge, and his teaching work took him to many different locations around Ireland. In 1931, he moved from teaching to the Government translating staff, and was based in Leinster House, in Dublin. He worked in the same office as Máirtín Ó Cadhain, translating Governments documents into Irish. My mother continued to teach in her native Mayo. I was brought up in Ros Muc, together with a brother, by my paternal grandparents. There were four of us children. My brother and one sister stayed in Mayo with my mother. One brother became a doctor, the other a dentist. And my only sister died, aged nineteen, of flu. My father died in 1971, my mother in 1962.

My father often spoke of Sean Phádraic Ó Conaire, who was a distant relation of his. Sean Phádraic spent a lot of his life living and writing in London. Born in Galway in 1881, he had one son and three daughters. His daughter wrote a biography of him and the son had a business in Cork. His wife died in an air-raid, in London, in 1941. Sean Phádraic himself died in 1928, in the Richmond Hospital, in Dublin.

My father knew Pádraig Pearse very well. Pearse was a kind, shy sort of man, and a great teacher. You see there were special courses for national teachers in Ros Muc in the Thirties. They came to study and do a 'teastas dátheangach', so they could teach in Irish and in English. Mr MacAonghusa, Colm Ó Gaora and Tomas Keogh used to teach there. Colm Ó Gaora and my father got on well. Ó Gaora wrote a book about the Anglo-Irish War, called *Mise*. My father was a staunch follower of Pádraig Pearse. He was upset when Pearse died. My father was in the IRB, sworn in by Sean T O'Kelly, but he wasn't in Dublin when the riots started. He carried the 'statutes'. The Irish teachers did that at the time. They were involved in 'The Cause'. My father was never imprisoned.

We had a simple enough life growing up in Ros Muc. The Irish courses did a lot for the area, bringing in quite a lot of money. There would have been thirty to fifty students on every course in Ros Muc. And they used to have a *céilí* twice a week during the courses. People used also go 'visiting' certain houses. These were known as 'visiting houses'. They didn't have any music or dancing, or story-telling, they just chatted away, non-stop. They had no radio, nor television, nor gramophones. With the modern technology the language is definitely going. And

I remember the 'fairs' at Maidcho Walshe's. He had a pub, and a Shetland pony that used go to Maam Cross to meet the Galway train and bring back the barrels of porter. But there was very little drunk at that time. The only people that drank in the old days were the Guards.

They used to make *poitín* here as well. The *poitín* then was real, good stuff, not like the poison they make now. They sold some of it to the people in Clare and some to the local *síbín*. That was like an illegal pub. A pub with no license. The *poitín* was cheap to make. All you needed was the equipment and a big sack of barley. Some were caught making it.

I went to College in Tuam and after that to Galway University to do a degree in Science. I studied Agricultural Science and when I started teaching taught general subjects with a bit of Agricultural Science, but mainly physics, chemistry and maths.

There were no lorries here until the Thirties. That's why you had so many sailing boats in Connemara. They used to come across from Leitir Móir and the islands on the boats to the big shop in Ros Muc. They sold timber and ropes in that shop. And the boats used to bring back fish from the Aran islands. This was salted and used right through the winter. The only people who ate meat in those days were the Guards, teachers and priests.

In Ros Muc they had no hearses. The coffins, lighter than they are now, were carried to the graveside. They made them themselves here, from the timber they bought in Gairfean's shop. They laid the corpse out in bed with a sheet over it. The remains were always taken direct from the house to Mass and then to the graveyard. They had those women who used to do the *caoineadh*. Some of them were very artificial. It didn't sound very good and it was very frightening for children. And they always carried the babies. There were no prams.

There was very little 'free' when I was young. Some sort of 'relief' for very poor families. They gave free meals in the schools. And there was the 'dole'. Roger Casement, who loved this place and used to come here a lot, gave his own money to buy food for the schoolchildren. And he left forty pounds with the Bishop of Carraroe, for 'relief' for the school in his will. I remember the hurricane 'Debbie'. It blew down the dance hall here in 1961 or '62. It's frightening to think it was in September. The storms we have now would have nothing on that storm. Afterwards they built a new National School and the old one was used for Mass.

There was quite a lot of death here, between TB and various traumas. There were quite a few who died of TB and, before my time, they had a lot of diseases – like typhoid and typhus, tied up with malnutrition. But during the time of the Famine, my ancestor's potatoes didn't fail at all. I never saw wheat being grown in the fields of Ros Muc. They had small fields and sowed oats, hay and potatoes. Although there was no employment there was a lot of work. The 'rotation' system meant a lot of work. They had to cut the seaweed and spread it on the little fields and then sow the potatoes. Then they had to mould them and pick them. I saw women carrying dung on their backs to spread on the fields. The women worked on the bog, cutting and saving the turf. If you had your turf six miles away it meant a lot of trips to bring it all home. And you used a lot of it then, because you cooked with it. You had to kindle it at night, and leave a few pieces lighting, so you could start it again in the morning. They were always up to go lobster fishing in the early morning. A fellow used to come from Clare, by boat, to buy the lobsters. In Carna they used to go to the railway station in Recess to send them off.

Leitir Meallán Festival: Formerly used for transport and fishing, hookers are now mainly used for racing and leisure sailing

There was a great drowning tragedy in 1908. My father was a survivor. There were five drowned, including the owner of the boat and his wife and child. It was a fine autumn day when they left Gairfean Pier. And the following year there were six drowned. Then we had a murder case in Ros Muc. I knew the murderers and the murdered man well. There was a book published recently about it. There was this man who used to visit Mrs Walsh and it was claimed it was him and Mrs Walsh who killed her husband. His body was found, three miles away, near the guards barracks, in Ros Muc. They'd never have found him, only he had two sisters in America who heard rumours about him. One of the sisters came home and started the whole thing going.

There was no such thing as tablets. If you were feeling low you had nothing to take but a glass of *poitín*. There wasn't a dentist either. You had to go to Galway to have a tooth out. There was a dentist, by the name of Miller, back in Cashel, and he came to Ros Muc once a month. And there was a man up here who used to pull teeth. He used to use a pliers, in O'Donnell's shop down the road. He'd have two fellows holding you down and he pulling them out. Some people used to drink *poitín* beforehand.

Nora Mc Cluskey

A native of Spiddal village who remembers selling at the Galway Market on Saturdays.

My brother Peter was the man who tended to the lighthouse. He had to fill the lamp with paraffin oil and he had to clean the revolving globe. You'd see it move if you were over on the beach. The lamp was erected there to direct the boats, especially the boats that come from Connemara. They used to come in with seaweed and loads of turf and stay overnight. They would go from here to Clare and Ballyvaughan, or such places, to sell their cargo of turf. Peter was so proud of his work that he would walk down to the end of the old quay every night just to see the light in the lighthouse working. The Galway County Council employed him. The lamp originally came from England or Scotland. And a fellow used to come over every so often to service and maintain it. Picture poor Peter climbing up his ladder to the top of the lamp, in bad weather as well as good. I forget what he was paid, but it wasn't very much. He might have been paid five or ten pounds every three months.

The pier was erected in the Forties. They got rid of the lighthouse when it wasn't working properly anymore, and they erected electric poles in its place along the pier. That was about 1965, after Peter had retired. He died in 1974. The light was a great guide for the poor souls that used to come in off the sea at night time. Spiddal was used as a

Nora Mc Cluskey

stop-over. They used to sleep on the pier overnight and go away again in the morning on the tide. They were making their living transporting turf and fertiliser and seaweed and fish. They used also bring in loads of goods from McDonaghs and Hynes in Galway.

It was a good old time and I growing up. Everybody was poor. But still, we lived and were happy. Even the doctor was badly off. The poor doctors were hardly paid at all half the time, because the patients had no money. There was a lovely man, Dr Loftus. I went to school with his daughters – Gladys and Lily, Kathleen and May. He was a kind man and, God love us, the payment he used to get! Often, just a sack of potatoes or a couple of dozen eggs. I remember his daughter, Lily, coming to my mother with some eggs, to put under a hen to be hatched out. That would give them chickens to rear. They were that badly off. And the poor doctor liked his *deoch*. They had just one boy.

We had a teacher by the name of Peter Greaney. His girls were at school with me too. One of them, Eileen, was in my class. She had the loveliest rich, red hair. The fishermen were always afraid of meeting her on the road, because of the superstition about it being unlucky to meet a red-headed woman, especially first thing in the morning. Wasn't it awful? There was Lily and Madge, Eileen and John Francis in the Greaney family. Everyone was fond of Peter Greaney. He came from Lochán, just down below the road there. He togged out Máirtín Ó Cadhain.

Canon McAlinney was another great man in the community. He started the *Gaeilgeoirí* coming here. He was a powerful, big man, but he'd fought in some war or other and had malaria. He used to get attacks of that very often. When he did he wasn't able to cycle his bike and my father used to take him round in the side-car. Whenever he was called to a dying person he would get this awful fear that he might not arrive in time to give them the Sacrament before they died. It was very important to him that the dying should be anointed. He gave a lot of work locally. The stations of the cross were erected by him with the help of my two brothers and Cóilín Walsh's father and Mike Hanley's father. Ned Walsh was very handy. He used to make the loveliest stone walls you ever saw, like outside the big shots' houses. The Canon had a lovely person for a housekeeper, an aunt of Nora Folan. She was a returned Yank. She was a lovely cook. I saw the brown bread she baked and it was a marvel. She was with him a good many years.

No more than the doctors, the poor priests never had much either. There was no collection in the church at all at that time. But when a person died at home there would be a table left out and everybody would contribute something. Usually it was half-a-crown or ten shilling. The rich might give a pound. It was hard on the priests. They'd charge for a wedding – not much – five or six pounds. I remember the Canon saying that some poor people couldn't even afford that.

There were all thatched houses then around here. I don't like the reeds they put on houses now. The reeds don't last as long as the straw. Very few had a trade at that time. My father had a side-car and used to take passengers to town. He also had a cart and used to do a lot of work for the Canon. We ate well on potatoes, vegetables and fish. We might have meat on Sunday. My parents reared two pigs at a time. One for killing, the other for selling. They'd always kill for St Martin's day in November. They used to spill blood for St Martin. They'd kill fowl as well. It must have been an old Celtic superstition.

My father used to sit in from the door and could tell the time of day by the way the sun shone. That was his clock. And when the cock crowed in the morning it was time to get up. People used to get up very early and go to bed early. They'd be tired and there was no electricity, only the oil lamps. They were expensive to run, especially in the winter. There were no prams in my young days. I remember when my mother used to go out working in the springtime. She'd have a basket with food in it. And she'd bring a can of tea. And she used to carry me in a basket on her back. 'Twas tied in with her shawl so it couldn't slip. And it used to be warm. There was a canopy on the basket. 'Twas a rocking cradle. Women going out to work in the fields or on the bog would have to take all the children with them, bag and baggage. We were always warm, because it was all woollen clothes at the time.

The shop belonging to Francis' was more a bakery in my time. We used to get a lovely 'high loaf', which was brown top and bottom. You'd put country butter and jam on them, hot. The country butter was beautiful. I used to make butter. That's another thing I've lost, the platters I used to have for making the print. They disappeared. And another item was a round piece of timber with a flower carved on it to print on the butter. I don't know for the life of me where they've gone.

I used to go into Galway on Saturdays. There was a woman there on Dominick Street and she always took the butter and eggs from me. She was Michael O'Flaherty's sister. I went on the side-car, but there were women who used to walk from here, carrying heavy baskets. Quite a lot of people in Galway City spoke Irish at the time so there was never a problem with the language. The O'Flaherty's people came from Ros a' Mhíl. They had a motor-car company and a funeral parlour as well.

I used to take part in plays. They were always play-acting around here. There was one that stands out in my mind for all the fun we had doing it. Bab O'Donnell, God rest her, Ciarán Mac's mother, Mary Kate's mother and uncles of the Johnny Báns were all in it with me. And Sergeant Cullinane was also in it. We rehearsed in Máirtín Mhichilín's house. In the play I was a maid for this widow woman. She was played by Mary Kate's mother and she fell in for money from someone who died in the States. It finished up, anyway, that it was all a fake and the whole thing fell asunder. There was a 'thick' in it, played by Pat Sheáin Tom, the Lord have mercy on him, and I had great fun showing him what to do. I was dressed up in a black and white apron, telling him how to behave in a lady's house. His mother, then, was the lady in the play. And I'd stand him there and tell him that when he left the room

Mike Molloy and donkey and cart

he was to bow. He hadn't a clue and there wasn't a pick on him. He'd make a cat laugh. He was very jolly. We had great times. That was the main social life for us at that time. Then, after the plays were finished, we'd be looking forward to the *Gaeilgeoirí* coming. They stayed two months, July and August, and I wouldn't be surprised if there were a lot of courtships started there.

After the First World War there used to be boats going out and blowing up the mines. I used to be afraid of my life at first. I thought it was thunder. Some of the mines were out there between the pier and the Clare coast. There was one mine that got into Lochán Beag and killed some people. There was only one survivor. He was a Faherty. He went to the States after, but got married to Biddy Ned when he came back. I remember the day of the blast well. It must have been the early Twenties. It was a Fair Day in Spiddal and we were living down in the thatched house at the time. We had jugs on an old-style dresser and the jugs came down flying and broke on the floor, when the mine exploded. It shook so much.

I remember the Black and Tans. I remember it was a summer's day. And there was a crowd on the bogs. About two or three lorry-loads of them came down from Moycullen. And maybe they saw people running, but they left the mountains and came down when they saw them. There was a donkey on the bog road and they couldn't shift it, so they tied it behind the lorry and pulled it. And the same day they came into Canon McAlinney's house, through the back door. And just a short time before he

The Lodge, Spiddal, currently owned by Bríd and Martin Lally

had cleared off out to the gardens. Only for that they'd have done him in. Didn't they do in Father Griffin. Father Griffin used to come and stay in the Canon's house for a week or a fortnight. And he was to come up to my brother's for the fishing rods, and he never came. Well, the Tans killed him. He was living in Galway with another priest and two of the Tans, dressed up as women, came on a side-car for him. They said there was a woman dying and they wanted him to come and anoint her. So he went with them in the car. They brought him out to Lenaboy, where they were staying, and killed him. My father saw him laid out in St Joseph's church. They used to be going around at the time, mad with the drink, looking for trouble. Another time they took Steve Feeney's father's horse and mangled it there on the road. The poor animal had to be put down. They were bad. They put the fear of God in you.

They were very clever too, were the Black and Tans.

There was a lad killed up in the mountain in Barna. And the Tans offered a couple of hundred pounds for information on who killed him. This was their way of shifting the blame from themselves. And they buried him in the mountain. But there was a good night's rain that night and they hadn't buried him deep enough. There was a young lad going up to collect cattle next day and he saw the coat fluttering in a stream made by the rain the night before. And the dead lad was only a young lad himself, who'd been collecting cattle the night before.

There was a well, or a small lake, out in Tír an Fhia, called Loch Tan. And years ago, a rich man with gold walking-sticks was cured of his arthritis. He was walking away delighted when he thought of his gold walking-sticks. Because they were gold and so valuable he went back to get them. And when he picked them up he was crippled again.

Tim Johnny's was the pub where the Crúiscín is now and it had a bar as well before Tim sold it to Johnny Kelly. They used to meet there. And Festy Conlon did his bit for the Royal Film on TV that was made there. They had a lovely bit about the area and its traditions and lifestyle. They had a *céilí* in Máirtín Mhichilíns. May Standún was there with the band. And when Festy was recounting afterwards, for the Royal Film, he explained about Tighín Johnny and the Cattlemart. And he said, '*Seo é Tighín Johnny. Ollscoil a bhí ansin.*' Which means, 'That's Johnny's house. There was a university there.' Sure, 'twas indeed a university, where Máirtín Mór Ó Tuairisc, Máirtín Standún, Máirtín Steele and Máirtín Ó Cadhain graduated!

May Standún

Musician, music teacher and businesswoman. A native of Mullingar, she lived in Spiddal from 1946 to 1995.

A music session in An Droighneán Donn, Spiddal. From left: Donal Standún, Patrick Simmons, Johnny Connolly

The trip down to Galway was a nightmare, because I took the bike on the train. Then, when I got off the train I had to cycle out to Spiddal. And at that time once you came to Barna there wasn't a word of English. And I had never come across people like that. My sister Kathleen and I met Cáit Neachtain from Spiddal at the Gaelic League and she came to live with us in Mullingar. She had invited me down to spend a holiday with her in Connemara. I was totally unaware of such a thing as a 'Gaeltacht area'. And there was a crowd of kids playing 'Ring-a-Rosy' and playing with stones and I got down off my bike and asked, in my best Irish – '*An bhfuil a fhios agat cá bhfuil Cáit Neachtain?*' And they only clapped their hands and laughed. So I went on. And the road then wasn't like it is now. It was a real donkey track, winding in and out. And finally I came to the little cottage that's still there. Cáit was away that day, but her mother, Kate Ned, welcomed me.

After a few days Cáit came back and her sisters came from Dublin. There was a little shop owned by an elderly couple Mr and Mrs Murphy. I used to go in there for a few things with my coupons. And one day I was chatting with them and telling them that Martin, my boyfriend, and myself, were saving up to buy a little place. Mrs Murphy, who was a great sport, said, laughing, 'Sure why don't you buy this place?'

So I wrote to Martin that night and told him about the place. Eventually he came to see the place here in Spiddal and we decided to buy it, even though we only had fifty pounds as a deposit on it. However it worked out all right and we came to live in Spiddal, to run the little shop. We got married and spent our honeymoon in Dublin buying things for the shop, using the coupons we had with us.

I wasn't long in Spiddal when the secondary school started off. And there was a lot of controversy. Canon Donnelly was threatening to excommunicate people who went to the technical school over in the college. He said it was atheist and had no religion. Then the nuns came along and told me they were stuck and wouldn't be able to take any pupils if they didn't get someone to teach music. So I agreed to go along to the convent to teach piano and violin, two days a week. And I used to go walking across the beach, winter and summer, to a quarter-to-eight Mass.

After Mass I'd get a cup of tea in the convent and teach until seven in the evening. I used to be so tired, especially when Dearbhaill, our second child, was an infant. Sister Anthony in the convent was great. You see the system was that the nuns didn't pay me. I was paid directly by the pupils. And Sister Anthony would always help me get the payment from the pupils. 'Twas badly needed to buy stock for the shop. Sometimes if some of them didn't pay promptly we were really desperate.

Because money was so tight we had to be sure that whatever we bought in for the shop was really profit-able. We used to buy nails, and 'Drummer' dyes and knitting wool. We used to cycle into Galway to buy the goods. And Eileen, who worked in the shop, used to cycle in on her day off, to put the money in the bank.

Set dancing in Spiddal Village for Currach Festival

We had a great mixture of things in the shop. Things were still on ration. There was snuff, which had to be weighed on the scales, and there were a few cigarettes. And the locals, like Festy Conlon and Johnny Morgan would be watching to see if there were any lorries coming. And they'd watch for the 'Carrolls' being unloaded. And then the word would spread that the cigarettes had come in.

You'd have to ration them out. And five 'Woodbines' would be the most you would give to any one person.

There was a lot of singing, but there was nobody who played music very much. There was traditional singing. Ant O'Donnell sang and Seán Neachtain in the college sang. Peadar Shéamuis Mháirtín sang. Mike Curren of Park, and Pádraig Folan, and Peadar Shéamuis Mháirtín's brother all played accordeons. And Festy Conlon played the tin whistle. Pádraig Johnny Bán, who was only fourteen at the time, played the mouth organ, and was very good at it. So we decided to form a band, called Beanna Beola, and we bought a set of drums. Seán Ard played the drums. Our bungalow, where we also had the shop, was the *céilí* house. And there were no strict 'shop hours'. You could come to the hall-door at twelve o'clock at night and ask for ten cigarettes. But then, you didn't just go away. You came in and sat down. And everybody played cards or sang songs, or played music.

Our band used to play at *céilís* over in the college. And we used to get a pound a night for playing at the *céilís*. And they used to go on until two and three in the morning. I remember well when we asked for more money – one fifty or two pounds. I was terrified. And the priest left the money in an envelope for me. And we all got the same amount. One fifty or two pounds, I can't remember exactly now. For me to get that much money was great. It meant that Martin and myself could invest in stock for the shop.

I remember we applied for a phone at that time, because we needed it for the shop. Séamus Ó Beirn's father was the doctor. He died young. He was married to a nurse. She ran the practice. The way you knew the phone then was – one ring for the Post Office, two for the Guards, three for the doctor. And we were five. If you wanted to listen in to people's conversations you could. But we had a sense of honour and we never lifted up the phone until it gave the five rings. And sometimes when you were on the phone you could hear someone breathing into it, listening to the conversation. And sometimes, he might even contradict you.

We had an open house always. Over the years, when Dearbhaill and Donal were growing up we had all kinds of well-known people come and stay with us. The Clancy Brothers, The Dubliners, the Keanes from Carna Strand, Mary O'Hara, Joe Burke, The Wolfe Tones. Mary O'Hara was very young at the time, only fourteen or fifteen, and she was playing in the Taibhdhearc in Galway. Like many others we invited her out for a night and she stayed a week. I can remember her playing hurley with Eamonn Johnny Bán, in her bare feet. She was afraid of spiders.

The only thing we ever bought on hire-purchase was a sewing machine. All the sheets at that time were made out of flour bags, which caused an awful lot of trouble in the

Road races in Spiddal for Currach Festival

shop. You got the bag for one and sixpence – eighteen pence today. Anyhow, we got word that, with coupons, you could buy calico in Guiney's in Dublin. So off we went and got a roll of this, and started making our own sheets on the sewing machine. We put a big advertisement in the paper and everyone was buying sheets. We made money on that. We then bought in mattresses and Martin learned to drive and bought a little van. He'd put three mattresses on the roof and go out and sell them, and then we'd order more. But I continued to teach the music, all the time, even on a Sunday. I'd be teaching 'til ten o'clock at night. I used to cycle, with the violin on the carrier, to the Franciscan College. The music made a big difference. Otherwise we couldn't have bought the place and run the shop. There was a funny thing with the mattresses. When we had them in stock we used to give them to people to sleep on if they were up late playing music for us. And then, if someone came to buy a mattress in the morning, we'd have to wake them up and get them off the mattress quickly and plump it up for the purchaser.

My mother and father had no music at all. But they

May Standún

were always interested in it and from the time we were four or five my father had bought a violin and we were sent for lessons. My mother believed that if a child was taught how to play music they would never be poor afterwards. Every evening we did our half-hour practice. My father loved 'The Blue Danube' and the National Anthem and we used to play them, over and over. They knew so little about music, but they loved it. There was a paper that came out every week with a piece of music in it, and my parents used to cut that out and stick it on cardboard and put it before us to play. They pushed us a lot, but it worked. And they were so proud when we had visitors. And so, when Donal and Dearbhaill were small I was determined they would learn music because it had meant so much to me. And we got so good at music that my parents had to padlock the drawing room if they went out at night. Because we used go into the drawing room, open the windows and shout out – 'What would you like to hear?' – to the people passing on the street. And we'd play tunes to the people on the street.

When we came here to Spiddal, the coffins were brought down on a horse and cart. And there would be the women with the *caoineadh* at the funerals. So we bought a station-wagon and turned it into a hearse, and used it for funerals. And in between funerals we used the hearse to take export parcels – mail order stuff – to the Post Office. And people down from Dublin were either horrified or amazed at our using the same car for funerals and bringing parcels to the Post Office.

Peter Mhichael Lydon

Retired Caretaker/Bailiff of that part of the Spiddal river owned by McDonaghs. Native of Spiddal.

There were six children in my family. The other three boys are dead and the two girls are alive. One of them is in England and the other one is in Kerry. The one in Kerry comes home now and then, but the one in England never comes home. They're all older than I am, and that's old enough. I'm not far from the hundred. I'm seventy-five.

I didn't go to school much. We had very bad teachers at that time. They were very strict. At that time you had to bring two sods of turf to school every morning. I often got ten slaps of the cane for going in without the turf. And sometimes the hand wasn't good enough. The teacher would take down your trousers and beat you with the stick. Some of them were fierce. The schoolchildren might have been wrong, but not that wrong.

There's a ghost near the old wall beside the cemetery. They were going to knock that wall, but they saw the ghost walking there. This was in the daytime. There were lads stealing apples from the tree outside the nuns' house and they used to see it every night. I don't think anybody has seen it recently. I never saw it myself, but I did see a ghost at the Ball Alley, where you turn up at Bothúna Road, at the bend. He was all black, like a nun, with no head to be seen and making no noise at all. I remember speaking to him, three or four times, but he didn't answer.

Peter Mhichael Lydon (left) and Taimín Tom Mhicil (right) in the Crúiscín Lán pub in Spiddal

There was another lad from the village with me at the time, Patsy Tim. That could be over sixty years ago. I heard that a lot of people had seen that ghost there. And that he was one of the Morrisses. It could have been the one that committed suicide.

There used to be pitch and toss and betting at the Ball Alley too. We mostly played 'heads and harps'. You'd throw up two ha'pennys and if they landed on what you'd betted, which would be heads or harps, you'd win. Everyone couldn't win. And the racket started when Máirtín Thornton used to have two special ha'pennys with harps on both sides. But people copped on to that real quick.

I didn't do much courting in my younger days. They didn't like me. That didn't bother me. Do you know what the Yank said? 'Dead man, no good. Dead pig, some good!' I used to go to the dances years ago in Coláiste

Chonnacht. That was about forty years ago. There was a girl from Barna going there at the same time. She never got married herself. But if she didn't see me inside, she would sit down at the door waiting for me. And if I came and she wasn't in yet, I'd sit down and wait for her. She never got married and we never went out together. We were a year talking and dancing and we never went out together. I had no bicycle or anything at the time and the journey was too long for me.

We had no money in those days, so we didn't go into pubs. The pubs didn't make much money in those days. When two men from Indreabhán, who had come back from America, bought the Crúiscín Lán, they only paid £6,000 for it. That was in the early Fifties. They were bartenders and had run two pubs in America. I never went to America. I never even went to Dublin. They tell me it's a big place. But I've no interest in travelling at all. Not even to town to Galway. I'd be more tired coming home from walking than from a day's working at home.

I gave up the basket-making a few years ago. There was no demand for them. We then started the lobster pots. And I advertised on Radio Connemara. And we got a call from the Aran Islands. He asked me what kind they were and I said they were the same as the old porter barrel. So

A lobster pot

he asked me to send him a few. And I sent him a few and then I got word from him that they weren't right. So I told him to keep them for half-price. They're harder to make than the baskets. There's a hole going down into the middle of the basket where the lobster goes in, and that has to be made separate. Then you have to break bits of mirrors and put them into the pot. So that when a lobster comes along and looks in he thinks he sees another lobster inside and goes in to talk to him. Then he's caught. We used the rods from the mountain to make them. The people making them now are usually blind.

A lot of strangers used to come here fishing – French, German, English and all. General de Gaulle came here, and Dr Adenauer was over here with me for a few days. This girl who organised it told me that we were the only people in Ireland who knew that the doctor was coming. I was waiting for him all week. And he came on a Friday and he went up the mountain and then he came down again. Then we went down and he put his camp down on the bank of the river. I showed him the river and I gave him plenty of time and we went out at ten o'clock fishing. That would have been thirty years ago. And when we were finished we left the fish out on the shore all night outside the camp. And the next morning when we came out the dogs had eaten them. And all the doctor said was 'Surely no foolish animal ever took salty fish!' We found the heads over at the house where the dogs had left them. Dr Adenaeur died a month afterwards. His wife and two daughters were with him and they all camped. The daughters were at school in England and had very good English. But his wife had no English at all. General de Gaulle didn't come up here at all. He just passed through.

Another man who came was the Scottish financier, John Sheehan. He came during the War, just for a week. He was a lovely common man, but a great gentleman. He used to come down to the kitchen in the morning in his pyjamas, and Mrs Flaherty didn't like that. We'd fish for two hours in the morning, from ten 'til twelve. Then we'd clear up. Then he'd go and have a game of golf in Galway. And every evening he'd have a chicken and a half-pint of whiskey. He used no knife or fork or anything. He was a real gentleman. We used fishing rods not like the ones you have nowadays. You'd tie the rods with a belt until you were going. You had a special way of tying it and you'd have to cut the belt to open it. And, on his last day on the river, we got two salmon.

There was another man here as well. He was a Count and he was Minister of Aviation in Switzerland. He stayed back in Cashel, but came here for a few days to fish. And Pádraig Flynn was here last year.

I did go out fishing in the bay sometimes. But it was heavy work. Especially when you caught mackerel and hake, four or five together. You'd drift away from the shoal and it might be half an hour before you'd drift back into

Peter Mhichael Lydon fishing on the Spiddal river

them again. And you caught them as quick as lightening. If you had twenty hooks, you'd catch twenty fish. That was in July. A fresh mackerel wasn't put on a pan. You'd put it on an open fire, with a tongs, and watch it sparking. It's better than any meat, to eat it like that. I used to take off the head and tail.

There was money to be made from *poitín* at that time. You could drink it then. It was good. There was nothing in it except the barley, the yeast and the sugar. Now they're putting too much through it. They're putting metholated spirits in it and parazone. The parazone is lethal. I asked someone recently how they keep the stuff clean. 'You get a drop of stuff from the chemist,' he said. There was a time when a man and myself drank a gallon and a half of *poitín*. The real stuff, before they started adding to it.

John and Corrine Millard

Residents of Kenya. Inver Lodge in Ros Muc was their summer home for many years.

The history of this house is that it was built by O'Hara. And he took on the fishing as a project not to fish but to sell the letting of the lakes and rivers. It was leased to the Martins of Ballinahinch. He started building in 1835 and the Famine was in 1845. So it gave jobs to people during the hard times. It was finished in 1940. Every brick and timber and mortar was brought over by boat from Galway. There was no road at that time. The boat came in over at Cill Chiaráin and the cargo was then manhandled on to these little row-boats to come over here. Scríb belonged to the Berridges. They bought it from the Martins. And the Berridges had it for some time. And then there was Lord Dudley and his antiques. He was a Lord Lieutenant and he had a place in Dublin. He came down for the fishing season for two or three months. He had this place and Scríb. His wife drowned near Scríb, off the rocks. There are a few ideas about that, because he was living here with Gerty Miller, the music-hall star. When we came here there were something like twenty or thirty models of fish pinned on the walls, and underneath a lot of them – 'Gerty Miller caught this'. The corrugated iron bungalow was built for the staff. Then Lord Dudley had it.

After that Captain Wheeler bought it. He had done a lot of travelling in the East and in India. He was a quiet

Corinne and John Millard outside Inver Lodge

man. He didn't really associate himself with the locals. My father bought this place from Captain Wheeler in 1941. Then he sold part of it to Guinness and we took over the remainder.

When my father bought it in 1941 there were the entire two river systems, thirteen lakes – all holding trout and salmon – twenty-six thousand acres of land and five houses. He paid six thousand pounds for it. People thought he was mad. It was during the War and they wondered why anyone would want a big place like that. My mother was mad for fishing. She wanted a place of her own. So my father bought this place. My mother drove down with my sister and I. I was just a child at the time. My father was too busy to come down, so it was quite a challenge when we three women came down on our own. We had no phones or electricity or radio.

When we were finished unpacking my mother said, 'Now girls, into your overalls and go and weed the dining room'. And she was serious. There was no damp-proof course here and there were things growing in the dining room. It had just been used as a fishing lodge, in season, and then forgotten. When we opened the sideboards we found old sandwiches and empty beer bottles in there, left behind by the gillies and keepers. They'd had it more or less to themselves before we came, as the Dudleys weren't in residence most of the time. It was quite fascinating for us as teenagers and for my little sister. We used to run around the bushes in the garden and we'd pick up silver plated salvers, copper saucepans, bowls and things that the

shooting dogs had been fed off. The butler used to put out the leftovers, roast beef and vegetables, from the dining room. And we would pick up the most extraordinary treasures, china bowls and things of quality china. It was a real treasure hunt from our point of view.

We lived in Naas, County Kildare. My father was Odlums Flour and Oatmeal. It was a family firm. He had mills in Portarlington, Naas, Waterford, Portlaoise and Cork. I wasn't old enough to know if it was strange coming from Naas to here. We only lived here during the fishing season. And it was hard to come across to this house in winter, because it was on an island. We built a modern bungalow fourteen years ago, which has a lovely view across the lake and has a gorgeous view of sunsets. We are letting that at the moment.

My father sold part of the estate to Guinness because it was so big and needed so much management. He just kept the Lodge and three lakes. The Guinnesses had the Zetland Arms Hotel at the time and all they wanted was extra water for fishing for their guests. The Lodge was a white elephant so they were glad not to have that landed on them. They wanted the three lakes badly – Lavine, Corrine and Inbhear Mór. Guinness agreed to maintain the fishery.

We'd been struggling to stay alive with a big farm in South Africa and my father didn't think we'd take on this. So at his death it was offered to my sister and myself. And that's how we bought it. We bought it in the Seventies. We left the farm in Kilimanjaro in 1977. People mainly fished here for white trout and the occasional salmon. It was a natural run in from the sea in those days. They'd go up to the mountain streams and spawn there. And then they'd go back out to sea again. It was a natural turnover. Then these fish farms came and polluted the estuary with the fish droppings and the food they give them. The fishing is absolutely finished. Scotland also had the same problem, but they saw what was happening here and controlled the number of cages allowed in estuaries. We've no clean water at all now, and they're also using chemicals. And it has ruined people's livelihood. There used to be grouse shooting as well, but that's gone now because of the burning of the heather and the grouse's natural habitat. You'd walk all day now and if you were lucky come home with a couple of brace perhaps. So, sadly, that has gone, but it has increased the grazing for the sheep.

John Millard and Kevin Macken beside a boat used to cross over to Inver Lodge on its island. A rope foot-bridge is also used in summer

We didn't have many people coming in the early days. The times were hard. We had the turf-range fire and dark kitchens and paraffin oil lamps. Even when I was here in 1945. We were going back to London on an airplane and it got bogged down in the mud at Baldonnel. An ambulance had to pull us out. We used to come by rail during the War, which was pretty tough. And we came once in a gas-powered car, with a big cylinder of gas. And I remember, I went to Maam Cross to catch the train on the postman's side-car. But you couldn't rely on the trains. They were running on turf. My father never trusted the train. When we were resident in Naas he used to ride on his horse to the train station at Sallins, and his groomsman used to follow on the bike with his bowler hat and his umbrella. Then my father used to take the bike and put it on the train, and the groomsman would take the horse back home. The train usually broke down, so my father would have to cycle half the way to Dublin to the Bank of Ireland. Then, at night, the groomsman would ride out to meet my father coming back.

Lady Dudley started the District Nursing here with the Lady Dudley funds. The clinic was halfway to Ros Muc. And then she came in here because of the pressure. The Dudleys weren't landlords, they didn't have tenants. Lord Dudley was the British Governor General in Ireland, with a house in Merrion Square. He used to come down here during the summer and bring his staff. It was different around here. There were no estates here. Only Scríb and Inver. It was a different set-up here, with no tenants. The owners here employed people to work for them. Crumlin Lodge is about five miles outside Spiddal and is owned now by Patrick Helmore.

I went to Wales first of all to school, and then to England. And when we bought this place I was working in London, and the War was on, and I was working underground. It's a pity that the fishing has all gone now. We kept the fishing private. We never let out any boats or fishing, because once you start that you have to maintain it, and have gillies standing by, and then people may not arrive. It's not a very peaceful situation. We used to have gillies employed. Now, all the fish have gone. We have plenty of bog on our land and we cut turf. We couldn't keep animals, because there wasn't enough grazing or dry land for a horse. There's a wonderful island on the Corrine lake, which isn't ours anymore. But it has a wonderful bungalow on it. And we used to sleep on that island when we had it. My daughter's birthday is the 21st of August, and she used to insist on us having a wine party up there. And we used to walk up carrying wine and food and a bit of bedding. There were

Screebe House which is now a hotel

often eight or nine of us. We got a boat across and unpacked and ate and drank. Very often we couldn't walk home so we'd stay by the fire. Captain Wheeler built the bungalow for his mother-in-law, who didn't like it. She was an artist. So he told her he would build her a house with a beautiful view, where she could paint.

We had music and lots of books. By the time you had worked in the garden and fished all day, and had a hot bath and supper, you were ready for bed. And the next morning came very quickly and you started again. It was a real outdoor life. And then you had the bicycle if you wanted to go to the shop. Then the phone and electricity came. That was a big deal. My mother made our clothes. There was more time to do these things. We used to do a lot of sewing and knitting and painting and embroidery. We had locals in to do our cooking. We never live here full-time. We spend the summer here. And we go to Kenya in the winter, although it is risky there at the moment. And if we sold out we wouldn't be able to take the money out. We never feel threatened here. We find it friendly here. We came here after the Troubles. There weren't any problems here. This place wasn't vandalised. Colm Ó Gaora's place was.

Nicholas Ó Conchubhair

*From Leitir Móir (Lettermore). Brought up in a family
business which now belongs to his sons.*

My father came from the parish of Killanin, in Moycullen,
and it's almost one hundred and fifty years since he came
here. My mother is a native of this place. She was a
McDonagh, one of the great names around, locally. My
father was the first O'Connor to come into this area. They
had ten children, seven boys and three girls. They're all
dead now, except me. None ever migrated, or emigrated.
We had a farm. My father bought a farm in Dublin in
1910 or 1911. It was in a place called Ballyfermot. And I
went to school in Dublin. Two of my brothers, Peter and
Michael, went to school in St Enda's College – Pearse's
place. They were there for a year or so and then were sent
to Blackrock College. My eldest brother qualified as a
doctor and joined the National Army in 1922, helping to
form the first Irish-speaking battalion. He was a Gaeltacht
man with Irish, so he could understand all dialects. It was
unusual in those days to go to Dublin to be educated.
There weren't many academics down here in Connemara.

My father had a shop here and he had the land in
Dublin. We had a shop and business and in those days
there were very few cars. I had a 1923 model that came up
from Cork. It looked like a truck. It could take cargoes
from Galway. But the boats were the usual way of shifting
cargoes. We had a Galway hooker. She used to go to

Nicholas Ó Conchubhair outside his home in Leitir Móir

Galway once a week and bring out anything and
everything that could be sent to Galway by train from
outside. In winter months the boat might be weather-
bound for a while. So we used to send the car to meet the
train at Maam Cross. The roads weren't great. Most shops

had their own boat. McDonaghs had two. The first bridges between the islands were built in the last century – Béal a' Daingin and Carraig an Lugáin and Cuigéil.

People used to walk to Galway in those days. There was a story of an islandwoman who got up at sunrise and walked to Galway. She had a bag on her back and was home by sunset. It's thirty miles each way. I remember that woman myself. She used to nurse.

There was a place called Trá Bháin which was great for fishing. They used smaller boats there. We used to eat a lot of fresh fish when the weather was good. And we cured fish. We used to get a fish from the Aran Islands called bream, which was a beautiful fish. And we cured mackerel. People were great for curing. That was like salting it and drying it out for the winter. They'd last about six months but the quicker they were eaten the better. My father would buy those to sell in the shop. The most frequent food in our diet was the potato. A lot of potatoes were grown and eaten here.

In our shop we had everything – groceries and flour, meal, meat, bran and timber. We had nailed boots and shoes and *báinín* and white flannel, and braiding to put on clothes. And we had leather. There was another shop further down the road, a Mrs Macken. That had a bar as well. And she had a blacksmith's forge and a bakery. There was a coastguard station here once, but 'tis gone now, stones and all. There was one in Spiddal as well. And another in Carna and another in Baile an tSléibhe, in Ros a' Mhíl.

The family was divided. Some of them living here and some of them at the farm in Dublin. My mother was here and my aunt was in Dublin and my father was to and fro between the two places. My father sold the farm, eventually, when he got old. My brother Peter was an inspector in the Dublin Corporation, and Michael, the next fellow, was in Customs.

The only thing I remember about going to school here was one of the teachers, called Catherine O'Toole. She's a hundred years old this year and still going well. There was an old custom that we used have to bring a sod of turf to school. They spoke Irish and English in the school. Back in those days they weren't even talking about advancing the Irish language. It was all English. Even when I did my Leaving Cert in Dublin it was supervised by Protestant ministers. It was still under British Rule. That was 1920. We had a Protestant church here at one time. Nicholas has a shop in it now. He converted it. The Protestants had a school here as well. And they used to give free soup to the very poor people, probably to encourage them to join. And some did convert, but it never really materialised. After the Protestants left the Church it was turned into a knitting centre. It was fitted out for these little machines. A lot of girls used to work there. It was there for years and they got modern machines. And some of them had machines at home and used to bring the work home.

I inherited the business from my father. I remember the First World War. That was the first time that things got scarce. Flour got very scarce. Things like boots and shoes advanced in price. Of course the Second World War crowned it, because prices doubled and trebled. And everything was rationed. You had coupons for sugar and tea and that. In 1941, you were only allowed half-an-ounce of tea for each person for a week. Where you had young children in a family things weren't too bad, because they had an allowance but weren't using the tea. But where you had one or two adults on their own it was very difficult. There was a lot of racketeering and marketeering going on. Everything was scarce, except money. Money was plentiful, but there was little to spend it on.

I remember, as a child, taking the train from Maam Cross to Galway. They say when that railway was being planned that the Killanins from Spiddal wanted to bring it along the coast to Derrynea and Costelloe and then shoot it up to Ros Muc. Instead it ran through Maam Cross to Recess. It failed because there weren't that many people living in those areas. The railways failed down in the South of Ireland for the same reasons. There was one in Loughrea. It was the Tymon branch. It was only twenty miles long and it lasted a long time. When there was no train the boats did a harvest collection. Then, when the trains came the boats lost the business. And in turn, when the lorries came along, the trains went wallop. That's how it all happened.

Some of the cargoes were too big for the railway so the boats had to be used. There was a big boat called *Máire an dá bhata*, because it had two masts. And that used to go to Galway. And that was how my father used to go to Galway. And that boat used to take paraffin oil in barrels, because there was no electricity at that time. And she used to bring in timber and herring in barrels. She used to be loaded down. One day they met this other boat near Black Head in County Clare, and the crew had tapped some of the barrels and drunk the porter. They were all lying around drunk. The next day when they were coming back they saw the same boat and this time, my father said, the crew were all sound asleep on deck, and the boat floating around. The publicans hardly ever got a full delivery, because their barrels were always being tapped. They could see where the barrels were being re-pegged but they could never prove it.

Poitín was plentiful around the area at that time. It was

Hooker near Carraroe

made in a lot of houses and it was lovely stuff. Anyone could drink it, it was so good, not like the stuff they have today. They put all sorts of chemicals through it now. In those days they were very honest fellows and were so careful making it that it took six weeks to make. And you could test it. The priest used to test it. There used to be lots of *poitín* raids here. There was a sergeant here by the name of Gleese. He came from Monaghan. And he used to say: 'They're the loveliest people here, but they're ruined by that stuff they make. You won't get anywhere in the world where they're as straight and honest.' He tried everything to get them to stop. And the DI did too. Youngsters started taking it in the end. The old people used to give the children a taste of it if they were at a wake.

In those days they used to make the coffins themselves. The carpenter would come. And they were very nice and simple. They also did the burying themselves. And the relatives used to help. They had big wakes beforehand. They used to have two nights in the old days. It was terrible rough. Then the priest persuaded them to bring the remains to the church for one night, to give them a rest. They used to stay up all night. Although some of them would have to retire. And they use to do the *caoineadh*. It was an old custom. Every woman that came in was expected to cry. Some of them were great criers – champion criers. And they used to come without an invitation. It was ridiculous, the *caoineadh*.

I remember the IRA. I was in the IRA. I was very young. I was about seventeen. I used help them collect money. And the houses here used to give them shelter. I didn't wear a uniform, because I had to be discreet. I was looking after people who were spying. And the police came here one morning at about five o'clock. My father didn't like the IRA, because he was in the Old Irish Party. But he agreed with me in a way. After a while the Auxiliaries came on the scene and they asked us where we were from. When we told them, they said, 'Oh, go home, sure we're just after being down there having tea with your mother!' The Black and Tans weren't too bad around here, because we had a lot of Loyalists and Protestants in Galway. I stayed with the IRA until the Truce. And after that, I didn't take sides. My brother was the doctor in the Irish-speaking regiment of the Army. He was in Macroom when Michael Collins was shot and was supposed to have attended to him.

I was sixty-seven when I retired. It was a hard life running the business. You were always on your feet, always on the go. I had the Post Office as well. I divided my business between the two boys. I have four girls and two boys.

Peter Canavan

A blacksmith in the family tradition. Native of Cill Chiaráin (Kilkerrin).

I was seventeen years in America. I was in California – I was in Santa Cruz. I went to America to live in 1974. I went on holiday, but I liked the country so much that I stayed. But I used to come home every year. All my family were grown up at that stage. I was working in America. I worked for about ten years in nursing homes. My wife had died in 1969, so it was lonely here on my own, with my youngest son gone to England. I came home five years ago. My family originally came from here.

A lot of strangers have come into Cill Chiaráin now and a lot of the older generation have passed away. There used to be the Nees here. There are none left now. There were a lot of Cooves in Cill Chiaráin, but they're on the decline as well. And my own name, the Canavans, were here. There aren't many left now. And there were the Walshes as well. There's still a few of them around. And there were the Connerys. Emigration is the main reason some names are gone. There were large families then, and they brought them up well. But they still had to emigrate to get work.

I grew wheat during World War Two, but wheat used to take an awful lot out of the land. The land would need ten years to recover after a year of wheat. The barley also takes a lot out of the soil. They use it the easy way now, for grazing for the cattle. You wouldn't even get a cock of hay off it now. When I was young we had to milk cows. You were never idle. In summertime you had to bring the cattle to the lake to water them. And you had your lessons to do as well. But we were better off to have something to do. The people in the cities envied the people in the country. We had a better life.

My father was a blacksmith and knew a lot about horses. So from an early age I learned a lot about horses from him. As a boy, I'd leave home at three o'clock in the morning on horseback to be at Spiddal Fair for seven. We used to buy and sell foals. I worked with my father after I left school, learning the blacksmith's trade. I had to learn a lot about the horses' hooves. It took me three or four years to learn the trade. My brother also became a blacksmith. It was dangerous work because you had to handle the horses properly. And the customers were good. After paying you they'd give you a present too – maybe a bottle of whiskey. And some would leave you a drink in the pub. Before World War Two it was five shillings for a set of four shoes, for a horse. Donkeys were around three shillings. The mules and the ginnies were around four shillings, because they were very vicious.

Six bars of iron, a hundred-weight, was only nineteen shillings. A hundred-weight of furnace coal, which was slack, was one and sixpence. And you had a bag to go under the coal. That was another sixpence. You could go to the station to collect all that, or you could send your order with the hookers. That cost another four pence. We didn't go to McDonaghs. We went to Hynes all the time. There weren't any blacksmiths after I finished. Then the lorries came along. So we used to make the cranes for over the fire and the pot handles. And we used to do the iron for the boats. There was quite a lot of work in those days.

Then there was the whitesmith as well. That was my grandfather. He used to make the silverware, the knives and the forks and the spoons. And he used to make locks and keys for doors as well. He also made trumpets. He used to put a silver six-penny bit in the trumpet. He was really gifted.

I retired from being a blacksmith twenty years ago. The need for them was gone then. I had a lot of my tools stolen from me. I used to do a lot of work with the branding-irons for the hill-farmers. You put the initials of the owner on the iron. And you had to thicken the iron up. I used to charge two and sixpence for them. I did that work for a lot of areas round here. They used the irons for the sheep and the cattle. They used to put it on the hooves of the cattle. It wasn't painful for the animals. They still do it with sheep.

I used to go to Peacock's in Maam Cross for a drink.

Cill Chiaráin Pier (Kilkerrin)

You got three pints of porter there for two and six. Today you wouldn't have change out of five pounds. I didn't go that often when I was young. Though in our trade you lost a lot of sweat and you needed the Guinness. I never went out if I was working. My ancestors were natives of this place. Our surname has to do with the O'Flahertys. The Canavans were, at one time, doctors to the O'Flahertys. Roderick O'Flaherty was a cruel man. Out in Moy-cullen, in Auganure, they put people to death there. There was a death cell there. He had a castle there on Loch Corrib. He owned most of Connemara in those times.

The stories that we used to tell at that time, around the fire, were mostly history, about Oisín and the Fianna. And there was no television or radio at that time. They used to tell stories to the children, and it was fantastic. There was a man back in my village – Eamonn Burke. He was a great *seanchaí*. And so was Col Ó Lochlainn. They used to go around telling stories. And now *seanchaís* are making money in Dublin telling stories. And in those days they got nothing at all for it. Eamonn Burke was probably one

At the Holy Well on the Feast of St Ciarán, 9th September

people of Connemara. It was theirs. They put so much work into it. That's why they value it so much. They used seaweed to fertilise the land and to sow potatoes in. They built the walls from stones, because there were so many stones. The barley used for *poitín* had to be good barley. They used to thrash the barley with a slasher. They then put it into a barrel. And they used to make their own oaten-meal bread. You had an old mill-stone to grind the oats. There was a hole in the middle and you put the grain down there. And they made the stone coarse for grinding. They used to make the *poitín* behind the big mountain, Cnoc Mordáin, and out in Loch an Bhuí and Loch na Brocaí as well. Everywhere around here had names – the mountains and the hills and even the rocks in the sea. The people had brains too and knew where the landmarks were and where the rocks were. And the current is very dangerous. We used to say, long ago, 'Always look before you leave on your journey.' And those islands were very dangerous, especially at night. There was a priest here, a missioner from the Aran Islands, who condemned the *poitín* making. He burned all the materials for making it.

The landlords here weren't good. We had Lynch here, and we had the Berridges, and we had Dr Foreman. He had the estate here. You had Hazell as well. He lived in Cashel. And there were the Blakes. And they were all cruel. Those with the Bailiffs were the worst. And there is an old saying in Irish – '*Is minic sliabhach bán ag maistir saibhir.*' And they used to evict a lot of people from their

of the best *seanchaís* in Western Europe. A lot of the people living here in the mountains came, during the time of Cromwell, from Meath and Kildare. 'To Hell or to Connaught!' was the order then. The land belonged to the

A view of Cill Chiaráin Bay

land, though that was more in my grandfather's time. The Lynches were out here. They had a summer home here. They came in the winter as well, for the hunting and shooting. There was no church here in Cill Chiaráin until a little over a hundred years ago. And in Carna they have their church about one hundred and fifty years. Before that the priest used come out and say Mass in a house. There was a tradition then that any priest who died in the Parish had to be buried in the parish. And there was a priest from Louisburgh died here and side-cars came to bring him back to bury him in Louisburgh. And they blocked the horses, and buried him in the parish. They used to bury priests at that time in vaults in the church. The first priest to be buried outside was Fr O'Flannery. He it was who built that bridge out there about a hundred and fifty years ago. Then you had Canon McHugh and there was Fr Adams. They were all buried in Carna.

The Quay was built around 1835 or 1836 and the British Government paid for it. There was a lot of trade with the boats at that time. It was women who carried the stones to build the pier. They used the smaller stones for paving the quay. They had a canvas bag, like an apron, to carry the stones. That was hard work. They had to carry everything in those days. They had a saying, that the Irish used to carry the weight on their backs and the Danes used to carry it on their stomachs. That's why the Danes were called the *Fir Bolg*, in Irish. The Danes built Dun Aengus, in the Aran Islands. It was built in the sixteenth century.

People used to carry babies in their shawls in those days. Some men were very cruel to their wives. They used them as slaves. When I was growing up women were very

Mass at Maumean on the first Sunday in August

badly treated. They had to work hard, carrying turf on their backs and drawing seaweed. They used to have to work like that even when they were pregnant. Even as a kid I thought it was cruel. And they had to rear the children as well. They had the 'handy woman' to help deliver the babies. The doctors were very scarce. And there were no nurses until Lord Dudley's wife started the Dudley Nurses. The English were bad in one way, but they were good as well. And now, our own people are just as bad as the English were. Nurses are treated more like slaves now. And the matrons are terrible sometimes. I used to hear them roaring at the young nurses. But at that time, it was a way of life to work hard. It was accepted that the man could go out but the woman had to stay at home to look after the babies. Just like in the Arab countries. In the old days the couples always stayed together, no matter what. And they were happy. But it was the poor classes that always stayed together. They had no money. They had no radio or television. They only had the candlelight or the bog-light that was used in the fields. During the War they used a lot of the bog-lights. There was no paraffin during that time. You could get newspapers all right. We used to play handball, and we did a lot of fishing and camping out at night.

We also had dances in the country houses. They might have one once a week. And there was young and old at the dances. They had good music. And they sang a lot of Irish and English. A lot of the songs were love-songs then. There were a lot of songs that were composed about a hundred and fifty years back. We had set-dancing and waltzes. And they had the foxtrot as well. A lot of matches were made there, in those houses. The match-making died out, although sometimes it was good. Though most of the time it wasn't. They were looking for a dowry. But at the dances, if you picked your partner, you weren't looking for a dowry. You married for love and worked for britches. Before the church here they went to Carna, or got married in a house where Mass was said. That's where the tradition of the stations came from. And that tradition isn't being carried out in any other country. The St Kieran's Mass has been here since the time St Patrick brought the faith. All the missionaries that were here at that time were in the mountains. You have Croagh Patrick and Maumean. And there were the holy wells. St Kieran's Well is over a thousand years old. They built those, because that was the penance they were putting on themselves to keep the faith.

A lot of old people around here were able to tell things. They were able to foresee things. I remember myself, one time, not that long ago, I was asleep. I had been in the hospital in Galway, for an operation on my kidneys. The funny thing was that, in my dream, I dreamt that my sister in America had died. And when I woke in the morning my daughter came to me and told me that she had died. And because of the time difference in America she must have died about the very time I dreamt it. People were closer to nature in the past and more aware of things that were going to happen.

If you had arthritis or rheumatism you went to St

Peter Canavan

Kieran's Well, and the cured people used to leave their crutches there. And there was Tobar Mhuire – Our Lady's Well. The parish of Carna used to be called Moyrus Parish, because there was a well there called Moyrus Well. In Irish it was called Tobar Mhuiris – Maurice's Well. But that was Moyrus Well. It was back two miles from Carna village, at the end of the coast road. They had 'jumpers' there. There was a Protestant church there at one time. All of the 'jumpers' that were around this area were in Moyrus. That was in my parents' time. King was one of the 'jumpers'. He was the bell-ringer. He was a local. They were also called the 'soupers'. They were around at the time of the Famine to convert people into Protestants. There was even a time when there was a crowd going around kidnapping children and taking them away. The 'jumpers' in Moyrus didn't have a centre there. They were in Roundstone. There were none in Cashel or in Ros Muc. They were in Spiddal, but the natives didn't deny their religion, especially during the time of Martin Luther. And the Lutheran Church is still in England, America and Russia. Anyone who changed their religion around here was ostracised by the people here.

Dr Noël Browne

Retired politician and Government Minister. Great lover of Connemara where he lived for many years at Cloghmore.

We have friends that come to Connemara and tell us that they will never go to Connemara again. They can't stand the poverty, with the barren fields, and the grey stone walls, and the sparseness. That was what attracted Phyllis and I – that and the sea. I love the sea. I love to watch the sea. I go down there every day and watch her moods. We were interested in the lighthouse here. Lettermullan is a spectacular place. If you go out there, up to the top of the mountain, you can watch the sea come roaring in. And you can see across to Clare and Galway. It's very sad that people deserted the islands in the area, and that there are so many empty houses left there.

We look at Ireland as it should have been, with fourteen million people. And then we look at all those empty houses around us here. And we conjure up a picture of how it was. But they had to leave because the conditions weren't very good. They were probably offered better land. There was a lot of snobbery here too. We met a man and woman one day and she said, 'I'm a Mac an Rí! He's only an old Cawford!'

There was a good scheme at one stage by Dev, where people went to Rathcairn in County Meath, from around here. But this lady came back, because part of her family grew up here – the Mac an Rí and the Currens. She's a lovely lady. And they kept the Irish and they intermarried, like the Jews. The Flahertys all had beautiful hands. They could do anything. The father was a *fíodóir* and a *táilliúir*. They would have been great craftsmen. And that brings you back to Rathcairn, where they pushed the land on you. And I was saying that to Mrs Cawford, and she replied, 'Oh, they wouldn't come. They wouldn't leave here.'

We started making films forty years ago, on Medical Education, with Pat Butler. Now, there's this awful antipathy to the co-operative movement. They could do with doing a cost analysis here, because there are five tractors on this one *bohereen* and they could do with a co-operative movement. And the people here should be educated to see this. They could get so much more out of life, like Connemara West. Connemara West is full of classes and courses and lectures and furniture shops. You can only grow cattle here, but you can't fatten them. Frank Aiken came here and organised the putting up of glasshouses, and they grew lovely tomatoes. The glasshouses blew down in gales and, instead of erecting them again – like they do in Jamaica, after hurricanes – they lost interest in them. The other thing was, they had no heat. But Aiken was ahead of his time. And that's what they should have done in Connemara. They should have done the same with the language. They should have nurtured the language and grown out from here instead of the Breac- Ghaeltacht. The people here were all so precious, because they all spoke the Irish language. They didn't treat it as a special thing, in a special place. That's

A view over the bay and Leitir Mealláin Cemetery

changed now, to some extent, with the RTCs and they are giving those who stayed a living. But the old co-operative nature of Connemara has gone. They now have tunnel vision, with a vengeance. The neighbourliness has gone. They're living in the city now and building there. It's an ageing society now, here. You see the children doing well in education and then they have nothing to offer them.

I used to tell them – the Government – to give them money on an uneconomic holding. And they didn't face the fact. And I don't understand why they didn't take more people out of Connemara, like they did with Rathcairn.

Or go to Connemara and teach them intensive farming, because the people here are very versatile, they'll do anything. And instead of that they threw them on the dole, Indeed, they bred them on the dole. When I was a Minister I had a great interest in Connemara. And I remember Mickey Joe Costelloe. He started the Sugar Company. He was a truly great man in his time. I asked him to come down to Connemra to see what we could do. And we had different ideas – like growing food on the grass and cutaway bog. But we couldn't get anyone interested, because they were all on the dole. And then

Mickey Joe lost his temper with them and left. The whole 'freedom' experience has been catastrophical. We used to send our people with a one-way ticket to America and they got a job and stayed there.

Connemara was ruined because of that. They had this idea that it didn't matter. You gave them the dole or sent them away and that was that. But now things are different, are better, with the RTCs. They've created a new kind of youngster and there will be changes. We're getting quite different boys now, like the McDonaghs. They're never going to work on the land again, like their fathers did.

I'm the only Irishman in the Browne family. They all emigrated to America. Una, my sister, emigrated at twelve years of age, by herself. She went on the boat from Galway, when the boats were still leaving from there. She was mad angry, and she wouldn't look to come back. She had this sense of rejection. There was a lot of that feeling and so people never came home again. When Una went, an aunt received her on the other side. She became a nurse. But a lot of girls went out and were received by people they didn't know. They could have been used for prostitution. Many Irishmen died making the Panama Canal. And they wouldn't even use slaves for that. We're past masters at selective amnesia. In my own life I had the experience of a brother who died in the workhouse. They experimented on him during an operation and he eventually died. And it, so easily, could have happened to myself. In fact, I very nearly went to Letterfrack. However, incredibly, instead of going to Letterfrack, I went to be educated by the Jesuits in Beaumont, the other extreme. I can't forget these experiences. I got my education accidentally. Strangers asked if I would like to be educated.

The workhouse was very much an issue fifty years ago. I was terrified of workhouses. There was a black van that used to go round Ballinrobe and I was terrified of it, because I thought it was designed to bring us to the workhouse. But, in fact, it was bringing dead bodies to a common grave. My mother was, shortly afterwards, buried in a common grave in London. I was about nine when my father died, and my mother died when I was twelve. That was the last time that I had any family. And so the natural progression would have been to go to the workhouse. But then, these extraordinary accidents started to happen. These wonderful people came along and offered me an education.

I see Peaitín now – a local lad – and he can make wonderful boats. But, instead of that, he's full of diesel oil. And I feel that he should be an artist of some kind. He should be working with his very gifted hands. And that's a great loss to society. The arts are another thing. There's very little here. In Galway we have nothing. And Dublin isn't that great. In Galway there's no College of Art. And it's a very wealthy city, with new shopping complexes opening every other week. And they've no College of Music. They had the option to include music as a course in the university since the Sixties, but they haven't done it. There's no opera, ballet, symphony music, or chamber music. There's no serious theatre. There's one in a garage. And there are wonderful young people trying to be artists, but they get no assistance at all.

My theory is that from the Norman conquests on, right through to the British invasion, we lived at that level that you now find in common Ireland; there was no room in our lives for the aesthetic side of our lives – the arts. We lived to survive. That was disastrous and we never developed an artistic ethos in our society. All the great music and art in Ireland stopped dead in the twelfth century and never re-emerged. And the result is we are still people of the eleventh century. The Irish people, as such, have little or no connection with the people who inhabited the island after the twelfth century. And we lost the opportunity to develop our music. It was not as developed as folk music in other countries. And the really big damage the British did to us was to impose a dark age on us for seven hundred years. And that's why we have so little to show in our art galleries and museums.

I was paying tribute, recently, to the Connemara people and their likeness to the ordinary Australian people. I asked Mrs Mac an Rí what she thought of 'The Requiem'. She said, 'Well, you shouldn't have included so much poverty!' But what else could you include in the seventeenth century. But these people are the original Irish people. I'm Anglo-Norman and my children have about six different nationalities running through them. But the original Irish people are like the Aztecs, So I likened them to the Aztecs and the Aborigines.

When we came here first the big difference to Phyllis and myself was when we saw a pram going down the road. That was revolutionary. When we came here first the boys were sent off to the Agricultural College in Athenry. And they threw them out. They said, 'If you haven't got thirty acres don't be bothering us.' They weren't prepared to develop the horticultural side of Connemara. They treated it as if it was County Meath or County Kildare and they tried to rear cattle there. Anyway, all of these boys are technicians now. They're skilled craftsmen – electricians, plasterers and bricklayers. That has upgraded the living standards. And they all have these dreadfully marvellous, eight bedroomed houses. And they're brilliantly resourceful. That has been a very dramatic transition. But that means that Connemara has gone in the way that we knew it.

If you want to get the real Connemara you have to go back to the past, before the changes. They're now doing intensive farming. The whole sort of co-operative nature of the Connemara home, where Mamó was the head of the house, and Mamó would decide who repaired, who gardened and so on, has all gone. Peaitín now drives the digger, Michael is a carpenter, the others are plasterers. Some of the women were powerful. You have the first generation poverty thing. They were so poor and then, suddenly, they prospered. When Máirín got married she was twenty minutes late. But that was tradition. It was the last time she would keep him waiting. That was the last of her independence. You have the older generation telling the younger generation to have another baby. Women didn't go out to work. A lot of them were actually illiterate.

Rathcairn is interesting because they've preserved the language there. I always felt, also, that the radio was trying to preserve the language. I always felt that it would be useful to get the *blas* listening to Connemara Irish on the radio. But because of the power of advertising you don't get that. You can't have people speaking Irish when you're trying to sell. And so we've sacrificed the language for that. It's a terrible failure. We've failed in everything. We've failed in the Six Counties. We have archives of letters from the 1886 Famine Committee. And they show a marvellous accounting of their gains and losses.

Recently Údarás established a course on film-making. There were about twenty students on the course and they got about £15,000 of a grant to start with, which isn't much. But there was one film made based on the archival material of the 1886 Famine. A Mansion House Committee raised an enormous amount of money to dispense. And there was an enormous correspondence between here and the Mansion House and it was raised in the House of Commons. So parliamentary reports and letters were included to illustrate the effect of the 1886 Famine around here – and Carraroe and Ros a' Mhíl. I did the voice-over for the film. I read the letters. We did it in the Jesuit place in Galway. So it's the students' attempt at illustrating the effects of the Famine. Pat O'Connor's daughter was the camerawoman. He's the local garda. And Leah, and Ciarán, our grandchildren, were in it. And out of that project, two grandchildren Glen and Ciarán, have started in animation. The idea is that more films will be made out here. It's a wonderful industry, with a lot of potential. The sad thing is that we were, as a nation, opposed to the development of film-making for a long time.

Festy Conlon

Well-known and well-loved traditional musician from Spiddal. Renowned for his tin whistle playing.

There was great music. My uncle used to play the flute and he used to play the whistle. I always heard music at home. My mother used to sing and my father played the fiddle. He played the fife as well. My father was Micheál Ó Conluain. And my mother was Kate Sheáin Tom. She was Kate Costelloe before she married. Her father's brother was a great flute player. He used to go around to weddings playing the flute. He played all over the country. He used to play a lot in East Galway and Loughrea. He didn't earn a living out of it. It was just for the *craic*. My uncle's name was Pat Costelloe. He was a great flute player too. He played up near Moycullen and Oughterard. He played at weddings and *céilís*. We all picked it up, by ear. I started playing over at the college at *céilís* and back in the houses and at the odd wedding. It was great fun. There used to be mostly pipers playing. I remember the likes of Séamus Ennis and his father playing over at the college.

My mother was from Baile an Domhnalláin. They were Costelloes. They had a thatched house. The house was burned during the Black and Tans' time. My uncle rebuilt it with slates and it's still there. I don't remember the Black and Tans at all. We used to have *céilís* in the houses every night when I was small. They were even in the old shed up the road. It was all sets then. There was a full-set and a half-set. And there used to be a big rock. They called it *Leathchrois*. We used to dance at that rock. It's still there. We used to go there in the summertime. Up in Baile an tSagairt we had a *céilí* every night. And they were over in Clancys and in Sweeneys in Sidheán.

And the priest stopped them because all the men and women were going to the *céilís* together. Of course they weren't up to anything. The mothers and fathers were there too. Canon McAlinney stopped them. And even Canon Donnelly stopped them. When we were small we could hear them dancing at the rock. Cóilín Neachtain had an old melodeon and you could hear it miles away. When the *céilís* stopped in the houses there was the college. The *céilís* started there in 1933. That was all right. There was no harm in that. They were great bands. The Kilfenora used to play there and the Climber and all the best bands. These *céilís* took place every Sunday. Half the village used to be there. They were on from nine 'til two. They were marvellous. You used to get turkey and ham and tea there for half a crown.

There was much music around this area. We had Seán Neachtain over here. He played the box. And Paddy O'Donnell played the piano and the fife as well. He also sang. That was in the Thirties and early Forties. I was playing when I was six or seven. I used to play the flute. My father had a fife. That was the first instrument that he had. I used to play with my father. He could write music. He just picked it up. And he was great at languages. I could pick up languages myself, quite easily, but I had no

Festy Conlon playing the tin whistle in Hughes' pub, Spiddal

interest. Even when I was at school in Athlone, I was the worst in the class at Irish, because I had it, but I didn't have the grammar. I adored French. I always loved French, but I hated Latin.

I went to school in Athlone, to a boarding school. My father was teaching in Athlone. He was teaching Irish in the Tech. He also taught around East Galway. And he taught in Moycullen and Oughterard and Clifden. My mother always lived here but he was all over the place. He used to give private lessons. My brothers got scholarships to college. I went to Athlone for the year in 1939, but came home then to mind the land, which was thirty or forty acres. It was all rock though. There was nobody else to mind the land. My mother and my sisters were the only ones at home. We had a few cows. I wasn't sorry to have to come home. I was happy. I came back and stayed here. I worked around in Galway, building houses in the early Fifties. The first real job I had was in the Regional Hospital in Galway. After that I spent some years working on the lifts in Dublin, Cork and Dundalk.

We had a great wedding. We had a fellow playing at our wedding and he had eighteen children. Pat was his

Dara Conlon, Festy's son, with lobster pots

name and he used to cycle from his home in Tír an Fhia to Cotts of Kilcock in the County Kildare to buy accordions. It took him two days and he'd always stay with us on his way back home. We had set dancing at the wedding. It was on in the family house. Usually they went back to the groom's house for the entertainment. At that time they had 'The month's visit'. Whoever got married they'd have the entertainment in the woman's house and the following month they'd go back to the man's house. 'Twas called '*An Chuairt Míosa*'. And that was the end of it then. The entertainment on the day of the wedding was in the groom's house. We used to drink bottles of porter and eat turkey and ham and whatever else was going. Usually there were forty or fifty at the wedding. And you always left somebody out.

The women had a tough life. They used to stay home with the children, doing their knitting and sewing. The men had an easier life. They would go down the shore fishing on Sundays. The shore down near Standúns used to be black with people on a Sunday. There were always twelve or thirteen people with fishing rods, and people carrying baskets of

*Sean-nós singing by Mattie Joe Shéamuis Ó Fátharta
as part of Pléaráca Chonamara*

seaweed and carrigeen moss and periwinkles. The bay was full of salmon but we never knew how to catch them. Except sometimes if we had some kind of net. I saw Lord Killanin take one haul out of the Spiddal River with a net. Four hundred and twenty salmon. The Killanins used to sell the fish in Galway and Dublin. They made money on the salmon. Lord Killanin was all right and so was his father. They had a few people working for them. They used to buy drinks for the locals in the pubs, and they had garden parties up to 1956. Everybody was invited. They'd have sandwiches and drink and you didn't have to dress up. It was a great time. But then, something happened to the weather. It must have been the pollution in the air. And when we had snow you could see the rabbits and they couldn't run in the snow.

Up until the War people walked around here barefooted. After the War boys wore britches. Before that the boys used to wear skirts. There was no problem with that. The mothers used to make the clothes. They wore skirts until 1939. We wore shoes. But there were women who used to walk barefooted from Carraroe to Galway and back, with eight stone baskets on their backs. Baskets full of eggs and butter and fowl. My father was a teacher and so we were never short. But some people were very stuck. They never went to the landlord for help. They always helped one another and nobody ever starved.

In the Fifties the *Fleadh Ceoil* started. I went to a good few of them, playing music. I went to Loughrea and Cavan. I was in Clare and Clifden. I went to Sligo and all around. But mostly it was the same crowd following the *Fleadh*, a little circle. There are very few of them alive from that time now. Connemara had a mighty tradition for the music, especially Carna. Carna still has. Every house you go to in Carna, they play music. The Canavans play and so did their parents. And the Folans play the fiddle. They're in the States now. They're gone since 1948 or 1949. They went to Long Island to a cousin. I play very little myself now. I play in Tigh Hughes sometimes. I was there last Sunday.

We had Santy at Christmas. When nobody else had Santy we had him. We used to get Meccano sets when we were around thirteen and fourteen. I remember getting a ha'penny in my stocking. We used to get train sets. We didn't play as much music at Christmas time.

We used to go to Standúns at Christmas for the music. It was a marvellous house. The door was wide open for everyone, with lots of eating and drinking.

You didn't see a woman in a pub much in those days. Only on a Fair Day, and then in the snug. They did as much work as men at the fair, minding the cattle. Sunday was the day people went to the pub, if they went at all. The people from the mountains used to come down to Mass and then go to the pub after Mass. They were lovely people. There was no music at wakes, just the *caoineadh*. There was music at baptisms and weddings. Usually the mother wasn't at the baptism. She might be in bed for a month after the birth. Or she might be out digging spuds next day.

The priests at that time were very strict. I think they had a bad effect on people. They made idiots of people. They used to preach about things. They didn't mention names but you knew who they were talking about. I used to go down to Standúns for music in the Sixties. There was always music there. There was no music in any other house. We used to hide from the priests when they came along. They used to call to my mother every day to listen to stories and songs. My mother used to sing *sean-nós*. My grandmother was a great singer as well. They were all in Irish and they were all love songs. They were passed on from memory. They were never written down. The singing went back for generations in my family. Cáit Ní Choisdealbha was my mother. The music hasn't died. My mother had the songs by heart. It's a natural talent. Anyone can read out something. But for learning, it's a talent. Some people have their own rhythm in the songs. Some people use the same tune for every song. I learnt the air that I play on the whistle from my mother. I love the old songs. I wouldn't know the songs, but as soon as I play I can remember and understand them.

Sean Ó Loinsigh (John Lynch) and Anthony Lee

Local historian Sean Ó Loinsigh (John Lynch) in conversation with Anthony Lee, owner of the Hotel of the Isles, Leitir Mealláin.

The land between here and Carraig an Lugáin Bridge and Cuigéal Bridge was an island up until 1892. It can be viewed from a rock at the top of Tír an Fhia. In the Thirties the older people remember how they played football here and used to leave their jackets and *báiníns* on the top of this rock. The reason that you have the landscape as it is is because of cutting the turf for the Aran Islands, that are nine miles out from here. And you had the hookers and smaller boats take the turf out and exchange it for fish, which we salted and used through the long winters.

There's very little bog left now, apart from that on the western side. People jealously guard that bog and cut it carefully each year. I'd say, in another five years, there won't be any bog on the islands. They'll have to travel fifteen miles out to Sheanadh Phéistin and around that area for their turf. Gradually that custom will die. People think when they approach Garumna Island that God intended it to be an island. But it's a man-made island. And the landscape is changing. There are ferns taking over the landscape. One or two of the lakes are there since the Ice Age. Loch Hoirbeaird is an example of a stone *crannóg* – a *crannóg* being a timber dwelling, a fortification on a lake. It was mostly for protection from wild animals and that, because we had wolves in those days.

The story about this *crannóg* is that the person who lived there had been banished because she had committed a sin. She committed some type of adultery. So she was banished to the little island. But that isn't the real reason why *crannógs* are common on the islands around here. They were mainly used by the holy people who built them. And they had an underwater path of stones which was visible at certain times of the day, depending on the tide. They were well protected by this, as there were no boats, as such, at the time. Another good example of that type of *crannóg* is at Loch na Scainimhe. It's before you approach Carna village. We can't be too sure if they were used as hideouts or as monastic places. But certainly on the lakes inland, the *crannógs* were used as fortifications and whole families lived on them. But around here they were used as hideouts or monastic places. There is no recorded settlement here before the sixteenth century.

This land was full of bogs and trees. And in the nineteenth century that bog was cut away. It was part of the economic development of that time, as well as fish. And as you can see, villages were built by the sea. It's only in the last century that roads were built inland, through the islands, and you began to have settlements alongside the new roads. And the pattern is still the same. Services tend to be where the roads are and people are moving from the coastal areas to where the services are. People had settled here because of the various extremes of landlords and evictions and having to move further west. If you look at the names here – McDonagh, O'Toole – they all came in from outside areas. The Flahertys were here longer. Then a lot of people came in at the beginning of the nineteenth century. They would have come via the coastguard, after the French Revolution, introducing names that weren't native to the area. They integrated into the area very well.

A hotel was built here around 1880, on the strength of the fishing. They had the best brown trout in the country here. Captain Odlum came here to fish. I don't know where the idea of building the hotel came from. It was Patrick McDonagh, who married Sabina, that started the Hotel of the Isles. He was a brother of Thomas McDonagh. The McDonaghs were well-known Galway merchants. One of them was a TD. A lot of Spanish and Irish agents used to be involved in smuggling. The harbour off Leitir Móir was known for brandy smuggling. In Leitir Móir, Tyrone House was owned

Droichead Carraig an Lugáin

by the St Georges, and they had agents and sub-agents. The O'Tooles were agents for landlords. And a lot of these agents called their children after the landlords. For example, there's Richard and Henry O'Toole, and their landlord was Richard Henry St George. Anthony's grandmother was a Comerford. So Henry's family are five times removed. We had Yeats here – Jack Yeats – that is. I don't know if Willie Butler Yeats stayed here. Roger Casement stayed here and also Horace Plunkett. Emer MacHale's mother was born here. She has the visitors' book from the hotel. The hotel had to remain in the McDonagh family. Another of them, Meta McDonagh had a pub across there, a thatched pub.

In 1847 or 1848, before the decision was made about the railway to Clifden, there were a number of people, including the MP for West Galway, who wanted to have the railway going from Galway to Leitir Meallán, to help out the fishing industry. And it would then run along the coast through Ros a' Mhíl. In Spiddal, in 1850, the MP, the Bishop and the people gave evidence on where they thought the location of the railway should be. And the big

The Hanging Rock on Garumna, where people left their jackets while they worked on the bog

consideration was the fishing from Aran. Eventually what happened was that it went from Galway to Clifden through Ballinahinch. The landlords around there had the cash and the voice and it served their estates. But there was nothing there, once you passed Oughterard, until you came to Cashel. So it only served the estates and the landlords and that's why it died, because it wasn't founded on any good economic reason. We had no 'pull' on our side, no political power. The landed gentry were on the other side. And it would also have been a lot more scenic, running along the shores of Galway Bay – along by Spiddal, Cois Fharraige and Ros a Mhíl.

Now, most of the landlords here were broke after the Famine, because they got no rents during that time and had to mortgage their properties to assurance companies, like Scottish General. The rent that the assurance companies got paid for the mortgage and the landlord got his money up front. And eventually, when the land

indexes were set up, the companies got their money from the British Government. The St Georges had Tyrone House. It was burned during the Troubles. And there is a lot of controversy now over stone and arches being removed. Delia St George was the last landlord and she gave the Murphy money to Casey. There was one landlord's house here, where Sinéad O'Shaughnessy lived. That's gone now. There was a castle there. Sinéad was the landlord's agent. And Pádraig O'Toole was her agent – a sub-agent. When the old system ended they were able to walk in and claim the land, around 1901.

And when the Land Commission came along the land was divided up again. It depended where you lived. You got the land adjoining your house, about six to eight acres. Then that was sub-divided by the families. The Land Commission didn't sub-divide because they didn't think that was good economics. The priest used to be involved in the sub-dividing. If you wrote to the Commission asking to sub-divide the land they would refuse. So the priest used to sign it. Then over a period of forty or fifty years the land was married into. So the land was still owned by the grandfather or great-grandfather. And now, if you want to build your own house and get a mortgage, you have to go back to the deeds, which is very expensive.

In the seventeenth or eighteenth century, monks came here from the Aran Islands. Again it was a retreat. There was no spreading of Christianity then. They built a castle back there. That would have been under Gráinne Ní Mháille. It was an out-station. Going further back, the

O'Flahertys were here in the fifteenth and sixteenth century and they controlled the bogs of Connemara, because that's all there was – bogs. At the end of the eighteenth century you had small famines and evictions, as Galway grew. People began to move toward the coast, to places like Anach Mheáin, being the middle bog and near the sea. The O'Tooles were the main family here then, they came in around 1801, from Coney Island. And they came by boat. And I don't think they set out to come here deliberately, but they got in their boats and they sailed and rowed and eventually they ended up here. And it was from that that they managed to gain

The Crannóg in Loch Hoirbeaird (Herbert's Lake)

a hold of their existing land. They needled their way into the system. They became the foremen, or people in charge. And they benefited from that. For the ordinary Joe Soap would have been dependent on the rent collectors, who were the sub-agents. And the sub-agents turned out to be the shopkeepers, and they owned a boat, which was a sign of wealth.

My great-grandfather had to emigrate during the Famine. He was a crew member on a boat sailing to America. And the boat was wrecked off Boston and he was one of only two survivors out of one hundred and ten aboard. The boat was around ninety feet and twin-masted. She was called *Brig St John*. The two survivors held onto planks until they were rescued by another boat. He married an O'Toole. And he had only one daughter who married one of the Lynches. Cattle raids were common then. The last real raid was when they drove the cattle off the cliffs of Aran. They did that so no one could have the cattle.

There was a Goggin here as a teacher. He was a good teacher. He was in Spiddal as well. In Leitir Mealláin, back at the beginning of the century, they were the best Irish and English speakers in all Connemara. That was because of Goggin's great teaching. He used to keep the children in until half-four. But if you knew your stuff you could go at three.

Gertrude and Martin Degenhardt

Artist Gertrude and husband Martin are German nationals passionate about Connemara and its people. They own a thatched cottage in Spiddal.

We've been coming to Ireland for eighteen years. But getting a house here was a result of certain reasons. Gertrude, my wife, wanted to draw for short stories. And she wanted to go to the country to do them, not in the town full of mines, in Germany, where we were living. So we came here in 1974, when Liam O'Flaherty was still alive and living in Dublin. And we were lucky with him and with the company that we kept. And we came to this region and Gertrude drew for a book which sold a lot of copies a year later. It was a very famous book. It was known as the *Hans Book*. It was in a competition and became a very famous book in Germany.

There was a revival of Liam O'Flaherty in Germany as well. Liam O'Flaherty was very well known in the Twenties with the German publication of his famous book, *Famine*. But then, he became unknown again until the Fifties or Sixties, when there was a Swiss editor who specialised in Irish literature, and a very famous translator named Elizabeth Schnack, who died four months ago at the age of ninety-four. She had almost the monopoly of translating Irish literature into German for the past forty years.

We first came here because of the music. Then we saw this region of Connemara and we were very inclined to this region and came here a lot of times. And this time we came and Gertrude did a lot of drawings and her collection was edited in 1989. We have an edition of our own of Liam O'Flaherty's *Farewell to Connaught*. We had an exhibition at Kenny's. It was a very small edition of 3,000 copies. And Kenny's sold eight or nine copies.

The Swiss editor only produced 2,000 copies of his short stories. They also produced small editions of other Irish writers, like Sean O'Casey. In combination with a student movement and the Green Movement, Ireland became this ideal of Europe where the soil was unspoilt and life and work are still together in art. Like where the farmers play Irish music and all the people played Irish music whether they are eight or eighty. So a lot of young people came to Ireland, because it became the focus of this unspoilt Europe. It too was our reason to come over. It was part of our feeling. So we tried to come here. It was 1976 when we bought this place near Spiddal. And I hope that we will stay here for another thirty or forty years.

Ireland has the yarn of the mouth – singing, telling stories, writing and playwrights. An example is Samuel Beckett. And there are great musicians. I think you must know that the people in the drawing are real. They are from all over Connemara. They are the faces of musicians. She sketches them as she looks at them.

The reason why Gertrude took the technique of dry-points. The dry-point is a form of etching while you have the plate in your hands. It's like doing the reverse first, like

A typical thatched cottage in Leitir Móir

the mirror. If you are sketching and you don't sketch the person as they want to look they sometimes get angry. We were thrown out of some pubs because of that. But we were also told by a lot of Connemara people that ours is the most sublime and true way of drawing. It's the behaviour we depict when we draw. We are selling the drawings of Ireland all over the world. Gertrude has collectors in Norway and Sweden who buy her drawings of the Irish people. She also has done drawings for the book, *Women and Music*. And there are Irish musicians in that and women from all over the world. She has been working on it for almost seven years. It is music that is central to the drawings. *A Farewell to Connaught* was a dedication to this region. But in this book, music is only part of it.

We have six or seven galleries in Germany as outlets. But most of the work is done by mail order, by our own edition, which I am running. And we have most of the things at home. A lot of people in Germany come to our house to buy. It's a small operation. Kennys are very famous and have a great name, not just in Ireland but all over the world. It is mentioned as one of the ten most famous bookshops in the world. If you are collecting old Irish books or first editions you have to go to Kennys to get them.

Gertrude has three exhibitions in Germany in November. But the drawings are shown first here in Kennys. She worked here for a few months and then in Germany for four months. We will probably stay longer here next year, depending on how things go. I always have the feeling that Irish people are very open and friendly to foreigners. In Germany they don't like foreigners in their country. And they don't like themselves. In Ireland the most important thing was to free themselves of the British. The Freedom Movement was a deep tradition. I see this from the outside. Sometimes you can see better into the inside from the outside.

This house is the oldest here in this parish. I think it was built in the early eighteenth century. We know this area fourteen years. We tried to restore this house by keeping it to tradition. Connemara has changed a lot since we came. It has to do with the EC. The old houses are part of the history in this country. And the new houses could be anywhere in the world. We are losing a part of our history and our identity because of this. If everything continues like this it will be like regions in Switzerland and Austria. The houses' façades should be traditional. You can have modern facilities in the interior.

Joe Steve Ó Neachtain

Award-winning playwright, also poet and actor.
Lives in Spiddal area.

I'm publishing this year – fourteen short stories. I've published some poetry and some *agallaimh beirte. Agallamh beirte* is a dialogue between two people. There wasn't a lot of that in my time. But a person that was knacky with the tongue and had a fast turn of phrase was very good at it. Every five years I like to change jobs. I like to start something new. I've only started publishing recently.

The Jacob's Award is for a radio play I wrote – *Baile an Droichid.* What we had were several story-lines running through it as you'd have in a 'soap'. But we used everyday language, and everyday occurrences, whatever is happening locally. We had Michael D Higgins and Máire Geoghegan Quinn on it 'live'. Or we might get a local garda to do a bit of acting on it.

You know, it's amazing how people believe that what's happening in a 'soap' is real. In writing the script I had one of the characters apply for, and get, a grant from Údarás to open a chip shop, or something like that. The Monday after the broadcast, Seán Neachtain, the Chairman of Údarás, got a phone call saying – 'We were refused a grant for the same application. And you're after giving one on the radio, and now we want ours.' The poor man spent ages trying to explain that it was only a story, only a 'soap'.

My mother was the most influential person in my life.

She was a great guiding hand and still is. She's eighty-two years old now and very ill. When I left school I couldn't write my name. And it was a big drawback. I wasn't able to speak English, but I was able to sign my name in English. So it took a long time for me. I was fierce shy about this handwriting until I started writing *Baile an Droichid* seven years ago. And then the handwriting got better, so I'm not ashamed anymore. But as I said, I like to change every five years and do something different. I asked for a change in the Údarás as I like to have time to write. So I just do three days a week work there now. Then I have this old ambulance that I use as a room for writing. I can drive it up into the mountains and write.

I was only nine at the time my father died. In such cases a lot of people gave some of the children to be brought up by relatives. And my father had promised my brother Mícheál to relations to bring him up. My father was only thirty-nine when he died. Pádraig was eleven and Mícheál was thirteen. He was buried on Christmas Eve. Máirtín Standún and his wife arrived at our house at Christmas, with a van, at nine o'clock. They had a huge box in the van, with a present for all the children. And that was a great gesture. My father had been in hospital. There was little wrong with him, but he had a haemorrhage and died.

My mother is a great woman, with very strong beliefs. And she never said no to us. She would borrow if she had to. One time I was acting in a play and I was going up to Dublin. She borrowed a coat for me because I had no coat. Then I asked her for ten-pence. And even if she had to go to Standúns and borrow it she gave it to me. From there I went to Cumann Drámaíochta an Spidéal. The first play that I was in was *Aoibhinn Beatha an Scoláire*. The next play was *The Black Stranger* by Gerard Healy. I loved that play. We went to English festivals with Irish plays. We did another one, *All Souls' Night* by Joe Tomelty. That was in the drama group.

When my father died my mother was getting thirty-six shillings a week to rear the lot of us. And a stone of flour was seven shillings at the time. She couldn't buy the bag because it was too expensive. So I started working for the nuns in Spiddal. I lit the boiler every morning, before school started, and threw out the ashes. And I worked the full day Saturday and the full day Sunday, bar going to Mass. I got a shilling a week. And every seven weeks we'd have the price of a stone of flour.

I often look back now with regret that we knocked down the old thatch house when we built the new one. But there was a good reason why we did. There was a grant for the new house and that was given only on the condition that

Joe Steve Ó Neachtain going fishing near his home in An Cnoc

you knocked the old one. The north gable of the old house was one solid rock. And I remember well that my bed used to be in under that gable. We never felt it damp. They had a great knack with placing the stones when they built the houses. And we never felt a drop of rain even though they weren't plastered. There was nothing holding the house together only the dry stone walls, the thatched roof and fire in the middle of it.

And there was a rope hanging across the middle of the kitchen, from side to side, and on that hung hundreds of dried fish of some sort. When the spuds were going down in the evening for supper, you'd pull down some fish and knock the salt from them. You'd then boil them along with the potatoes and after that on their own. Getting the fish ready for drying was work that was done in the summer. When the mackerel were running you'd be talking about thousands of fish. And the old people in each house used to sit and gut them and wash them in water. Then, to brine them, they'd cut their backs and dip them in the coarse salt. They were then put in a barrel for four days. Then they were taken out again and washed and dried. The children's job was to make sure that no birds or cats got at them while they were drying. The dried mackerel would last for a year. We preferred to eat the rockfish fresh. Then there was a bigger fish called pollack.

Usually there was one house in the village that the people went to. That was where the entertainment was. That was the visiting house. This house, in our village, was the one next to my own. It was Páidín Choil Ruadhrí's house, and you went in there every night and there was a lot of storytelling going on. Especially ghost stories. Stories of people returning from the dead and the like. And Bartley Sheáin Mháirtín was a very truthful man. And he was a fellow who got up at four in the morning, every morning. They were going to Galway at the time with the turf and whatever. They walked along the shore to Galway when there was no road. And they wouldn't use any bit of the land for a road because they needed it to sow potatoes. And the sick house was west of Spiddal (which comes from *ospidéal*, Irish for hospital).

Now, when Bartley was going back with horses to the blacksmith, he'd have to cross over the Crumlin River. And the ghost of a dead relation, Pádraig, would always be there to meet him. However, this morning, Pádraig wasn't at his usual spot. When Bartley came to Crumlin Bridge didn't he see a ghostly crowd waiting, and the horse reared up and wouldn't go any further. And Bartley knew every one of them and saw that Pádraig was with them. When they saw

the horse was stopped they all moved across the river and on down to the sea, waving their caps as they went.

Now, I don't believe much in these things, myself, even though I had an 'experience' once. I was walking home alone, one morning about four o'clock, from a *céilí*. Usually Cóilín Mháirtín Choilm, a neighbour, would be with me. He was getting on in years but you knew he'd always have a story, or a joke to tell coming home. However, Cóilín had died, a while before. I missed him greatly. I was coming by Spiddal Wood, where Killanins is, when I heard something behind the wall. There were twigs breaking. I moved fairly fast to the middle of the road. I wasn't thinking of the dead. Indeed, I said to myself that I was only imagining things. There was a gate on ahead and I heard the gate open and footsteps coming along beside me on the road. So when I got past the wood I wasn't scared, still trying to convince myself it was my imagination. But the footsteps were still coming along beside me. I stopped and the footsteps went on for another four or five steps. And then I knew it was Cóilín, the man who had died. I was fully sure, for some reason that I can't explain. And I wasn't afraid. I knew that he wanted something from me. So I decided I'd talk to him when I got to my house. And I stopped now and then and the footsteps were still there. And when I got to the house I opened my mouth to talk to him, but nothing came out and he just walked on. I cried as the footsteps faded away. So I had a Mass said for him. I'm convinced, to this day, that he wanted me to talk. There's another story told of a

Fishing for mackerel at Spiddal

woman who died in childbirth. The man was left with the children. And every night he used to make a cake and put the embers over the lid. And after a while she used to come in the night and turn the cake. And the baby used to be crying and she used to tend the baby and feed the baby. She did that every night while the baby was small.

My sister married in America in 1968 and I went to the wedding with my girlfriend, Máirín. Máirín and myself got married in 1969. While we were in the States we bought two walkie-talkies, because we were told they had a six-mile radius. She was living in Barna at that time and we thought it would be handy to be able to talk to each other. There were no phones at home. But sure, the walkie-talkies didn't work for six yards, never mind six miles. Anyhow, we went to a *céilí* in Coláiste Chonnacht. The mother of a friend of mine had died and after the *céilí* Máirín was going home and I was going to the wake. As I was leaving her I said to Máirín, 'We'll try the walkie-talkies and see if they work.' She was going over home to Barna and I told her I'd ring her at twelve o'clock sharp. I went on up to the wake, but at twelve I decided I'd better not let people see me on the walkie-talkie, or they'd think I was talking to myself. So I went out into the middle of the fields at the back of the house. And I could hear nothing but crackling on the thing. But the next thing I heard this fierce, lonely cry over the house I'd just left. And it wasn't human, or animal, or a bird cry. So I headed back to the house where the wake was. But inside everything was normal and nobody was crying or wailing. Then, I remembered, the banshee always cries at the deaths of families with a C in their surname. And this house was O'Connor's. And my mother, who is still alive, says she often heard the banshee. And I know a teacher, Tom Sally, and he says he actually saw the banshee, in the form of a big black hen with only one wing. He was young at the time and he heard the cry coming from the big black hen. People were also afraid of what they called the *scread na maidine*. This was a fierce scream always heard just before dawn. It was supposed to be the cry of a soul going to hell. That was the worst of all, a real bad curse.

I remember the Mission. The Mission was a big thing. And when it came to Spiddal you dropped everything. There was a famous missionary by the name of Fr Connolly, from the Aran Islands. He was a huge man and he certainly didn't need a mike. You'd get hour-long sermons. He put up a wooden cross outside when he came and it's only lately it rotted away. He put it 'against *poitín*', outside Séamus Ó Cualáin's. It was about ten feet high and six feet wide.

Seán Cheoinín (Jennings)

Boat builder and sailor. An islandman.
Native of Fínis Island.

The Jennings lived here. My mother's family also lived on the island. They were the Ridges. I was brought up here. We made our own boats. I worked for years with the Caseys who had a boatyard. None of my own family carried on the tradition of boat-building except myself. One of my brothers has a trawler. My mother used also make sails. I got married in America. The name of this village is Leitir Ard. I lived in Fínis for years. There's nothing there now. There were about twenty or thirty families there in my time. When I was nine years old the school closed. There were only a few left going to school at that time. The last teachers there were Miss McGorian and Miss Kelly. And Miss Malley was teaching me. Years before that there were forty two children going to the school. But people had started to leave at that stage.

I'm told I went from Fínis to Carna in a currach to be baptised. I'd hardly remember that. There was a sailing ship here at half-mast. She was built by the Stantons. I was born on the first of December. Today is my birthday. It was bad weather when they took me out on the boat to be baptised. Mary was the oldest in the family. She's six years older than me. Then there was Jim, Pat and Máirtín and Colm.

My mother used to sew. She used to work in Carna. She used to sew by hand. She made sails for the boats. And the needle was huge. It was very hard work. She made stars too, for the races. They were pieces of material put on the sails. They had a star on each side of the sail. It was a real work of art. Pat used to sew the sails as well as a boy. Pat used to spend all his time up on the sail loft. He'd be left up there for weeks until he'd finished them. He was around nineteen at the time. They used to sew by paraffin light and it was very hard on their eyes. My mother used to sing away all the time while she was sewing. My mother used also knit a lot for us when we were small. My sister made clothes as well. Boys and girls wore the same clothes when they were small. No boy wore pants until he was four or five. They all wore the same type of dresses, the boys and the girls.

When my father was making the big sail he was like a baker, because he was full of flour. There was a starch in the material. It was called baffety. Calendo. 'Twas a cotton seed. You were white, like a baker, after handling it. There was Russian tar, a kind of grease. You boiled that and rubbed it into the sail so it wouldn't rot. They used also rub it on a cow if there was something wrong with her. There was a man up near Casla and he had a hooker. And he was the first man around here to use a calico sail. The sails were black. The Russian tar made it black. There was a Stockholm tar and it was red. You could buy it in the shops. The tar had to be as warm as cow's milk. You rubbed that into the sails. They used to cut the sails better than they do now. You might need seven sails for a big boat.

You made the biggest sail first. We did it on a triangle and folded a bit back to get the proper shape. They marked it with a blackened stick from the fire because it had to cut though the flour. Then the boat was tarred. That did everything. It protected and covered it. The sail wasn't any good unless there was borler around it. You had to buy the string. There was some on either side of the sail

Seán Cheoinín near his home in Leitir Ard

to pull it up and tie it. It's hard to do it now with the nylon.

I used to build the boats with ash and with oak. It would take a fortnight to build a boat. If you had a chainsaw it would be quicker. The hookers took longer, but they weren't built around here. The *Black Adder* was built around here. She was sold to Casla. She was lost at Black Head. The *Ark* and *Cúchulainn* were also built here.

The Caseys and the Clohertys in Máínís lived on boat-building. There were great traders there on the island. They had the best shoe-maker, the best weaver and the best cooper on Máínis. There were tailors and blacksmiths as well. That was before my time. The Greenes were the blacksmiths. People used to come to the weaver with their wool. You used to get sixpence a yard for the wool. That's two and a half pence now. When Martin Casey was building the hooker for Pádraig Hower, Pádraig was making as much on his weaving as Máirtín was making on the boat. The weaving was famous in Máínís. People used to come from the Aran Islands to have their wool woven in Máínís.

If you went out fishing you might get about six tons of fish and you got about eleven pounds for that. There was an old lady in Galway who used to buy and sell the fish. She bought it from us and sold it to the farmers. Her name was Delia Lydon. She had a bar where The Quays is now. She had a lovely niece who used to be there often. The niece used to chat me up. Delia wanted to be the middle woman. She had to get to The Quays first, in case the farmers would get there before her. She lost out a few times. But she used to give us porter, or a steak, or a pound of sausages, to get the fish before the farmers. We got good money from her for the time that was in it. Five Woodbines were five pence and a pint of porter was ninepence. And you got a lot out of half a crown. I remember when you got twelve or fourteen sweets for a penny.

We used to cut our own seaweed and bring it in to sell. We used to take it to Galway by boat. It took three hours to get there if the wind was strong. If there was a light wind it could take nine hours. We used to spend the second day there and the third day coming home. We did that all the year round. There was a rowing boat – *Bád Uí Choilm* – and it used to go from Tóin Fhínise to Tigh Warren in the Aran Islands six days a week with seaweed. That was the Casey's boat.

I was more of a sailor than a boat-builder. Though I did build some currachs. I was twenty when I started that. I used to go to Galway every weekend. I used to go to the docks. Life was great there, and the people of the Claddagh were lovely. When the people were out fishing at night they'd make signs, using fires, so you wouldn't go near their nets. We used to cook on the boat. And we'd have parties on the boat. We had bunks to sleep and so we stayed overnight on the boat. Sometimes it was bad if the weather was bad. Your clothes got wet. The trousers were bréidín or tweed and they soaked up a lot. The people of Galway were very nice to us. We used to have a pint together. There was Flaherty's pub at the docks and Peter Greene's near the Spanish Arch. They're all gone now. We never had any accidents on the boat. 'Twas an open boat with a half-deck.

The McDonaghs were a very important family. Monica McDonagh had her own letter-heading. And she supplied the shops in Galway with ladies lingerie, nightdresses and that. The *Erin's Hope* and the *Catherine* were her boats. She had nine trawlers in all. And her brother, Tommy, had only seven. And she had a lime kiln in Galway. Her father was born in Mason Island, near Carna. They moved into Galway. Monica was Máirtín Mór's aunt. She started the business. Now, there was a man called O'Brien in Galway who, when he died, left all his worth and belongings to Thomas McDonagh, because he had no family. Monica used to supply all the shops around the area and they sold artificial fertiliser. That's how they made most of their money. They were very industrious.

There were some great boats built in Galway around that time. The *Mary Ann* belonged to Pete Green's father, and she was bought by the McNamaras of Ennistymon. And they used to sail her from Aran to

Hooker in the Claddagh, Galway

the painter, Augustus John, and was used as a houseboat on the Thames. And eventually it went on fire. And in the books there were women who wrote about their fathers, and the capers and carry-on that took place on the *Mary Ann* with their fancy women. It was the biggest of all the hookers. The *Erin's Hope* was built in Galway as well. And it was so big and heavy that it took some of the quayside paving with it when they put it into the sea. The Caseys built that and the *Mary Ann*. *Erin's Hope* was built for Monica Mór McDonagh. There was also the *Ark*, the *Russel Gun* and the *Camper*. And the Caseys built one for my grandfather. Then they built a boat called the *Trinseach* for this fellow called Trench over in Kinvara.

Richard Murphy wrote a poem called 'The Last of the Galway Hookers', because he thought that he had the last one. But he didn't, because they were revived. There's another poem of his called 'Sailing to an Island'. And it's about Cloherty's daughter finishing the building of the boat when her father dies. Women didn't traditionally build the boats – they made the sails. But Máirín Casey used to make the oars. The best of the boats were built by the Caseys and the Clohertys and most of them were built in Máinís. Máirtín Ó Laoi was another boat builder. The nicest boat of the lot was the *St Patrick*, built for the Conroys. It went to America. And it's gone to the North Pole now. The *Airc* was a big boat that disappeared in the Bay of Biscay. Harry Calleia had insisted on taking her to the Mediterranean.

Doolin. The *Mary Ann* has been mentioned in a literary context. It went to London after that and belonged to

Marcella O'Toole

Publican/shopkeeper's daughter, from Spiddal village, where her family owned the famous Droighneán Donn pub.

I was born in 1923. My father was one of twins and his mother died the day the twins were born. My father was a butcher, the only butcher here at that time. His family owned a lot of land in the Spiddal area – and in Furbo, Barna and Rahoon. My father's mother was a Kelly and Frank Kelly is a first cousin of mine.

There wasn't 'dole' at that time. Instead of 'dole' they gave out free beef, and I remember signing hundreds and hundreds of vouchers for the beef. Oh, it was the most ridiculous thing on earth. My father supplied them all with the meat.

There was a lot of heckling and haggling over land in this area at that time. When I think of, for instance, the school. That land was sold for a song. You see, the woman who owned that land was dying in hospital and didn't the canon go in to the sick-bed to see her and buy the land from her. My father nearly went crackers. A woman dying and the priest heckling her over a piece of land. But I suppose it was good in one way. The school is very convenient where it is.

I looked up the history of my father's family in the library to see where all the Kellys came from. The Kellys originally came from Mayo and from Kells, around that area. They were in Furbo too. Daddy had three aunts in Furbo, opposite Pádraig Pearse's college.

Marcella O'Toole outside An Droighneán Donn

Dr Noël and Phyllis Browne outside their home in the Ros a' Mhíl area

Lord and Lady Killanin in their Dublin home

Barna Pier, rebuilt by Alexander Nimmo in the 1820s

Barna Woods

Old schoolhouse in Boluisce area, Spiddal

Cottages in Seanadh Gharráin overlooking Boluisce Lake

Spiddal House, former home of the Morris Family and Lords of Killanin, designed by architect William A Scott

A view of Spiddal Beach and Pier

Camus Church is Séipéal Mhuire na Deastógála (Mary of the Assumption)

Flora in Camus

Mass being celebrated on Oileán Mhic Dara on the Saint's day, 16th July. The Priest in the center is Fr Éamonn Ó Conghaile

Pléaráca Chonamara Festival at Cill Chiaráin (Kilkerrin)

Hookers at Pléaráca Chonamara Festival

Stations of the Cross at Maumean on Good Friday

The Pattern, Rossaveal, 9th June

The Screebe Fishery

Views over Screebe

A view over Sheanadh Phéistin

Horses grazing in Sheanadh Phéistin

A lake near Maam Cross

Bogland beside Carraroe

Leitir Calaidh (Lettercallow) where there is a monument to Colm de Bhailís

A sheep bridge near Costelloe

Gertrude and Martin Degenhardt outside their cottage in Spiddal

The Twelve Bens

An early medieval chapel called 'An Teanpaill' in the area of Tír An Fhia

Más Pier near Carna

Teach Furbo belonged to Michael Ó Droighneáin. He was a teacher and his wife was a teacher. Actually Michael came from Cré Dubh. He's Maidhcín Dan's uncle. The McCambridges bought their house from the Blakes. There were also Blakes outside Tuam, in Ballyglunin. They were all the one crowd.

Daddy was born in Spiddal. His name was Bill Kelly. Daddy broadcast from the University in Galway. He brought a lot of his friends in to take part in the broadcast too – Mrs Conlon, Pádraic Casey, Brídín Clancy, Winnie and Mike Clancy and Paddy Nee. I was only small at the time. I never heard the broadcast, because Mammy wouldn't allow us to have a radio. She used to say, 'You have enough of *píobairín* (the piper) in yourselves!' because my father used to pick up the accordion at any hour if someone came into the house. Especially McCarthy. McCarthy used to drive an oil lorry and he was a great dancer. He'd be out at half past ten in the morning and he'd come in and say, 'Bill, give us an oul' tune on the accordion!' And of course, they'd be off. And they'd call on Mrs O'Donnell's husband to join them for a jig and a hornpipe. Then McCarthy would lead with 'Right! I'll see you and leave you!' Whatever that was supposed to mean!

We had a Poorhouse here. I don't remember when, exactly, because we never wanted to dwell too much on poorhouses. We wanted to look ahead, not be looking back. History's okay, but sad things like that you didn't want to bother to investigate. But down where the present school is, that's where the peelers had their barracks and it was burned down. So was Lord Killanin's house burned down. My mother was great for jotting things down. A great woman for history. And I gave a big ledger she kept to my son, Sean. She had every priest and doctor and guard written down in that book.

There's great history about the O'Donnells and the Palmers. The O'Donnells worked for the Palmers in the past and that's how they got the land and the house. That's what people did in the past. That's how they got things. For instance, the only people who could afford to send their children to college were shopkeepers. If you had a shop here then you wouldn't come on another for maybe twenty miles. So they had it all to themselves, the shopkeepers. Money talked. And it was the same way when they went looking for jobs in the bank. They had no problem.

I thank the Lord for a great father and mother. He supplied the music and she supplied the history. It's great to have an interest and I love it. And then back in the secondary school there were what you'd call the 'jumpers'. They were Protestants and people used to give them soup. They were so poor at the time and yet so happy. It would amaze you. There was so little to be had. Style in clothes was a thing of the past. You had something for Mass and you made sure you took it off when you came in from Mass. And you had something for school. That was it. That was the sum total of your wardrobe. You could hang it all up on one nail. People put some of the money they made away. They didn't spend it in the pubs. Most of them only went to the pubs on a Fair Day. I often wondered how the publicans survived. But I suppose they made up for it on a Fair Day, including my father. They really drank on a Fair Day. They also drank *poitín*, even though they couldn't get that in the pub. I often wonder how they made it.

The only thing they looked forward to then, the same as now, was the summer trade and the visitors – the *strainséirí*. It was these strangers who spent the money. The local women never went into the pubs, except the odd alcoholic. They were outside and their hands on the window sill, listening to the music and the songs. And when the guards would raid us we saw fun in everything, except when a row would start, and then we would run like the hammers of hell. We were scared. But there was this lady who worked for the guards, long ago. She was an alcoholic. She was the chief bottle-washer in the barracks. She was great *craic*. Now the guards used to raid different areas looking for *poitín*. The *poitín* they found was emptied down into a little gully. And didn't your woman get wise to this and hid a saucepan underneath the gully so it filled with the spilled *poitín*. And all the time her employers – the guards – used to wonder how she managed to be footless drunk so often. It was so funny. I'd say they tumbled to what was happening, but sure they didn't give a hoot. That's the way they were long ago. They were entirely different. Women used to have the odd glass of wine. If it was a fierce cold day they'd go in with the men, because if they

didn't the men would spend the 'rates money' on the drink. And the women would pull their shawls right over their heads in case anyone would recognise them. And they used to stoop and put their heads down. Oh, now the day the sailors flocked into the North and the women started going into the pubs was a bad day for Ireland. That's how it all started – prostitution and everything. Then sailors came into the South, on the big ships, into places like Cobh. So you don't know what the Maastricht Treaty is going to be like, what it's going to bring.

There were lots of medicines and cures for ailments when I was growing. Some of them worked and some of them didn't. The dandelion was a great cure for warts. You took a bunch of dandelion and squeezed out the white, milky juice from them and dabbed it on the warts. The warts just disappeared and never came back. My mother was a very strict woman and I once made the mistake of calling dandelions 'pissy beds' in front her. She was shocked. 'My goodness,' she said, 'don't talk like that!'

And the liquorice, the plain black liquorice. That was great for a sore throat. I used to suffer a lot from sore throats while I was trying to give up the fags and took to sucking liquorice sweets instead of smoking. I found it cured a sore throat I had. I've always sucked liquorice since, every so often, and I've never ever suffered from a sore throat.

Then, before shampoos came in at all, they had great ways for cleaning the hair. My mother always used paraffin oil. Yes, paraffin oil. She'd put some in a jar and then dip

Waiting for the Currach Festival Parade in Spiddal

the comb – or the rack as it was then called – in the paraffin and comb it through the hair. Then she'd let that lie for a bit, and wash it out with good hot water and a little soap, and the hair would be lovely and shiny. But after she'd combed the paraffin through it you'd think your hair was going to fly away, 'twould be so full of electricity. And other people broke eggs and massaged that into the hair. If you look at old photographs of the past you'll always notice how healthy looking the hair was. The women, especially. The women would often wash their faces in buttermilk to keep the skin soft.

And there was no such thing as 'excercises', or whatever then. I think, myself, that cars and too much television have us ruined nowadays. We're constantly sitting down. In my young days the women would work as hard as the men. They went to the strand for the seaweed and they went to the bog for the turf. They often worked with the baby strapped to their back.

Stiofán Ó Cualáin

Musician, dancer and retired schoolteacher. Native of Carna. Taught the accordion to the now famous Johnny Connolly.

I had a very happy childhood because I was born into a family of musicians. I was the youngest in the family. And I had a brother, Dara, Lord rest him, who went to America in 1929. I was born in 1925. And what he left to me and to the family was a beautiful accordion. So we had the accordion, a flute, a tin whistle and a violin in the house. We had our own band. We had music every night in the house and I used to go to bed at night and the music used to put me to sleep.

My parents didn't play music, but my father was a lovely singer. He was born in 1866 in Inis Ni, near Roundstone. And he ended up in Carna, where my son was born in 1966, a hundred years later. My brother learned the violin by ear. When I was about four I used to play a small melodeon. And then, after that, we had our own band. And I used to dance with the band as well as playing. I used to do the 'Blackthorn', and 'The Jig', and 'The Reel'. And about that time my sister Mary came home from America and said, 'Stiofán, would you like to go to secondary school?' And I said, 'I'd love to go.' I was around fifteen at the time. In those days you went to secondary school a bit later than nowadays. So my sister Mary and my brother Dara, between them, sent me off to St Mary's. They paid for my fees and the other two sisters

Stiofán Ó Cualáin at his home in Moycullen

paid for my books. So all my mother had to do was pay my fare to Galway.

So I was very lucky. I liked school. You went to secondary school and then on to a training college. I went to Limerick training as a teacher. I had been teaching in England before that, but the pay was bad, so I came back after a few years to do the training in Limerick. I really enjoyed

*Johnny Connolly, well-known accordion player, with Inis Bearcháin
and its deserted schoolhouse behind*

Nearly everyone there had ten or twelve children. I remember having thirty-five enrolled at one time. And of all the children I taught, for eighteen years, which is a lot, you could count on one hand now the number left here in Connemara. They're out in the States, or in Huddersfield, London, Preston, places like that. Huddersfield is a great place for the Irish. It's like Boston.

doing the new curriculum training in Limerick. I found it hard on Inis Bearcháin, having to teach all the classes in a small, one-teacher school. They came to me as babies and left me as grown-ups. In the morning you taught maths to fifth and sixth class. At the same time you had to try to fit in the others with reading and writing and history and geography. The inspector only came once or twice a year.

I came to Inis Bearcháin in 1952. There were a lot of families on the island then. They were all large families.

They always made a lot of *poitín* on Inis Bearcháin. Not so much in my time, but in the olden days, before that. I heard a lot about them. The men who made the stuff were called *stiléirí*. There were at least six *stiléirí* on the island in those days. They stopped making it around the late Thirties or early Forties. The Gardaí were after them and it wasn't worth it.

The thing I remember most about my first days on Inis Bearcháin is how self-sufficient the people were.

Colm Ó Ceallaigh

Born in Camus. Retired schoolteacher and writer, he published several novels about the Irish diaspora.

I was born in Camus, but I left there when I was ten years of age to go to school in Roundstone. At that time it was common practice for the eldest daughter, or the second son, to go live with their grandparents, or their relatives. And they loved their grandparents and relatives as much as they loved their parents. It was an accepted thing that went on all over the country. It was a Celtic thing that went back centuries. And the grandparents loved them as their own, because their own children were gone. And when these children grew up and went to America they used to send money back to the grandparents to come over for a holiday to the States. It was a new experience for me to go live with my aunt. My aunt had three sons of her own.

I left Camus where it was all Irish and went to Roundstone where it was all English. So I learned English. I had a great teacher. I remember being out at four in the morning in Roundstone Bay, taking up a net. And I had no shoes and the currach was going up with the waves. That was fine. But when it was going down again I had to wrap my toes around the timber of the currach to keep myself in the currach. I liked Roundstone. I still have a lot of friends there. One of my best friends was Festy Lenihan. He lost an eye. And when I called to see him lately, he was totally blind. He'd had another accident. He was a big man. I hadn't seen him for fifty years.

I came back to Camus in 1941. The War was on and people were moving around a lot. But you couldn't go to England unless you had a passport and a job to go to. During that time we cut turf all summer. There was no oil and no coal, so people were making money cutting the turf. As a boy I was cutting turf and had my own donkey. That way I was able to earn more than a man cutting turf on his own. I was getting three pounds, thirteen and fourpence a week. The man was only getting three pounds, ten shillings. I was beating him by three and fourpence, by getting paid for the use of the donkey as well. And I was getting an allowance of oats for the donkey too. I was fourteen at the time. That was before I went away to school in 1942. I came back in 1944 to cut the turf again. Camus was the big place for cutting the turf then. So were other places where you had good bog – Scríb, Maam Cross, Sheanadh Phéistin.

Camus was kind of an historical place. About two hundred years ago there were very few people there. The O'Flahertys were there and I think the O'Sullivans came in later. The O'Sullivans retreated back to Camus after the Battle of Kinsale. They fought all the way up through the country. The Normans attacked them and the Irish attacked them and some of them came across the mountains into Connemara. The Kellys came across as well, from beyond the Corrib. As far as I can go back it was Máirtín Ó Ceallaigh who first came to Camus. He had four sons. And one of them was my grandfather. He was killed in 1900. There were ruins of houses there. Then

Pádraig Pearse came and put Camus, like Ros Muc, on the map.

It was three miles to school and we had to cross the mountain to go to Mass. It was a fierce thing to climb. We had no shoes at the time. We got a pair of boots for Christmas. Times were bad but times were good. There was no money, but everyone was happy because they had

Colm Ó Ceallaigh from Camus, a retired teacher and writer

nothing, and didn't know what it was like to have something. The only strangers that used to come to the place were the Berridges. They were the original landlords and used to come here shooting. When the Land Acts came in around 1900 nobody had to pay rents to the landlords. The Berridges weren't big landlords. They were then just part of a group that owned the fishing and shooting rights. I remember seeing Major Berridge and the sister and brother coming around with their guns, shooting. They were nice people. They were very friendly. They used to go to Mass regularly in Camus. They had a car to travel. When the War started they stayed in

England. But they got work in England, for people from Camus. They were very good people. An interesting thing about Camus church is that the Sanctuary lamp was put there by Pádraig Pearse, and is still there. The church is very old.

The first church was on the southside of the mountain. Fr Moran said Mass there a few years ago, in the ruins of it. The walls are still there. The walls of the priest's old house are still there also. Then there was a change in the approach to education. It didn't come in for the benefit of the Catholics. It came in for the benefit of the British, because they needed men for the Army and the Navy. They needed men with a little bit of education who could read and speak English. The Irish were joining the British Army a long time before that, but, for promotion, it was an advantage to be able to read and speak English. There were no Protestants in Camus at that time. Not that I know of. There could have been landlords' agents or game-keepers. But I don't think we had any 'jumpers'. I think we had a few 'soupers', but that was during the Famine. They put soup kitchens all over then. During the week it was vegetable soup and on Friday they had meat, because they knew no Catholic would eat meat on Friday on account of the temptation. Seamus Welby was teaching in Muiceanach idir Dhá Sháile. And there was a Valentine Lennon teaching in Camus. Seamus Welby then married in Camus, and his salary for the year was six pounds. Valentine Lennon was only getting two pounds. They were teaching in a *scioból*, or a shed, from home. And in Camus it was actually part of the house itself. There were four Catholics going to school – three boys and one girl; and eight Protestants – six boys and two girls. There was no patronage and no Catechism taught. This goes back to 1836 or 1837.

We had slate pencils in school, and quills and pieces of sponge and black ink. And if you didn't want to buy the ink, you could make ink yourself from the stuff in the bog. It was black stuff, like coal, and you had to dig it out and let it dry on a rock in the sun. Then you put it into a jar and poured water through it. That was way back before my time, probably in Welby's time. And for brown ink you got the moss and boiled it. The same as the dye for the wool. They could get red ink from rose-buds and purple ink from heather. They didn't have to go into the shops for anything. Chalk was a piece of stone. A pencil was a stick burnt in the fire like charcoal. Paper was the skin of an animal.

They were good at improvising. They made their own clothes, like *báinín*. There were weavers. There was a weaver and a tailor in every village. But there was also a travelling weaver and a travelling tailor. They'd come and stay in the house while they were making the clothes. They might stay two weeks or a month. And they were boarded and fed by the family. They weren't single but they were kept busy. That's the reason that you have Mac an Táilliúra and Mac an Fiodóire. It was only natural. They didn't see anything wrong with it. It's only in the last ninety years that things have changed. Things changed when the workhouses, during the Famine, were opened up, and the single, pregnant girls were sent there. There were two in Galway. There was the Magdalen. But before that there was nothing said and the child was brought up like any other child. There was nothing said to the tailor or the weaver. It was pure natural.

But we got uppity after the Famine. There were a lot of men who went away to work and stayed away for a long time. And he might have had two children when he left, but he might have four when he got back. And he couldn't say anything. So there were five before he left to go away again. And he mightn't come back for another five years. And these things weren't questioned at the time. And if the husband died, if he had a single brother, then he went in and lived with the widow and family. And if the brother was married he took the widow and children into his own home and raised two families. It was quite like the Arab tradition. And the more you look at it the more Moorish it was. They didn't think of the cost. They had no money. They sowed potatoes and vegetables and they fished. There was no such thing as a shop. It didn't cost any money. And look at how much fun it was! It wasn't that common, but it did happen between Tully and Spiddal.

And another thing that happened was, that when both parents died, the uncle would take the family in and have another family with his nieces. That was very hard, very rough. There was no question of getting husbands for the nieces. Though, sometimes, they were matched up with a bachelor who lived up the mountain and had a thousand sheep. There was no such thing as love. I remember it. I remember my father getting out a bottle of *poitín* and a man coming to the house late at night. They had a few swigs out of the bottle and then they went to this other house to meet the girl and the match was made. And that was less than fifty years ago. And no one objected. The man or woman had no choice. Once she was married she was his slave. She had no rights whatsoever. The women slaved and worked very hard. I saw them with baskets on their backs. They sowed potatoes and they put out turf. I saw many a woman with a child on her back, wrapped in a blanket, working away.

I was a student in Coláiste Éanna in Salthill. I got second place the first year. I went on to training college, and then I came back here to teach in Leitir Meallláin school. It was a mixed school. Mrs O'Sullivan's son was a priest out west and he used to come here on holidays and say Mass. Helen Flaherty left here in 1900 because she beat up the RIC. She became Mrs Sullivan. But there were four or five brothers and sisters in the family. And they used to make *poitín*. There was no road there at the time.

But the RIC came along and raided the house. However, they couldn't find the *poitín* because the mother was in bed. And she had the jar of *poitín* in under the blankets with her. And modesty prevented them from pulling down the blankets. Everything worked all right until they were going out and one of them made a grab for the daughter and she hit him. The others turned back then and started wrecking the house. They came back next day but there was no one in the house except the mother. Whatever way the Sergeant looked about he saw the brass button under the table and he said, 'Ah, this is my evidence of the assault on my man.' But by that time, Helen and Mary and the other sisters were all on the liner to America.

Helen got involved in Irish societies out there. She was involved in collecting money for the 1916 Rising. She sent weapons and everything over to Ireland during the Rising. She brought some of the IRA out on holidays and looked after them. I came across a lot of things about de Valera as well. But I based my story on that and brought it up as far as 1923, and then I had several hundred pages. That was in 1971-72. Then I did a lot of research in England, America and Canada. And I discovered that I wasn't teaching history. It was manufactured history. There was a lot of knowledge and information that was kept from us. We got a lot of it from an English point of view. That was one thing about the English, anything that happened here, they wrote it down and you can still get a copy of it, whereas, if you want information about

A view of the pier in Roundstone

your own people, especially between 1916 and 1921, it's not available. It's there, but you won't get it.

Because I was a teacher I was considered a stranger. It was the same with the priest and the policeman. The pub next door opened in 1972 or 1973, and when I went in there for a drink nobody would bother with me. It wasn't that they didn't like me, and they were the kindest of people. But they kept their private lives at a distance. It's only in the last six years they have started to let me in. It

was all due to the way the English and the peelers treated them. Then the priests came along and bullied them, and the teachers beat them in school. And that grew — that fear of authority.

It was terrible. We went to national school with Protestant children and they were our best friends. Then we went to secondary school or college and we were forbidden to even speak to them. There were three girls from Roundstone and I knew them from schooldays and they were in school in Dublin when I was in Dublin. I used to meet them on the train going down home and couldn't even speak to them. It was against the rules and regulations of the Bishops. I'd have been expelled if I'd spoken to them. I wasn't allowed into a Protestant church. I was fifty years of age before I entered a Protestant church.

This area is very historical. It was a transit area for the saints. It was a seafaring place. It was a transit area for the O'Flahertys and the Joyces, on the rampage into Aran and down into Clare. It was a stopping off point for the British Navy and for ships going to America and Canada. It was a compass point. It was a loading and unloading and storage point for British ships there at the back of the church, going back maybe three or four hundred years. The records are somewhere. A lot of documents were burned in the Customs House in 1921 and 1922. There are two other places in Dublin with archives – the Four Courts and Heuston Station. The archives in London are all on microfilm and have been stored in the West Country by now. A lot of documentation was lost in the poorhouses in Loughrea and Oughterard. They were considered to be of no value. Just pieces of paper. We've missed out a lot on our heritage. It's only now that we're starting to get it back, on computer. But we're only going back to 1950. It would be great if we could go back to 1850.

After I wrote *Sclábhaíocht* I sent it to a publisher who said it wasn't good enough because it wasn't 'standard Irish'. And I gave it to Micháel Ó Conghaile who sent it to France. They came back and said change this and this, but I wouldn't. Eventually I had it published and it's been a good seller. It's about the Irish in England. I spent a whole year in England four years ago. And I used to go to England working, during the summer holidays, over a period of five or six years. I worked on night-shifts and day-shifts. I worked on the dock-lands. I worked in Waterloo and in Gretna Green. I worked in two jails and in a hospital. I worked as a carpenter. I worked in Wales as a machine driver. I worked as a plumber and an electrician. I worked as a jack-of-all-trades, so I could see what was going on, to get my material for the book. When you're on holidays you don't see anything. You have to be working and out at all hours to see what's going on. I saw people working, I saw homeless people and I saw those who sold their bodies. It concerned the Irish crowd in England, and I brought all this out in the book. The same thing applied in America. I went to Canada and California. So this new book, *Deoraí*, is about America – the Irish in America. There's a lot of our history lost and it's almost like we don't want to know about it. We don't seem to care.

Cissie (Bairbre) Bean Uí Chonghaile

From Gairfean, Ros Muc. A great authority on its local history.

My family name was Walshe. My grandfather came to Ros Cíde from Leitir Móir, across from where the Berridges live. And he built a house there and lived there evermore. My father lived to be three months short of a hundred. We lost a lot of information. All we can remember is what he told us. And he could read and write and that was unusual. He said he went to a night school and that's how he was educated. Everyone in the family was well-educated. The primary education was excellent at that time. That was up to the time that I was going to school.

I had five children, three boys and two girls. And there were five in my own family – two boys and three girls. Joe and John, my two sons are living just down the road. And Michael is managing for the Conneely brothers. My two sisters and a brother emigrated. My brother and sister are in San Francisco. They're twins. And I have a sister in Pittsburgh. There were usually big families around here, maybe ten to fourteen in a family. And half of them emigrated. I think that the people who emigrated didn't do so well. They had to work very hard. My family had cousins in America to go to when they emigrated. My sister in San Francisco qualified as a nurse in England before she went to America. She nursed in England during the War. She

Conroy's Pier in Gairfean, Ros Muc

started a nursing home for old people in San Francisco. She had one girl and her husband died young. She worked hard and did well.

There was a man called Tom Joyce in South Tuam. We used to bring our shoes there to have them fixed. You had to go to Mayo to have the shoes made. The others were just cobblers who did small repairs. They didn't make shoes. But a lot of households were handy themselves with the shoe repairs. They'd have a last and a hammer and tacks and thread for sewing. And we had a few tailors locally. John Lydon was a very good tailor, in Camus. He did the Gardaí uniforms. He was deaf and dumb.

And then we had the weavers. Four of them. Two in Turlach, one in Inver and one in Glinn Ghatha. The Glinn Gatha weaver was a lady – Mrs Duggan. Then there was Tom Kane, Bartley Mannion and Michael Mannion. People used to bring the thread to them and they'd weave it. They'd do the warping at home, on the pens with two scraws. And you'd bring that to the weaver for making blankets and grey flannel and white flannel for their clothes. They made lovely tweeds. They used to colour the wool. It was lovely. They used natural dyes. They even used the gooseberries. They got some kind of mineral water from the bog and they put that on first to help keep the colour in. And they used the *scrathach*. That came off the rocks. That was a lovely colour – a kind of maroon. But they used to buy some colours in the shops. You'd buy an ounce of it. Some of it was like ginger or a crystal red. That was used for the red petticoats for the women. The red petticoats were worn for many years. Petticoats weren't white for ages. The flour bags were made into sheets. They made the petticoats out of the white flannel. Some women wore two – a white one underneath and a red one on top of that. You'd need the two in wintertime. But they always wore the red one, summer and winter. And going to Mass they might wear a skirt made of a bit of material they'd bought. We used to call that material serge. It was a blend of wool and cotton. They'd have nice colours, like navy. Conroys didn't order suits at that time. You bought the material and the lining and the buttons, and the shoulder pads. Everything was there. Then you made it yourself.

You didn't have to buy the sails for the boats. The material was all there again. They had rows and rows of calico material. The calico was around fourpence a yard. Then, it got dearer and dearer and dearer. They don't use it anymore. It's nylon they use now, or terylene. But, of course, they're not doing anything now with the boats, like they used to in my time. There was nothing else but boats in my time. It was like living on an island. In my time they were taking turf to Aran and Clare and Galway. It was all boats, boats, boats. Then it was the trains and when they stopped it was the lorries. And things improved. People were happy.

When the boatmen went to Aran with the turf they could be paid with fish. They'd come back with fresh fish and sell it in the shops. You were delighted to get fresh fish. You could get salt fish all through the year, like rock-fish and pollack. And there was ling, a big, long fish. That was very plentiful, especially during Lent. Fresh mackerel was only a penny each. And they had salted herring in big barrels. That could have come from Scotland. Some of them could be very salty, but if you steeped them overnight they were very nice. And when you were cooking it, if you put in a small bit of bread-soda, it took away the salt. But it didn't do the people any harm. They lived to be nearly a hundred years. The meat was very scarce, until you could afford to kill a pig yourself. Or, I used to hear them talking of 'tiger', which was some kind of salted bacon. And it came from Russia. It was Russian boar. And they said it was just a big slab of fat. They were buying that until around 1916. They said that when you put it down with some cabbage it formed a froth on top. But they found no fault with it and it didn't kill them. And they were healthy.

They didn't have a second set of clothing except the bit they put on going to Mass. And they had to be out in the hail, rain and snow. And they'd come home and sit in their wet clothes and dry them to the fire. And you could see the steam rising up. And they didn't have lumbago or arthritis like they have now.

Conroys had a bakery in the shop. There was another bakery in Turlach, but that was years later. They had a boat, a *púcán*, that went around the islands delivering the fresh bread. And the first stop that it had was Cill Chiaráin, across the bay. And then he went round by Leitir Mealláin to whatever shops were there. And then the boatman came up by Béal an Daingin, by the swing bridge to the quay, and landed there at all hours of the day and night, just delivering his bread. And the old lady who lived next door to me when I got married told me that the people used to race each other to the shop to get the hot bread. They used to call the 'Vienna' that they sell now a 'Grinder'. And they were nice and hot, indeed. But it was a luxury to buy bread then. It was expensive. At that time they might only buy bread once a week. A loaf cost three or four pennies.

The Conroys was one of the best shopping centres from here to Galway. They had everything and anything. The people came in boats from Cill Chiaráin, Carna, Leitir Mealláin and all around. And even on a Sunday they were open, and you'd see a rake of boats coming across to the shop. The boats took the material – flour, bran, sugar, tea, pots and pans from Galway to the shopping centre. The *St Patrick* was the Conroy's boat. But at Christmas time he got two or more extra boats to have the place filled up with anything the people would need. There was another shop – O'Malleys – that started after the Conroys. It did a good trade as well.

PD Conroy was an agent for the Cunard-Canadian Line. He gave a framed picture of a boat to my husband's mother. Then Michael Conroy was agent for the flight companies. So the shop was a travel agency as well. PD himself would leave on a Sunday and travel all over Connemara to meet people in certain places. People who would want to go to America or somewhere else. And he'd get them going. It cost about twenty pounds to go to America at that time. That would have been around 1928 or 1929. And Conroy was a good man. He paid their passage and did everything for them, until they could earn it in dollars over in America. Then they would send back the money to him. You could always trust them to send back the money.

Then the O'Malleys were agents for the airplanes. The O'Malleys had two horse-carts 'til they got the lorry. Then they used to deliver to the houses all the way to Carna. They used also go as far as Maam Cross and load up from the train. The train came through Maam Cross to Clifden until 1935. I never saw the train coming or going. I never went on the train. The first train I saw was in Galway. Of course, at that time, Clifden was the capital of the West They had boats docking there

Part of Conroys' shopping complex in Gairfean, Ros Muc

in Clifden. And they used to sail from there to Scotland in the olden times. They would walk up from here or down from Westport to Clifden to travel to England or Scotland for the potato season … the Harvest, as it was called.

The dispensary was right beside Conroy's shop. And the doctor used to come across from Béal an Daingin. He was based there until the 1950s. And he used to come across on the boat, especially in emergencies. He may have had a car or a side-car, but in an emergency it was always the boat that took him and brought him back home. In maternity cases it didn't matter if it was rain or storm. There was no midwife until Lady Dudley started it. She started the Lady Dudley Fund. She took up two

rooms in the Post Office in O'Malleys, and her-self and her two daughters helped run the place. Then the service spread out and was all the way down the western coast from Donegal as far as Cork. Her husband was the Lord Lieutenant in Ireland. They had two houses here. She lived in the lodge at Scríb and he lived in the house at Inver. Mrs Odlum used to collect money for the Lady Dudley Fund. The Fund continued for years, until the Board of Health started the nursing organisation. There was a hospital on the Dublin Road in Galway. Then there was the central hospital. That was an Army barracks before that. They had babies at home in bad conditions. The mother and baby could die before the doctor would reach them. The babies weren't buried in consecrated ground, because they weren't baptised. There are hundreds of them buried below near the sea. There's a little graveyard there. They were buried there up until the Forties when the Church laws were changed.

Anthony Mannion

From a farming background in Ros Muc, he studied
agriculture and worked all his life for the Land Commission.

My family are from Ros Muc. The Battle of the Boyne was 1609. And the Battle of Aughrim was in 1691. And Aughrim was Mannion territory. And after the battle they were driven out, practically the whole way to the West.

There were six in our family, three boys and three girls. Two of my sisters went to America. In my young and teenage years every post office and every shop displayed large coloured posters of the White Star Line Ships, and later of the North German Lloyd Liners. They looked very attractive and the young boys and girls looked forward to the day when they would join these ships and enjoy the happiness and glitter the posters portrayed. Along with the profit to the shipping line the shop or Post Office through which the passage was booked also gained. A very popular song then, which you heard at every gathering, every cross-roads and every shop-corner, was, 'I'll book my passage to New York and gain my passage free. / And be my Love's companion in the Land of Liberty.' The American wake was a regular feature of the emigrant's departure. They stayed up all night. The neighbours came. They had music and sang songs and cried and danced all night. When morning came there were the goodbyes and the crying. In all it was a sad occasion. I was at one, as a child. That was when one of my older sisters

Anthony Mannion from Ros Muc outside his home in Galway

went to America. I was young at the time and I feel that I would not like to be at one again. I was at a second American Wake in my teens and it was the same feeling. Their song was a sad one too.

I understand that I first went to school when I was five years old. My sister Barbara brought me. And she played a joke on me. On the way she took me into a little disused farmhouse on the side of the road, saying that this was the school. We got to the real school, eventually, having taken a shortcut across the bog. The schoolmaster was Patrick Connolly, a native of Glenamaddy, in East Galway, an area which was native Irish-speaking at the time. He spoke Irish and English equally well. He was a good, hardworking teacher. He was a passionate lover of Ireland, its history and its people. He taught Irish history with a great passion. I felt this emotion one day when he was telling our class about the treachery of the clan that attacked the Munster side, (the Fitzpatricks) and they returning from the Battle of Clontarf. He was very much involved in the politics of the period of which I speak. He was a very close friend of Patrick Pearse. And in the long winter nights he would meet a few of the local people in Teach an Mháistir. And he talked to them and listened to their stories. I remember, when I was eight or nine years of age, carrying a small bag of grass for the Master's cow on my back. Having got rid of this mighty weight I went into the kitchen, where my father was, with two or three other neighbours. Night had fallen at this stage. Thinking about that in later life, I figured that it was similar to scenes in other homes, in other places, where Pearse, on his travels, talked to them and listened to their stories. As I said earlier, the Master was very much involved in the politics of the time. Now, he lived only three hundred yards from the school and passed the barracks every day going to and from the school. He was active in Pearse's drilling and marching and possibly looked on as an enemy by the police. And eventually, it was tantamount to open warfare between them. As far as I remember, the policemen in those days were Sergeant Hunt and Constables Feeley and Murphy. I remember, one day playing pitch-and-toss with other boys, for buttons. Policeman Murphy came along and played with us for a three-penny bit. I won the three-pence.

I remember them training the workers – the little farmers. They gathered and started out in a place called Cloch an Leachta. And they marched on toward the church. I have a recollection of the marches. Pádraig Pearse was in front. My brother remembers him a bit better, and he's two years older than me. My father told me that my sister and myself used to copy Pearse marching up and down, up and down. But I don't remember doing that. Anyway, I'm told he had a very strong effect on everyone. I remember where he lived. Later the old teacher lived in it. It's known now as 'Pearse's Cottage'. We were fishermen, and we used to fish every day, even after Mass on Sundays. In those days no one, young or old, ever missed Mass on Sunday. So we'd cover about five-and-a-half miles going to and coming from Mass every Sunday. On fine Sundays we used to come back through the mountains and have a picnic with my mother. And often, on the way home in the evening, we'd take a short-cut through Pearse's plot. And believe me, that was some enchanted place. I felt that feeling, which I used to get in later years, about Pearse. He had that effect on everyone who met him, especially the people of Connemara and the Aran Islands. He wasn't a great talker, but he'd listen. He used to visit the local teacher, Connolly, and the local people would come in to meet him there and tell stories. And they all agreed that he was a great listener.

Later, I could see his ideas in his books. But I was only two years old when he was last here. All I remember of him is through my parents. At that time the people here were ninety-nine per cent behind him, or perhaps more.

They shared his vision for the country, his respect for the culture and respect for themselves. And there is nothing like our own culture. I saw this culture in my youth. What they set out to do they did. And what they promised was fulfilled. Pearse used to train them how to walk. They didn't have any arms. And they used to stop at certain places for him to address them. For instance, he used to stop at Cora na Móna. He would say, my father told me – 'Courage! Have courage! There's nothing in the world that will defeat you if you have courage. Focus on that!' And he was awakening that courage, and they had it.

A great friend of Pearse was a woman called Lil Ní Dhonnacha. Lil first came to Ros Muc in 1929 and stayed in our house. She it was who showed me the *Irish Times* advertisement for scholarships for assistant agricultural engineers. I got the Exam and entered Athenry College on the 4th of February, 1930. I was twenty years old on March 18th that year. Athenry College was my Alma Mater, and started me on my career.

Later, after the Easter Rising in 1916 the Black and Tans with their high-powered lorries and Crossley tenders, came to the area, terrorising people and raiding houses. Anyone who was a friend of Pearse was a target. First of all, local men who were in the struggle with him, had to take to the hills. Master Connolly had to go 'on the run' for six months, and slept at night in the most isolated part of the parish, Tigh Choimín Pháidín Dónaill. Those in the arms struggle were led by Pádraig Ó Gaora.

I remember the night the Tans burned Patrick Pearse's cottage, Colm Ó Gaora's house and Master Connolly's house. Firstly, there was a roar of lorries as they approached from Scríb. There were beams of light from their headlamps. Then the noise of the lorries died down as they reached their targets. And then there was a volume of flames as the houses went up. We, as children, slept under the stars that night. It was about two o'clock in the morning, as far as I remember, when the houses were set on fire. We had a clear view of everything from where we were lying on our mattress and hay. I forget what we had over us. We were there for safety. That was the only night we had to sleep out. But they raided our house one night. I didn't hear them, so it must have been in the middle of the night when they came in. The girls were asleep in one room and the boys in another. And mother asked them not to go into the girls' room. And they respected that plea and didn't go into that room. It showed the human side of the thing. There was a group of them in the kitchen, and there was a cake that my mother had baked beside the man at the back. And he took a piece of the cake on the quiet. That night we had to sleep out was a beautiful night.

Sometime later the Tans called again. In those days a pig market was held in Turlach Beag once a month, and there was usually a big gathering. Well, the Tans entered the market and hammered, with the butts of their rifles, a number of men who were holding their stocks there. The men had done nothing wrong to deserve such an attack. Our next-door neighbour, Michael McDonagh, was a close friend of Pearse. And often he did not see eye to eye with the police. He was the local shopkeeper and butcher. And he was travelling to the market, on his bicycle, when a bullet whisked by his ear. He felt he had a close shave with being shot dead. Another day I remember, as if it were yesterday, was when the Auxiliaries were ambushed at Doire Bhanbh. A racehorse which was kept at Lord Dudley's estate at Scríb, was ridden as hard as ever I saw a horse being ridden, to the local Post Office, O'Malleys, to phone the Black and Tans' base in Galway.

I was reared at the end of Ros Muc. The house was on the right-hand side, beside the garage. It's the first house there. There's an old ruin there. That's where my grandfather had the Post Office. And the hedge-school that the O'Malleys had there is supposed to have been the last hedge-school in Connemara. That was the Grace O'Malley group. It's where all the smuggling went on. There's a place called Siléar in Ros Muc, and a place called Bradley Harbour in Leitir Meallláin, and they're all associated with smuggling. One of my ancestors, on the Mannion side, was the captain of a boat called the *Cutter*. The *Cutter* was a Government yacht chasing hundreds of smugglers. Bradley Harbour was one place they landed in and also in Siléar and Foirnis. I know that there were pirates off Belmullet, but I never heard of piracy off the Connemara coast. But possibly they went to Spain and brought it back from there. They

A boreen in Ros Muc

were great sailors and the seasons were better out there. The McDonaghs might have attacked Spanish ships. It might have been the reason they became so wealthy.

'*Buailé*' is a Scottish term. '*Buailé*' meant a period that you'd spend in the summer. You'd go out into the wilderness with the cattle. And you'd spend time there with the cattle. Around here, they used to go to the mountains near Recess.

Coan was telling me about this. And he said to me that we'd go off and do that some summer. So we did. And he was old at this time. He was getting the pension. There was a little hut there in the mountains, used by fishermen. It had walls of stone and a thatched roof and was about eight feet by five feet. The bailiffs who protected the fish used to go there. But anyway we set off and took the cattle. We had about ten apiece, calves and everything. We had no bed or anything. It was almost sunset when we got there. And away up ahead of us we saw the little hut. And Coan told me to rest the cattle and let them graze. He was going on ahead to make a fire in the hut. I was to come up when I saw the smoke rising. Anyway we had our tea and then we settled down to make our beds. We used bags of heather. Coan was telling me how that was how they used to do it when he went to Scotland in the old days. I slept like a dog. We used heather for building the fire. One night Coan got a severe pain and sent me to get some *poitín*.

Jack Toohey

A Jewish businessman who was raised in Limerick City. Retired to Connemara to live in Costelloe Lodge, former home of Titanic designer, Bruce Ismay.

I came to Connemara about twenty-five years ago. I made up my mind then that I was going to retire here when I was sixty, and I would have a cottage and a hundred yards of fishing. Now that I live here, I don't drive around Connemara unless I have a relation here. There is something about Connemara that you don't get anywhere else in the world. I remember, years ago, going from Dublin to Galway in an hour and three-quarters. At that time there weren't very many cars on the road. I always had a big car, so I could go fairly fast. But always, after I'd gone through Galway city, and coming to somewhere like Roundstone, I'd drop to about ten miles an hour and relax.

You can sleep well here. It's relaxing. I was a good golfer when I was young. I had a handicap of nine. And I was good at motor-racing and I was a good bridge player. And I packed it all in for work. Now I need the golf. I could do with all those things now, but I gave them all up.

This house was built in 1925. But they neglected it. It was terrible before we bought it. The windows were bad and draughty. There was no heating in it. It was a summer-house. But that was all right. I knew what I wanted to do with it. But I decided not to build on the garden and trees. It was a twelve-acre site. We'd never lived

Jack Toohey outside his home, Costelloe Lodge

in a city – in Dublin or San Diego. And I often think, when we're here and the weather is bad, that we should move to the sun. But we're better off here.

Ismay came here originally in 1913 and he bought the house and the fishery for six thousand pounds. I think, maybe, the fishery was extra. But he came over here, every year, with his crowd of twelve, for the fishing, until he died. And his wife came over even after that. The original house was burned in 1922, during the time of the Troubles – the Civil War. And then he built this house. He died in London. A couple of years ago this oldish man and woman were staying at John Joe O'Toole's, the postmaster. And he rang me up and said that they would like to walk around the place, because they used to work for the Ismays.

He used to be the valet and she used to be a kitchen maid. So we welcomed them. We brought them into the lounge and the funny thing was that, in all her time working there, she had never been inside the lounge. The old valet told me about the *Titanic*, which Mr Ismay had designed. He said they were after what sailors call 'the blue river', and Captain Smith was increasing the speed of the engines every day. And Mrs Ismay wasn't on the ship. And I heard that a lot of the life-boats went away empty because the emigrants who were down below couldn't get up to the upper deck, where the boats were, because they were locked in. They were locked in to prevent them getting up to the Second or First Class decks. There were, in those days, two routes across the Atlantic – a summer route and a winter route, And the winter route was longer, to avoid the icebergs. But the Captain took the summer route. The question was, should he have been on the summer route in April. The Valet said he was on the wrong route. The *Titanic* was part of the White Star system. She hit an iceberg.

Pat Herdman lived here before me. I was part of the syndicate in the Costelloe Fishery. Then I sold it. I had the Zetland and two other fisheries. I came here when Billmeyer had it. And a Colm Ó Lochlainn owned it before that. I bought Costelloe Lodge in 1983. When I bought it I was twelve months working on it. The garden has improved a lot. We've done a lot to it over the years. I've been coming to the West of Ireland all my life. I've been coming here since 1947. I was a fisherman. I used to fish a lot. I don't anymore, though I have fishing rights just outside here. The Costelloe syndicate have the fishing rights to the fishery. We were in California for three years before we decided to live here. I had the Inbhear fishery, but I sold that a few years ago. Luckily I did, because the forestry people were ruining the spawning beds with the trees. Odlums used to own the whole fishery but then they sold it to the Guinnesses. I came back from California and took a house in Millards, about a mile from my fishery. And I used to go fishing every morning, but after two or three weeks I got sick of it.

I'm the son of a Lithuanian, Jewish refugee. They'd never heard of Ireland. I think they stopped off in Ireland, in Cobh, or Waterford, on the way to America. And they

A Connemara cottage, not too far from Casla (Costelloe)

were so glad to get off the boat that they never went back on it. I was born in Limerick, because that was where my family ended up. I left Limerick when I was very young. Toohey is not our real name. The locals couldn't pronounce Tooch in English, so they called us Toohey. Most of my relations went to South Africa and they called themselves Tooch. I never went there because of the situation with the blacks. My family all had wonderful lives there and got to be very wealthy. And the black people had damn all.

My parents didn't try to arrange a marriage for me, even though it was still being done at that time. All my

sisters had arranged marriages and they all lasted. Their husbands are all dead now. They outlived their husbands. I married a Jewess. That marriage lasted ten years. Then, I divorced her, which was the best thing that I did, because she married two millionaires afterwards. I didn't really associate with Jews. I spent more time with Christians. I was into motor-cars, and I was involved with racing-cars. I might have associated sometimes with Jews, just playing golf and that. I used to go out with a Christian girl, but she wouldn't marry me because I was Jewish. And my parents were always at me to marry, so I met a nice-looking girl and I married her. But I wasn't making her happy, so I told her that the best thing for her was to divorce me and marry a fellow who would make her happy. We never had a fight, there was just no real bond between us. It was a stupid marriage, really.

Then I married Agnes, my designer. I was associated with her for years. She was a fencer on the Olympic team. She designed the uniforms for the Olympics and was on the Olympic Council. She's not a Jewess. But she was born in a Jewish quarter in Dublin, in Clanbrassil Street. I come from a very Orthodox family. They were alive when I married Agnes, and they didn't object to it. I had a very good relationship with my parents. I'm not a practising Jew, but I'm very conscious of being Jewish. I had ten relations killed in the Holocaust. I'm an Irish Jew. I'm not taken for a Jew in business, even though I have a 'Jewish' nose. They have a funny idea of Jews. There are very few Jews left in Ireland. A lot of them have gone back to Israel. And others, who are qualified, have gone abroad, like other Irish people.

I think my father was a peddler when he came to Ireland. The Jews were trusted. So he made a few bob and he started a furnishing shop. He even opened a mineral factory in Cork. Then he had a clothing factory, which started as a work-room in Grafton Street, in Dublin, with just a few dozen workers. But he was never a businessman. He wouldn't own a motor-car. He always walked to and from work. And he gave away everything. He made money, by accident, in shares, and he gave it all away to charity. And my father went to Israel and when he came home he hadn't got a penny and I had to keep him for two years. I brought him home and put him in a good nursing home. An orthodox Jew believes that a certain amount of money should go to charity. He is buying a sure ticket to heaven. But my father also tried to give my money away. For himself, he lived a simple life. He had a comfortable life and lived to be ninety-four. So it is in my genes that we live long.

Mary Kate Waters

A native of Spiddal village. Spent several years working in Dublin, before returning to Spiddal.

My grandmother died on the 10th November, 1938, and she was the last person to be buried in the old cemetery in Spiddal. It's closed now. There's a legend that St Enda came to Spiddal. And that's why it's called St Enda's church. There's a stained-glass window in the church and it's written there that the Saint came to Spiddal. Lord Killanin has two seats there, near the tower. He donated them to the church.

When Canon McAlinney became parish priest, every house had to donate ten shillings for the stations of the Cross. The Canon was a great man. He was the first person to bring the *Gaeilgeoirí* to Spiddal. He told the people to do up their old sheds and houses. He even helped them and showed them what to do. And the people moved out themselves to live in the sheds, when the *Gaeilgeoirí* came. And the Bean an Tí used to come into the house and cook for the *Gaeilgeoirí*. And the Christian Brothers used to come and about twenty of them would stay in the house. And they had *céilís* in the college. The summer college used to run for two months, July to August. Seosamh Ó Murchú was the first step-dancing teacher. There were usually eight staying in the two-bedroomed houses. It wasn't a big change for them coming here, because they were nearly all country students. They were all trained teachers but had

come to the Gaeltacht to improve their Irish. I think that they got a small grant as well.

Lal looked after Spiddal village for the Holy Communion. Every family used to give a shilling a year for the Holy Communion. And that's how Canon McAlinney paid for the Communion bills. Everybody could use

Lal's Cottage

the Killanins seats when they weren't there. They used to have visitors, sometimes, who would sit in their seats. They used to have state balls in the old Killanin House. My uncle was brought to London by the Killanins. That was how he ended up in London. They used to have lovely tennis courts and lovely walks in the grounds. And you could go up to the grounds and walk around. But if royalty came from London, Lord Killanin used to tell the villagers not to come up, and he used to close the gates until the royalty left. The Killanins started to grow tomatoes and they were the first people around here to own a car. And Lady Killanin used to give presents. They gave a lot of work to the locals.

Lord Killanin had a sister called Miss Rose. Her face was disfigured and she always had a nurse. She was a dummy as well. They used to come on their holidays. They had their own generator and electricity. They had a bathroom in the house. The water had to be drawn from the well in the garden. At Christmas time they had a ball for the people around. My grandfather and my uncle both worked for Lord Killanin. And my mother worked for him as well. They used to dress-up for dinner and they always had lovely dresses and hair-dos.

There was a Protestant church here too. And the secondary school was where the 'jumpers' were. They used to steal children from other places in Ireland. They used to put them under a hay-cart so nobody would notice them. They used to teach them and feed them. There used to be about twenty of them there. The 'jumpers' were there in the late 1800s. My mother told me these stories. And she said the 'jumpers' were always beautifully dressed. They were educated there. They had their own tutors. They had two factories in Spiddal. And my mother worked in one of them. They made beautiful crochets. There were five or six girls working there. Then they had to get out of there and move down across the road. They had a little factory there as well. But they didn't have as much luck after the move.

Mary Kate Waters at her home in Spiddal

My mother had wanted to be a nurse, but the rest of the family had gone to America and she had to stay at home. I never found Dublin different. My uncle used to come on holiday here twice a year. When I was around thirty-five or -six I got tired of Dublin. I brought my mother to Dublin when I got a job. She was lonely here and she had a thatched house that needed fixing up.

When my uncle died, my mother and myself moved back to Spiddal. Indeed, I met my husband at a *céilí* in Spiddal. He was working in England at the time. I hardly knew him and we got engaged. And it was the best thing that I ever did. My uncle left me the shop. The shop was always in the family. My grandmother came from Park. They were descendants of the terrible O'Flahertys – Roderick O' Flaherty. And she had two sisters and no brothers. My grandmother had no fortune. Then Da Cooney came home from America and he had sovereigns with him. They say that he had two boxes. He'd been to Tasmania as well. Well, when he came home he was looking for a wife and he married my grandmother. He was about fifty-four and she was twenty-four. And he was very good to her. He paid seventy pieces of gold sovereigns for the shop. They moved in to live there and reared seven children there. She used to get the dried fish from Aran. There was a lot of bartering there, as there was very little money in the area. Things were so tight then. One of my uncles came home from America and he bought a bike and toured Ireland. And that's how my grandmother came to the village.

Old Cemetery in Spiddal

When the nuns came to Spiddal Canon McAlinney got the nuns to gather money to buy the Sacred Heart. I remember going to a party that Lord Killanin gave when we were children. He was very good to his tenants. When the new pier was being built my grandfather got a job building it. When the Killanin's house burned there wasn't anybody in it, but they managed to save a lot of it. Part of it is still there. They used to have afternoon tea on the veranda, which is still there. The Black and Tans were down in the barracks, where the old school is. It was an old coastguard station, and they renovated it. But they say that the primary school is sinking because the sea is underneath it. There are ruins of an old monastery there by the cemetery. The walls are still there. They had a church there as well and they used to sleep there.

Uncle Peter had the shop. Then he got married and had no family. He used to sell fishing gear, leather for shoes, screws and nails and everything. And he always had paraffin oil. He kept that outside. He had tea and sugar as well. And he wouldn't sell that to you unless he liked you. He had been told the War was coming and he had got all that stock in. He never worried about coupons. There was a Sergeant there at the time and you had to close on a Monday in Spiddal. And they used to check for weights and measures. Well, one day the Sergeant was coming around to get a pot of jam to check for weights and measures, and Peter wouldn't give it to him unless he paid for it. Peter had a dog and he had the dog trained to go up to the convent to get the paper. And it had to be the *Independent*. And one day when the dog went to the convent the Sergeant was there and he tried to give the dog the the *Press*, but the dog wouldn't take it. It had to be the *Independent*.

The tenants used to have to pay one penny sterling, but the Cooneys never collected it from us. And Lord Killanin never evicted a tenant. They had a barter system and they used to bring vegetables to Lord Killanin, and they used to work for him as well. My grandfather on my father's side worked for him. They lost a lot of money when the house was burned. If they weren't stolen, the pictures, and other valuables, were burned. The Black and Tans were stationed a good while in Spiddal. Some of them were okay, but a lot of them were convicts and that.

The system of education was fantastic here. We had a great music teacher. She was marvellous. And we used to have concerts in the college. People thought they were fantastic. Education was compulsory then. We never got a half-day. Even in babies we had to stay in until four o'clock. We only got a day off if a nun died. And on a Saturday we got off at three o'clock. We used to have to do the preparatory exams. And there was a nun who was related to the Joyces who used to send girls to another school to see how the other half of the world lived. These were girls and boys with no background. She was a great nun. When you came home from school there was no such thing as going out to work. The children who went to college were treated properly. They worked hard at school during the year and didn't have to work when they came home. But when the boys and girls came home from the national school they had to work. They had to draw water and prepare the food for the cows, and hens, and chickens. And they had to double the food on Saturday for Sunday. They had no day off, just Sunday. And they got sixpence to go to a *céilí* if they were lucky.

In Memory of Ruaidhrí Ó Flaitheartaigh

Going to Mass on Sunday was a big event. You always went to first Mass. You weren't allowed out on a Saturday night. At six o'clock on Saturday night my mother used to put away the machine, light the candle and we all said the Rosary. And on Sunday night I went to the *céilí*. But, before I went, we said the Rosary, even though there was also Rosary said in the church. Then a whole crowd of us went to the *céilí* together, and we came home together afterwards. It was all Irish dancing. There were no waltzes or sets. It was the real *céilí* Irish dancing. It was very strict. And we were allowed to play handball and pitch and toss. They started a football club in Spiddal, and I remember my mother had to wash all the shorts and shirts. And she used to have to go to the well to get the water. My father worked on the roads. He built the bridge in Barna.

139

Peadar Bhill Greaney

A blacksmith in the family tradition. His ancestors came to Furbo with Blakes, the landlords.

Bill Greaney was my father and Johnny Greaney was my grandfather. A barrel of rum came ashore and it killed some of them, and it killed my grandfather. My father was young to know about blacksmithing at the time, so he went to Oughterard to learn the trade. He walked all the way from Doire an Locháin to Oughterard every Monday, and back again every Saturday night. After three years of that he started his own business, as a blacksmith, where the old forge is.

My great-grandfather, Bill Greaney, who came from Dun Sandle, near Loughrea, was also a blacksmith. He was the first of the Greaneys here. He might have been working for the landlords, because they took him to na Forbacha, and built him a house on the south-side of the road and a forge on the other. It's called Greaney's Hill. That's where my grandfather first worked as well.

Then my father built a new forge in Furbo, and that one's still there. It was a thatched forge, but I slated it later on. It has ivy round it. The chimney is still there and there was a boiler-house there. Where the glasshouse is now is where my house was. While my grandfather worked for himself, my great-grandfather worked only for the Blakes. He used to shoe horses and make gates and all that. The Blakes had a big place then, around

Furbo, back in the nineteenth century. They would have had eight or nine horses. At that time the only motor car on the road around here was Lord Killanin's, in Spiddal. The landlord was law at that time.

I went to school in Spiddal. That time children would go to school at six years of age for eight years. Times were bad. I had to walk all the way, and go bare-footed in summertime. It was very hard. You had to learn English on account of the landlords. When they went they started teaching through Irish.

I remember working by candlelight at night. I worked with my father until I was eighteen, and then I went to Coogan's Forgery in Galway City, to learn the trade. Coogan was a very good blacksmith. Fintan Coogan was his son, and it happened that Fintan and myself worked together. And there were one or two other fellows who came from England and Coogan taught us all to be proper blacksmiths. And we were learning at the Royal and we were there for half a year. In the end they wanted all the smiths to come. And they all brought their own tools. And you had to make a shoe and drive it on the horse, and rasp it back again, to finish the job. McDonaghs was the big supplier – the iron, the nails, the core were all there.

You had to learn about the anatomy of the horse. You had big bags of bones of the horses, and you had to learn the names of the bones. Then you had to put the bones together. I started learning them and I was doing well. I put all the bones together and the fellow in charge told me I had done well, and wanted me to go to England with him.

But I couldn't go because my father was at home and couldn't do anything. You see, my two brothers and a sister had died of flu. Michael was twenty-one, John was nineteen and Ellen was sixteen. The three of them went in two days. My father wanted me to go to England, to learn more, but sure I couldn't leave him. There were eight girls in the family, but I was the only son left. So I worked with my father 'til he died. He died at seventy-five.

The people from the place were all our clients. Some people had horses, some had mules, and some had jennets, and there was a crowd of donkeys as well. It was normal to

Peadar Bhill Greaney's forge in Furbo

have a horse if you had a bit of land. The people that used to come to the forge with an animal used to do some of the work themselves while they were there. They used to blow the bellows. At that time we got long bars of iron. Some were fourteen or fifteen yards long, and they were an inch and seven-eighths thick. You cut that then for the shoe. Then you turned that to one side and put four holes on the outside and three holes on the inside for the

nails. The heat was fierce. It was an awful job.

And then when the horses were going and work was scarce for them, the shoes came, made and all. You just had to drive them in and put a little clip on the front. The horse's hoof has no sensation. It's very hard. But you had to be careful that you didn't drive the nail right through to the leg. If you did the horse would be bad for a while after. They used to say, long ago – '*Súil an Ghabha, coinnigh ar an tairne é*' – 'The Blacksmith's eye, keep it on the nail.' Inside the hoof is the frog, in Irish they called it *an bradán*. The horses had different sizes of shoe, and you used to have to make the shoes for the mules, jennets and donkeys. The mules were very wicked. They were always kicking.

There was a fellow who came from Bearna with a mule, to the forge. And the mule wouldn't stop kicking. And the fellow wanted me to take a bar and put it around the car at the back of the mule. And when the bar went on him the mule couldn't lift himself to start kicking. There

*Furbo Church and the
Blake family mausoleum*

were a lot of Connemara ponies around in those days. I remember, in Furbo, when things were getting better, people used to have a horse and a pony. They had the horse for working at home, and for sowing potatoes, spreading manure and for hay and that. And they had the pony for running into Galway. They had a small car for the pony and a big one for the horse. They didn't plough on this side of the country, because it was all stones. They used a spade for that.

When I started, before I went to Coogans, all I got was five bob to make a set of shoes, drive them in and do the rasping. And you had to buy coal, and iron, and nails, out of that. When we played pitch-and-put we used buttons sometimes, because we had no money. I used to make cranes for fireplaces. This crane was used to hang pots and pans over the fire. And I made the hooks to hang the pots on too. There was this young lad at the forge one day and he asked me what I was making. I told him I was making a crane and then he asked how long it would last. I said I thought it might last as long as myself. 'Oh, a damn good job to be in, says he, laughing, 'that job won't last long.' At first I thought he was just insulting me, but I thought about it afterwards

I thought he was right. That's when I decided to leave blacksmithing. There was no future in it anymore.

Now I used always do a bit of work in the garden, because of the heat and the smoke in the forge. So when I was seventy, I closed the forge and got a glasshouse to grow vegetables. The horses were nearly all gone at that stage. A crowd of donkeys would come in and all you had to do was put two front shoes on them. And all you got for the lot was around ten shillings. And the donkeys' hooves might be very twisted, so you had to work on them as well.

The grand gate at Furbo is the main entrance on the main road. My grandfather made that gate and all the other gates around Furbo. The gate between the Blue House and the house at Cnoc na Gréine belonged to Major Smith. There was an old 'squadron' going around Furbo and they used to work a day here and a day there for people, but they weren't very welcome.

I have two sons and four daughters. Kathleen is married to Willie Feeley in Moycullen. And Mary Ellen lives in America. Billy is teaching in Furbo school. And Paddy Joe used to be a great 'rambler'. He couldn't stay long anywhere. He's in America now for the last seven years. They're all married so I couldn't ask any of them to come back and carry on the blacksmithing tradition. There's no work for it now, anyway. And I amn't sorry that I can't carry it on. It was too hard.

I enjoyed working on the land. I used to grow onions, potatoes, cabbage, carrots and parsnips, and go to the

A glasshouse heater

market to sell them. It was better money than shoeing horses. I had a fairly big glasshouse with an aluminium frame, fifty feet long and twenty-one feet wide. But I gave that up and gave it to Billy. I got that glasshouse from a Government grant. They gave out twenty glasshouses from here to Ros a' Mhíl. There was a place back near Lochán Beag that had a fellow going round gathering up the tomatoes to sell. I used to sell to him. But sure they could give you their own price, and they were making a lot of money. The year of the big storm took away all the glass.

The church in Furbo is about fifty years old. There's a small church beside it. Blake, the landlord, was buried there, left in a coffin on a shelf. There were four other coffins in it. They were all on shelves around the wall. His wife, or sister, is there too. And they weren't long in it when a crowd came and smashed down the door. It was an iron door. And they broke the door, took the coffins out, stripped the covers open, took all the valuable and then left the coffins there. It was my poor father who had to fix up the door, and put the coffins back in. They used to call that *Tomba na mBlaca.* 'Twas a long time built before the big church. After that Blake left money and land to build the séipéal. Now there was another Blake behind in Tully. And he was terrible. But Blake of Furbo was a good man.

Máirtín Standún

Well-known, much-loved founder, with his wife, May, of Standúns Center for Irish Fashion and Crafts in Spiddal. Brought up in Liverpool by Irish parents.

I was born in 1918, in Liverpool. My father died in 1919. He died from appendicitis at the age of forty-three. My sister Mary was born in 1916, and another sister, Eileen, was born six weeks after my father died. Life was pretty grim in the Twenties and Thirties. My father and mother had been quite poor people. They didn't own any properties or anything. They didn't even own their house.

My mother was a very independent woman. She went out to work when we were quite young. And she left us well-provided for while she was out working. We were quite happy. Things were tough but we had a good upbringing. We all left school at a very early age. I left school at fourteen. There weren't very many prospects for working-class people in the Thirties. I didn't want to stay on at school while my mother worked, so I got a job in an office when I was fourteen. However I got the sack at the end of three months. In desperation I got a job as a delivery boy in Liverpool. There was a lot of heavy work involved. It was really bad. I'd have a rope around me, pulling this big, heavy flat. And when I came to a hill I'd have to wait for some kind person to come along and give me a helping push. Groceries can be very heavy – tinned fruit, sugar, items like that.

Máirtín Standún outside his shop in Spiddal

I worked for practically two years at that. And then, at sixteen, I was promoted to work behind the counter, to start learning the trade. In those days you had to serve three years until you went up to the provisions counter. I got on pretty well in the shop, but then I decided to come to Ireland. My mother had reared us to believe that we were only in England for a while and that our real home was Ireland. The strange thing was, that when I was only four, my mother had said just that to me, in Irish!

When I was sixteen or seventeen I joined the Gaelic League. I was determined to learn Irish. I was doing well in the class when I was transferred from one branch to another in my job and so that made it impossible to attend classes anymore. I then joined the Republican movement and was sort of hounded by the police for a while. So I eventually came to Ireland in the summer of 1939.

I had a job in Dublin until May 1940, when I was arrested and sent to the Curragh. I was there for three years, until 1943. While I was in the Curragh my mother got sick, so I came out, on parole, in 1941. A sister of mine was interned in Mountjoy, so I went to visit her. That was when I met May Mulready, who was a great friend of my sister. She lived in Mullingar and she used to cycle up to Dublin to see me. We decided to get married – sometime. We couldn't say when, because I was only on parole again and had to go back to prison. In the Internment Camp at the Curragh there were thirty men to a classroom. We were locked in every evening at four o'clock in the winter, and didn't see the light of day until

eight o'clock the following morning. And some of these men were very boisterous, having pillow-fights. And others were very morose and in a bad mood. There was nowhere to go. We just had to put up with it. Privacy was very important. Then in 1943 my mother got ill again, and I was allowed out on parole again.

Eventually I went to work in Dublin. I worked in a grocery shop and the wages were very poor. But it was a job. I got on well and got promotion to be manager of the shop. May was teaching in Mullingar and we were saving all we could to get married. We were determined to get a place of our own. That summer May happened to be on holidays with a friend in Spiddal and saw a little shop there. It was part of a house. After a lot of negotiation, we bought it.

One of our big problems in getting started in that little shop in Spiddal was the barter system. It was still very much in existence there at that time. There seemed to be a glut of eggs in the area and almost every customer who came in bartered eggs for tea and sugar and other groceries. The trouble was trying to get rid of so many eggs. I often had to stand in the marketplace in Galway trying to sell these eggs. I used to go in on a Friday evening around the shops. Quite a lot of the shops were already supplied and quite a lot were having to work the barter system themselves. So it was slow, to say the least. I used to dread Christmas because I would end up with cases and cases of eggs. It used to spoil my Christmas. I often took cases of eggs up to Dublin when things got really bad. But eventually things eased off as people didn't seem to be keeping as many hens.

The people of Spiddal and all that area were very, very honest. We used to give credit to everyone. I don't think we ever refused anyone. Whether or not you could do that now is very doubtful. It was wonderful to see such people. Some people might be slow, but it was not their fault. They might have to wait until the turf was dried to pay their bill. But they were very faithful customers and very honest. There was a great pleasure in dealing with such customers. It was a lovely place to live in, because of these honest people around you. There was great friendliness and neighbourliness. And if anyone in a townland was in trouble everybody was concerned about them. It doesn't exist anymore. Not to the same extent as it did.

When we came to Spiddal first there was a bus that went into Galway at eight o'clock in the morning and came out at eleven. Another went in at two. The eight o'clock bus didn't make much of a difference unless you wanted to go in to do some shopping. But the bus at two was important because people used to come from five to ten miles away from us to shop at our place. When things were slack we used to stand at the window and watch the people coming off the bus. Some of them were very big buyers, from big families, and they were great customers altogether. Then you were ready to dash to the bank with the day's takings, to keep the bank manager happy. There were turf lorries at the time, and very often, when a person missed the bus, they would get a lift in a turf lorry.

We had no transport ourselves, so I bought a little van in 1948. It was a second-hand van. I got it from Larry Crawford, who worked for Calor Gas. I had never driven a car in my life. I said to him, 'I'm buying this van and I've never driven in my life. I don't know what I'm going to do with it. I don't know how to drive.' 'Ah,' said Larry, 'there's nothing to it. Sit in there.' So we went through the village and we stopped at a little pub, then Marcus Dick's, now Tigh Chualáin. Still run by the same people, though Marcus is dead now and the son runs the place. Anyway we had two pints and Larry told me how to drive. 'It's very simple,' he said, 'nothing to it! Look! This is the clutch and this is the ignition key. That's very important, because it starts the car. And this is the brake. Now, you just keep your eyes concentrating on the farthest point ahead of you. You'll notice forms on the way, on the side of the road. But don't be trying to make them out, watching for the aged and the young. Just leave enough room for a man to fall off his bike.' Actually I took that advice and did that and still do it and that's why people, to this day, complain that I pass them on the road and don't pretend to see them. So Larry wasn't a bad teacher.

From the start the emphasis in our shop was on Irish goods. Boots went and wellingtons came in and that hit a blow to leatherwear. Then plastic boots came in and finished the tanneries all over Ireland. You had ready-made suits come in and replace the made-to-measure suit. Penneys came into the country and sold garments at a price we found impossible to compete with. You had to be a step ahead of the posse all the time. The business end itself became difficult, with the Value Added Tax – VAT. This involved buying office equipment and dealing with various things. I only had the rudiments of such things, but we managed well enough. We always kept our books up to date, even though that often meant working until two and three in the morning.

It was only lately that we got the mains. Festy and I have the gift of divining water. There is nothing as important as water. When Donal was twelve, I rigged up a little pump from the stream coming down from Baile an tSagairt. Later we built a house beside the old house and discovered a well which was invaluable from 1963 to the 1980s.

After we got electricity we started the ice-cream parlour. And that was a great success. From the start we had this great belief that you should get anything you could manufactured locally. So a local schoolteacher, named Donal Dempsey, made the tables for us. Money was tight, but we did up the old shop. The ice-cream parlour was something different. The people used to enjoy it. The women especially used to enjoy coming in. They'd say how different it was to be able to come in and sit down and have a chat and some ice-cream. We did practically everything to try to push up the profit. But we had no time at all to ourselves. We worked every day, including Sunday. I often regretted opening on a Sunday. I think we should've had at least one day to ourselves. Most people have two. I suppose that eventually we'll have a four-day week.

Things went well and eventually we had to employ staff as we couldn't handle things on our own anymore. We were very lucky with staff. They were all very devoted. We had Sheila Curran and we had Tess since 1956. She was great. They were all very loyal. We built a big kitchen and extra rooms and they all lived in as part of the family.

Pat McCambridge

*Owner of fine food & wine shop in Galway, and
the former landlords Blakes' estate in Furbo.*

The place was bought by my family sometime in the mid-Fifties. Before that it had been owned by the Tourist Board – the old ITB. They had rigged up the old house as a hotel and put it on the market. That was just after the War. At that time a lot of places were being sold, places like Ashford Castle and Ballinahinch. And it had been condemned. They had had a survey done by an uncle of my wife. That was before I knew my wife. A man by the name of Kennedy condemned it. The basement was under water level and it had a fair amount of damage. One bit that is still intact is the porch.

It belonged to the Blake-Dalys. There was a famous character there in those days, a Mrs Drew. And she owned this place (premises on Shop St), and Roxborough House as well. After we bought it, not a whole lot happened. My father built a little bungalow, where I live now. We've done very little with it. There were no damp courses on the walls so there was a lot of fungi. There were stables there as well. They were left intact. There was a famous, or infamous, Blake, who used only come out on Sundays. He was in a lot of trouble; he owed money and that.

Now Cnoc na Gréine House belonged to the Blakes as well. There's a book of names, compiled by the ICA in Barna, which deals with the Blakes. There was a Blake

over there and he was short of cash. Now his sister was the Reverend Mother in one of the convents, and she gave him a hundred pounds. And for that she got the deeds to Cnoc na Gréine.

There seems to have been a lot of different types of Blakes. There were Blakes in Menlo Castle, up the river. He was the one who only came out on Sundays. But even though he owed a lot of money, he cleared his name before he died. Then there was a John Blake. He was a great character and he had magnificent handwriting. He lived out in Oranmore, where Eamonn Lydon is living now. The Blakes seem to have been scattered all over Connaught. There were Blakes in Claregalway. The Blake woman who was born there ended up as Mrs Drew. She was very good-looking and a notorious character. There was a Prince killed in Limerick, in a motor-racing accident, and it is reputed he was driving her car. She was in London during the War and she married two or three times. She got hurt in the Blitz and was disfigured. There is a story that some solicitor wiped her out in London. Then she came back here and tried to re-possess this place. We had just moved in. This was in the Sixties.

When I was growing up we lived in St Mary's Road and I used to go out to Connemara, fishing and shooting, at ten o'clock on a Sunday morning. And I was always back for the family lunch at one o'clock. At that time I could only fire one barrel. I wasn't fast enough for the second barrel until a year later. My father used to go out there a lot to talk to the young lads, but I went out there to fish and shoot. That was Crumlin Lodge I used go to. On one occasion I went out there for a week. And in the week I collected fourteen trout and eighteen sea-trout. And the following year I did the same thing. Then I was able to drive and get around more. I got eighteen trout and twenty-two sea-trout. But I never sold anything that I caught, or shot. It was against my principles.

Crumlin Lodge was a lodge going back a long time. Mrs Burke-Cole owned it. Her husband and herself lived a lot of the

The ruins of Furbo House, former home of the Blakes

time in St Kerrin's in Blackrock. She had two sons, but they weren't interested in the place. The place was very secluded and very beautiful. That was back in the late Forties. Stanley Lowe was a great man to go out there. People came from England to fish. Crumlin Lodge was just a two-storey wooden lodge.

I never heard anything about the Blakes of Furbo. But then, you never heard anything about the good Blakes, only the bad ones. Lord Clontarf of Ballinasloe was a

gangster. I never heard anything good about him. Teach Furbo was a bit big for a hunting lodge. Now, there were other lodges as well. There was Fermoy Lodge. But most of the lodges have changed hands. Fuller stole the name of 'Teach Furbo'. That was originally Marino Lodge. And some people called it Thornton's Lodge. When Fuller first came here, he came to us and said he wanted to buy Furbo, or part thereof. Well, he called the other place, which is the Connemara Coast Hotel now, Teach Furbo. He bought that from the Thorntons in the Sixties. It was a biggish house. There were Christian Brothers in our house for a while. They had an Irish College there. Old Judge Ford lived there for a while, as well, way back in the Thirties.

The original house was built in 1820 or 1830. I think the Blakes built it themselves. It was a mixture of limestone, granite and brick. After that they added on and put in a toilet. The Blakes gave the ground for the church and the old school. The vault up there was the Blake's family

Cnóc na Gréine (Knocknagreena), Furbo

vault. But that was pilfered and desecrated around the War years. The vault was there a long time. A lot of what was on the deeds was in handwriting and it's hard to read.

There was supposed to have been a ghost in Furbo House. I remember Sean Forde's father telling me that, one night, there was terrible howling. It was a windy night. And there was an old well at the back of the house. It was very hard to get to it. But he went out with his torch and his dog, looking for the ghost. A lot of local people wouldn't walk up there at night.

My father never lived in the house. We only used it as a summer-house, until I got married, in 1962. The house was then little more than half the size it is now. I added on. Before me, Jimmy Ward lived there for a while. My mother gave him the house while he was building his own. For some reason or other my father never moved in there. But then, he was getting old at that time. My mother, even though she was an invalid, did stay there for periods. I have an agreement about the

sanctuaries. I don't bother to shoot anymore. I like to look at the birds now. I have about a hundred and twelve acres now. It was divided, way back in the early 1900s. I'd say that there was a lot of mountain there at that time. There wasn't much of a mention of tenants being there at all. There was a caretaker there all right. Walter's father was the caretaker there for many years. And Walter was with us for years. He had the Gate Lodge. His father was a very nice man. Jimmy Greaney used to work on the estate as well. He's Darby Greany's son. Another of Derby's sons worked for us in the old days. And the mother was a brilliant woman. She was very intelligent and very good with her hands. And Mrs Curran is another person worth talking to. There's another Greaney up where she is, as well – Bartley Greaney. There was a toll house there beside Cnoc na Gréine. There was a toll collector in Barna, and I remember paying tolls. Barna was located inside the Rahoon district of Galway, in an area called the Liberties which terminated at Liberty Stream, beside Liberty Point where tolls were collected. Tolls were to maintain the city walls and were put on produce sold at the market.

My father was working for a Protestant man in Newry. Now there was a Black and Tan in the area one night and he was quite drunk. And the Superintendent came to him and told him to move on. But he had his revolver, and wouldn't. However, my father managed to disarm him. My father worked for the Powells. The Powells had a pub and a grocery shop. Paddy Powell was in the Aran Islands. Jack Dolan worked for him as well.

John O'Connor

Farmworker in Willis Park, near Oughterard, a three-hour walk from his home, in Boluisce, Spiddal. The farm where he worked is now Oughterard Golf Club.

My mother used to make all our clothes when I was growing up. She used to use flannel and *báinín*. She used to put the thread on a thing like a little ladder and tie it up. But that thread went to the weaver and he made the flannel, about ten or twelve yards. And you had to get it washed as well. She didn't make the pants or the shirts. The tailor used to make the suits. But she was good with the needle.

My father used to make the baskets. He made them from sally rods, or hazel rods. He got some of them in the forest here, and some in the Seanaghurráin Wood. And we used to sell them, every year, for thatching houses. My father used to thatch the house. A good coat of thatch would last five years. But he put a 'comber' and a new layer of thatch on every year. My mother made the butter by churning it. The bowl was wooden, with a handle in it to churn it. After churning for a while you got a lump of butter forming. You then washed the butter and wrapped it in paper and sold it in Galway. The women were stronger then and weren't as lazy as they are now. Some women worked harder than the men. My father never brought anything to Galway. My mother did all the work. My father used to cut the turf. My mother used to flatten it and put it together.

I was sixteen years old when I went to work for the Willises. I got ten shillings a week. I got accommodation as well. His name was Robert Willis. He wasn't a landlord, but he owned a big farm. During the War I went to England to work at the building trade for a couple of years. With the 'blackout' you weren't even allowed to light a match outside after dark. You couldn't see anything at all.

When I worked for Mr Willis he had four horses, four cows, a bull and some sheep. The horses were half-bred and we used to go back to Roundstone and Ballinrobe and we won a few races. And we went to the Claddagh, in Galway. There used to be races there as well. And it was very hard to find a lad that wasn't too heavy for the horses. I used to look after them. I used to be up at six o'clock in the morning. I used to bring them round two or three laps of the field. I fell a few times. I used to milk the cows, as well. And we used to go out on the Corrib, fishing. Willis was a decent man. The horses were just half-breeds, half-common. They were never in the Galway Races.

Robert Willis had a family. His daughter used to live with him. She was fairly old. She never got married. She used to have a lot of visitors there and they used to play the piano. I wasn't living in with them. I had my own house, so I could come and go as I pleased. It might often be two or four in the morning when I came in. They had a girl working for them. She used to do the cooking and the daughter used to help. They had nice furniture in the house, armchairs in the parlour. They had a big press packed up with books and they used to sit around the fireplace, reading.

John O'Connor at his home in Boluisce Uachtar
with turf basket made by himself

Before Willis, I worked for a man called Lee. Lee came from Knock and he bought a big shop and a pub in Galway city. When I worked for him things weren't so good. He used to buy *poitín* back in Connemara and sell it in the pub. The police caught him, anyway, and he was fined. Folans had a lot of pubs in the city at that time, but didn't they sell the lot. A family called Francis bought one. Anyway, when Lee was kicked out of Galway, he bought a place in Oughterard. He didn't have tenants. He used to have people working for him. And he didn't pay that well. He had no horses. He had cows for milking. He never let me go out with the cattle in case I met somebody, and they might advise me to get out of it. I was there for two years. I was sixteen then. I just left home and went over to Oughterard and asked for work. That's how it was. You were tied down all the time. He wanted to keep me there. And then he wanted to cut my wages, so I left.

I used to go card playing at night. There were pubs as well, but I didn't go into them at that time. Or I didn't go to the dances. Most times we just went to other houses playing cards. We played for money, and at Christmas time we might play for a goose. We used to play twenty-fives.

My family, on my mother's side, were always here. They were Clancys. My father came from Leitir Meas and moved here when he married my mother. We used to go to school in the summer. And in the wintertime we could be at home for three months without going to school, because there was no path down the mountain.

They didn't sow much, just vegetables – cabbage, parsnips, carrots, potatoes – that's all. And my mother used to sell the eggs in Galway. She used to carry a basket with eggs and butter to Galway. She went over by Leitir Péic and over the mountain then toward Moycullen, and into Galway. She used to walk the journey bare-footed, with her shoes in the basket. And then she'd put on the shoes when she got to the city. The teachers that used to travel and teach didn't come out as far as here. They went as far as Leitir Péic. If someone was sick, or having a baby, if it was a question of living or dying, then the doctor might come next day. You had to meet the doctor out there with the boat. Someone would give him a lift as far as the end of the road.

They carried the stones to build the houses before the roads were built. Joe Curran brought the stone by boat to build his house. And you used to be afraid the boat would sink with the weight of the stones. He built that house even before the road was built. It was about twenty years ago.

They used to visit one another and they used to go to Leitir Meas as well. They played cards and told stories. They didn't have music, or singing, or dancing. They used to drink *poitín*. They made it in the mountains. You used to get a bottle of *poitín* then for two bob. They used to make it from barley and oats and brown sugar. You had to malt it first. And then you spilled it on the floor and burned it. Then you left it for nine or ten days, turning it every day. You had a kiln and you had to keep a good fire going. It was hard work and it was dangerous. They used to make it in the houses. That was risky. It would spoil the house with water. You were better off to make it in an out-house, or below on the rocks. They made

A poitín stil

poitín out on the island. But that was very hard work. You used to have to spend the night watching for lights coming and the guards. I was working in Oughterard when they stopped making it. They were making it in Oughterard as well. And if the guards came along they used to burn bushes and say they were clearing the land. But they weren't as strict in Oughterard as they were here. They were very strict here. If you were caught with the *poitín* you were fined six pounds. Or, if you couldn't get the money you had to spend six months in jail.

The priest used to come up here to say Mass. He had a season in every house. And then he used to go back to Leitir Fir. There were two houses there all the time – John Walshe and Michael Walshe. There's a road going there from Knock – a bad, old road. When the priest said the stations Mass they'd have a great day that day. There would be a meal as well. The stations were twice a year, and after the priest was gone, after the meal was over, they'd have a great sing-song. They'd have an accordion. The priest used to come up in a boat, up the lake, and then he'd walk over. They used to pay the priest some money, but not much though.

If somebody died they used to put the dead body in a coffin and carry the coffin down along by Bothúna. All the people used to walk behind the coffin and they'd have a wake as well. They used to lay the coffin outside the house and the women used to come out and do the *caoineadh*. They used to beat on the coffins as well, because they were so sad after the person dying. They used to pick out three or four women that were able to cry. And they could cry, no problem. Festy Conlon's mother used to do a lot of that crying. They used to have two nights of a wake sometimes. They'd leave the body two nights in the home and then bring it and bury it.

Pat Ó Droighneáin

A blacksmith from Spiddal, known locally as Pat an Gabha (Blacksmith). Sat beside writer Máirtín Ó Cadhain in school.

There were only four that lived in my family. The others died in infancy. I have a sister in America. And I had a brother who was a very quiet and shy man. He was a fine man. None of us became blacksmiths, like my father. Though we helped him when we were growing up. It was too hard a life. My father was eighty-five or eighty-six when he died. He used to put the shoes on horses. And he put wheels on the carts. He made carts as well. I remember him making a little cart for our own donkey.

I remember once, my father had twenty-two tyres to put on and the water had to be carried a long way – five barrels of water. But I helped him myself. And he used to go where the fire would be most hot. If the wind was blowing from the east he'd go to the west. And it was very hard work. There were lots of horses around in those days, and at that time of year they used to be very thirsty with the weather. They used to have to walk across Boluisce Lake and bring bags of heather across the ice, it was so cold and icy. And my father used to be up 'til two in the morning, sharpening the horses' shoes and putting in frost-nails. He was a strong man. That would be around eighty years ago. And my mother used to go to Galway with a horse and cart. I remember once we met my mother at Furbo gates and the horse was trotting along. And she told us she couldn't stop, because the horse might slip. But my father always had our own horse in such a way that my mother was safer than anyone else. At one time he had the contract from Pat McDonagh. He owned Conway's – it's called Hughes now. And my father was dressing tools for him for a long time. The Conways had two shops – a bakery shop and a grocery shop. They were very good people. They used to give credit. And they said that everyone paid them, except one man. It might have taken years for him to pay them, but he did pay them. After twenty-five years, he sent them a cheque for £25 from America.

My father, in spite of his drinking, was a fine man, and a good provider. He could do anything. For instance, he was very good at the fishing. He was able to bait any line and have the tackle always right. He fished from a boat out in the bay and he never, ever came home empty-handed. And he used to go out on very windy days, fishing for whiting. We always had plenty to eat. There was no such thing as selling the fish. He used always give some to the neighbours. Sometimes we salted the whiting. I don't think we ever salted mackerel. The Feast of St Martin was the 11th of November, and we always killed a pig for that Feast. We used to share it with our neighbours. We'd give them five or six pounds of bacon.

My mother had to work very hard to keep the family. There was a long, thatched house here at that time. My mother was a very good cook. She made the best of bread and best of butter, and so on. And at that time we had hens, ducks, geese, turkeys and everything. And the priest asked her if she would keep the strangers, the *Gaeilgeoirí*. Things were bad at that time and we had a lot of the rafters in the house falling down, so we had to cover them with plaster. And then my mother got cancer of the liver. My eldest brother went to Canada. He was really trying to make his way to the USA, illegally. But he got caught and he was jailed. And it was a long time before he got out. He was in prison for six months.

My grandmother, that's my mother's mother, lived to be one hundred and four. She was still alive when my mother got the cancer. My mother bought a shroud for my grandmother, but sure it was herself who wore the shroud. Then I had an aunt living with us as well, and she was semi-blind and not as well-up as the rest of the family. The night my poor mother died, my grandmother who didn't understand things at that stage,

Peait Ó Droigneáin, better known as Peaitín an Gabha, at home in Coilleach, Spiddal

was shouting at her to get up and make a cake.

Now we'd been used to the students, the strangers, the *Gaeilgeoirí*, staying with us since 1912. By 1928, when my poor mother died, the gentry of the country were coming and staying here to learn how to speak Irish. There were judges, solicitors, barristers, doctors and university professors coming. They were very nice, good people and were treated as such by all the locals.

I remember well, more that ten years later, when the War started in 1939 and 1940 there was a great shortage of fuel. And people of my age were all out cutting turf on the bog from morning 'til night. And then when the War stopped things got better. The Social Welfare for single people was stopped from March until November. So you had to get work for those months. I used to walk out to Boluisce to work every day. I was the blackguard of the family, very independent and wanting to earn my own money. And my mother had bought me a new pair of boots. There was no tar on the roads at that time, so after a week of walking to Boluisce the boots were in a bad way. The wages were eighteen shillings a week. After a week the boots were gone. My mother wasn't pleased at all.

I don't remember the landlords, but an aunt of mine, who went to America, told me all about them. She remembers them from growing up here. In her day everybody had to give three days work every week to the landlord. But she got tired of that and went off to America. It was said that the Lynch family, landlords of that time, fathered a lot of children, I don't know any of the girls who became pregnant. But the landlords, generally, were very cruel. Lord Killanin was a landlord, but he was nice. He had a lovely house that was burned down. It was a three-storey house and it had lovely rockeries. And everyone was allowed into the grounds, to take walks. But the Lynches weren't nice. They lived in Coláiste Chonnacht. They had a coach-house and a driveway. Joe O'Brien's grandfather, Nicholas, worked for them. He drove for them. I don't think they came to my father to get the horses' shoes fixed. It was before my time and I don't think my father was qualified then.

That time was a time of poverty. It was a nasty time. People were burning down places. They were blowing up bridges as well. The Irregulars burned down Lord Killanin's beautiful place. It was a very foolish game. I think the world has gone cracked. I was foolish myself. I remember people coming here at night and knocking on the door. My brother left Ireland and went to Canada because of the way things were going. And he had no friends in Canada. I thought that Michael Collins was a fine man. He was a great man. He was sent to England and de Valera stayed at home. I visited Béal na Bláth where he was shot.

Séamus Ó Beirn

Medical doctor with practice in Spiddal where he was born.
Great interest in the history of medicine.

Medicine was on my father's side. My grandfather and his brother were from Tawin, an island near Oranmore. Both brothers did medicine. My grandfather's name was Séamus and his brother's name was Bartley. And subsequently, all of their families went into medicine. Then my grandfather married an O'Malley, and practically all of her family were into medicine also. So both sides of my father's family were in medicine.

Now my grandfather was a very colourful character, and he was interested in culture as well. He was away ahead of his time. He pioneered a new concept of preventative medicine. In 1905 or 1906, he decided that there must be a way of eradicating typhus and TB. And he set about doing that. He took his bike and cycled around Connemara, and gave people classes on sanitation, and how to approach sanitation. One of the hardest things for him was trying to convince people not to have animals in the house – like a calf, or a *banbh*, or a sheep. Another thing was that they had no windows, because they were taxed on windows at that time. They only had one door and a chimney in the house. The GP in Spiddal died of typhus and my grandfather came out to Spiddal. He actually met the funeral on his way to Spiddal. He was here for a year and a half and then he

went off, as a ship's doctor, to New Zealand. He became a great friend of Marconi, and was a good friend of Roger Casement as well. Casement wrote to him a lot. He had a great interest in the Irish. My grandfather was a very complex man.

On the question of hygiene, some people used to bring big animals inside. They used, literally, to bring pigs into the parlour. The pig lived there. They didn't understand hygiene at that time. Even the medicine of that day had no interest in it. And the people wore a lot of clothes. They wore five or six layers of clothes to keep them warm. And they slept in these clothes. They sweated in them and they smelled. Some parts of the country had worse conditions than others. A lot of deaths were caused by lack of hygiene. The infant mortality rate was very high, and there was no sterilisation. People didn't understand about bacteria at that time. There were women who thought they were good midwives, and the women they attended were lucky if they were hygienic midwives.

They used natural herbs in so far as they were available at the time. Of course, some of what was available became the best medicines later on. It was just that they didn't know how to use them then. But the biggest advance for mankind in medicine was the improvement in hygiene conditions. You need to be clean. You need to realise that there are bacteria and there are ways of avoiding them. The people at that time wouldn't have washed themselves. The only time they might have washed themselves was in summertime when they were down at the beach collecting seaweed. They also had open fires and the toilet facilities were outside. There are little things that we tend to forget. Trousers didn't have a zip. They urinated through them, so there was always a smell.

They had a poor diet. They didn't have a staple diet that was consistent, other than potatoes and fish if they lived by the coast. We always feel that they fished during the Famine and so wondered why so many people died. But potato was the main staple food. They ate very little meat. And they only ate one meal a day, if they got it. So food and hygiene were the main causes of death at the time.

A cottage in Ros Muc

And there was space as well. People needed breathing space in their houses. This also helped to prevent community illnesses. What we tend to forget is the disastrous focus on medicine in the eighteenth century, and then in the nineteenth century they tried to focus more on medicine in a scientific way. But now science has swung too far in theory. So now, a lot of holistic methods have become popular.

But back in my grandfather's era he would have seen a lot of changes. My mother was the District Nurse. She was originally from Ballygar (East Galway). And she had the choice of Bray or Spiddal. She had never heard of either, but she picked Spiddal. She came here around 1940. She hadn't a word of Irish and she found it hard to communicate at first. There wasn't a great deal of English at the time. She got by, but it was a tough life. The Dudley Nursing Scheme in Ireland at the time was British-based, set up in the late eighteenth century, for impoverished areas. The State didn't set up a scheme until much later.

Lady Dudley left a great deal of money to a very worthwhile cause. She built cottages along the west coast, as nurses' houses. My mother lived in one of these cottages and she found it a very comfortable place. Then my father came during the War. All maternity services were district-located at that time. There were no maternity services in the hospitals. They didn't develop until later on. So the hospital, even still, carries a stigma for the older generation, because you only went to hospital if you were dying. That was the way they perceived it.

My mother would have been twenty-two or twenty-three when she came to Spiddal, which was poor and far away. She worked very hard. Then my father died when I was young and she carried on working. She had to leave us, sometimes, at night, to deliver babies. Most of the babies born in the area between 1940 and 1961 were delivered by my mother. The transition between the 1920s and the 1970s was massive, even though the country was impoverished. There was more of a perception about hygiene. They didn't begin to realise until then that fresh air was good for you. I knew most of that generation and I know how difficult things were for her. The area that she covered was as far east as Furbo, to Cnoc na Gréine. Then she went west to Baile na hAbhann. When she got married she left that place and went to live in Spiddal for two years, and then they built the house. My father died in 1951 and she moved back to the old house and I lived there from the age of three. She held on to the new house for a while, but found it hard to look after it, and had to sell it for less than it cost to build. 'Twas sold during the depression in the Fifties.

She was only in her thirties when she was left on her own. She had a local girl come in to look after us if she had to go out at night. I remember being put to sleep in the back of her car, in the wintertime, when she had to travel to Sheanadh Phéistin. I was about five, or six at that time. My mother used to encourage the women to breast-feed. She was proud that she had been trained. In the Fifties the hospitals started to take over, and mothers used to be confined for ten days to two weeks. And the mothers liked this because it was just like a holiday.

I recall one thing. My mother was very naïve. She had bottles of *poitín* and she thought it was Holy Water. People at that time were very religious. And I remember

her telling us that my father saw the bottles of *poitín* and he asked her what it was for. She told him it was Holy Water to bless herself. She had a very tough life. The nursing was a true vocation. And because we were a one-parent family, it was difficult for us. But it was the obvious thing for me to follow in my parents' footsteps. I would have got the tradition more from my mother than my father. I saw my mother working. I decided to specialise in rheumatology. Well, that's what I was heading into, but I had a change of mind,

I suppose, like everything else, human development is a slow metamorphosis. The attitude toward mental illness was very poor. It was the age of lunatics and strait-jackets. There was a great lack of understanding.

The main illnesses of psychiatry existed in those days. The big ones, like depression, were there also, but were never treated as problems. At the time people were very self-reliant. There was a surgery and people came on certain days. It was free during my grandfather's time. It was the English system and the doctors were paid a Government salary. In 1948, my father was paid a salary of £150 a year by the Irish Government. My grandfather was paid by the British Government. My father had private patients to supplement his salary.

The interesting thing was that, at the turn of the century, the life expectancy of a woman was fifty, so the menopause didn't really exist. A lot of people just didn't survive to middle-age crisis. At that time a woman was a second-class citizen and was taught to keep her mouth

Séamus Ó Beirn outside his home in Spiddal

throughout the world. The only place that really had preventative medicine was France. They had sheets of lambs' intestines in use as condoms in the prostitute houses there. The women in the West of Ireland knew a little about their own cycle, but knew nothing about the phases of life. It was an era of producing babies. The whole development of medicine and factual knowledge, especially in the past twenty years, has been phenomenal. But, in the whole development of man, medicine has done very poorly in the metaphysical realm.

In the early part of the twentieth century the life expectancy of people here matched that of Third World countries and Africa. The average age of a girl marrying was thirteen. Down's Syndrome existed at the time, but was related more to older women. A lot of children with psychiatric problems were sent to mental institutions. Those who had minor retardation problems were kept at home, but were sent to the parlour when anyone came to visit.

The doctor, teacher and priest were the pillars of society. They were the only ones that were educated. And the whole community depended on them to a much greater extent than we realise. They wrote letters for them and dealt with official business for them. My father moved to Bofin for a while, in 1939 or 1940. His first posting was in Bofin. He used to write to my grandmother. He spent two years there.

The biggest problem for my mother was that she had no Irish. I spoke Irish outside and English to my mother.

shut. This was the end of the Victorian era. There wasn't a lot of obstetric care at the time, especially in the West of Ireland. People didn't know anything about how to prevent becoming pregnant. There was a great ignorance,

161

When my father died he left my mother badly off, with debts. He had a car accident. We didn't go hungry, but we weren't well-off. I don't think that kept us apart from the community in any way. The other thing is that, in a close-knit community, the people confided in the doctor, and he, in turn then, had to speak to them in confidence, had to be part of their trust. And that perception included certain norms. So you do conform to certain norms because they trust you in confidence. I would know a certain amount about how to deal with difficult problems. We have developed to an extent that we do understand the causes, and we have developed psychologically. Now we can now relate more to spirituality.

My role now is different to that of my father and grandfather. They had to deal with crisis medicine, and we've gone past that. Our problems now relate to people's own self-perception. People are more aware now that things in their lives affect their well-being. So there is more psychology now. The trouble about medicine is that it's largely about compassion, and the more you give the more you want. And when you give compassion the patient wants more, which can become a problem if you feel too much. It's bad for the patient if medicine takes on responsibility, because then the patient becomes dependent. I would like to see medicine pass down in my family. But it's a hard life. The points system can be a problem, but it's hard to find a system that's correct. The worst thing is that the points are so high for medicine and everybody tries to attain them. But they may not be cut out to be doctors. It helps to have rapport and communication skills, and to like people, to be a doctor. And you have to have a listening ability and be intuitive.

My grandfather wrote a number of plays. He wrote a bilingual play. He didn't have any Irish when he met my grandmother and he always had great fun trying to speak it. He thought it would be a great idea to have an Irish-speaking theatre in Galway. He and a few others got together and formed the Taibhdhearc. Mícheál Mac Liammóir acted there. And my grandfather was its first chairman and produced plays. He did a lot of producing and directing. My grandfather's uncle had a business and he gave that business to his two nephews. It was called Fahy & Co.

Father Éamonn Ó Conghaile (Eddie Bheairtle)

Fr Eamonn, Parish priest in Tír an Fhia. A widower, with six children. Late vocation to the priesthood. Comes from a family of Seanchaí. Traces the Catholic religion from Celtic times.

They still follow the sun and the sea as much as they used to. It's still very much part and parcel of their lives – going out, leaving the harbour – in their boats. They go along with the power of nature, with the sun and the seasons. And they used to bless the boat. The first Saints sailed in here – Éanna, Colmcille, Mac Dara. And they still practise the old Celtic traditions. They gave us a lot of prayers. If a dog had rabies, you took the poison out of the tooth. Colmcille gave us that one. But with the new Catechism, that was all banned, the good and the bad together; because there was some bad as well.

These changes happened when Maynooth started. And some of it was abused. And this called the Catholic Church to banish it all. They used to say that *piseogs* were evil, which is not true at all. *Piseogs* were the basic psychology of the people. They had no schooling, really, but they had an education, and a very fine one at that. I took a great interest in it, even though I finished school forty years ago. There were many *seanchaí* around here. My father was a great *seanchaí* and, like other *seanchaí*, he

explained things very well. There's a difference between a *seanchaí* and a storyteller. A *seanchaí* is the custodian of tradition, and there are various types. There are the Ó Conghailes who go back through generations of people. They go back several thousands of years. There were several different tribes belonging to the one group and the one family were the *seanchaí*. There were various tribes that were here with the Bolgha (meaning 'dart from the mouth' because they used poisoned arrows), who later became referred to incorrectly as the *Fir Bolg*. There were several tribes with the Bolgha.

There were two sects of the Ó Conghailes. The Ó Connallaigh were another tribe. They were trainers and breeders and handlers of greyhounds. And others were trainers and handlers of the watchdog. This is going back to two to four thousand years before Christ and before that again. There were only two tribes that could not be traced here, that were here before the rest of us – Muintir Uí Nia, Nee, which means a spirit, and Ó Madáin, the Maddens, who were referred to as good people. And nobody knew where they originally came from. They had certain gifts in their names. I got all this information from the old *seanchaí*. I took great interest in that. I was interested in their healing powers, and how they used their magic, and the two types of magic. There are three, in fact; and how they prepared to be able to perform that wonderful magic. They had to get special training.

A person had to start on the lower branch of Crann an Eolais (Tree of Knowledge) and graduate to the top

163

Waiting for Féile Mhic Dara to begin

branch, where the magic powers were. Again, this is where confusion arises in the minds of people about witches. There were witch doctors in Africa, and there are witches in England and Ireland now. The Church was always very hard on them; anyone who had a gift of knowledge, or any gift, was branded as a witch. And they were really very good people. There was a woman in Clifden who was great. I never heard a bad word said about her. But the priests were pretty hard on them. Indeed, all the Christian Churches were hard on them. But they were very fine people.

A lot of them were probably getting their powers directly from the Holy Spirit. And they had an understanding how to do that. They had a 'recipe'. In some cases it was a natural power. People used to go to these so-called witches when they were ill and needed healing. If a woman had a sick child, the cure was got from a rider on a white horse. This was the cure, this was the cure. These people, with this special knowledge used to tell them what to do, and whatever it was, it worked. The healers knew about the power of the soul and the power of the spirit to heal, and to get that the spirit had to be good.

Now, through Confirmation in the Catholic Church we are given the seven gifts of the Holy Spirit. These are seven great gifts. But do we really receive them? We are given them, but do we actually know them? My belief is that we are too young to know about them, and that we should be over twenty-five before we are confirmed. And then we should be really enthusiastic about them, asking for them and looking for them.

I was with the Coiste Béaloidis of Connemara, and we were doing sessions in Áras Uí Chadhain. Pádraig Ó hÉalaí organises the *seanchaí* sessions. Religion was discussed by the *seanchaí*. And if one of the *seanchaí* was worried about some little aspect, or part of, the *seanchas*, they used to go to one another and discuss it. And that was called '*ag ceartú an tSeanchais*'. A direct translation of which is 'correcting the *seanchas*', but it doesn't mean just that. However, a lot of the old *seanchas* has been left unwritten, a lot of it was kept untold. They wouldn't give it to anybody. And the reason was that the people who were gathering it sometimes didn't understand it. You see, a lot of people don't understand what *piseog* exactly means. And if they have a good look they'll see that the Catholic Church itself has its *piseogs*. Like blessing yourself with holy water.

Say, for example, that a woman lost her husband, and she was very worried, because there was no State Aid and she couldn't feed the children. She was very shook-up.

And they go through a very emotional stage and come to a pitch where a power can be used, because it has gone to the extreme. It's almost the same thing as learning how to use magic. You have to bring the mind up to a stage where the spirit can work. It's the same as prayer; that people can bring their lives to a stage where their prayers are answered. And this really does happen. And it's really the power of one's own spirit. And I don't think that supernatural powers, or evil powers have anything to do with that.

The old Celtic religion was a part of what was passed on from one generation to another. There was the early Christian religion, which we had here before Saint Patrick came to Ireland. However it came here, I don't know, but it did. Mason Island, which was not really an island, is just beside Oileán Mhic Dara. And there was a time when there was a church there on that island. And the people living on the island did it up. And there was a brand-stone with the sign of the cross cut into it. It was like a cake. This was what they used to commemorate the Last Supper. They broke the cake on that. This was used instead of Communion at that time. Also, the sign of the cross, when breaking the bread, came from that. St John's Night is the bonfire night. There are two different traditions to that. There's the Pagan tradition and the Christian one.

There is a cross on Oileán Mhic Dara which is probably the oldest cross in Ireland. I was on the island for St Mac Dara's day and I met an Egyptian priest who was telling me that the granite of the cross was not local granite but granite from southern Egypt. There were evidently four crosses in the world from the beginning of Christianity. The one on Mac Dara's island was possibly brought to Santiago de Compostela in Spain by the Apostle James and from there to St Mac Dara's island, which was seen as being on the edge of the Western world. Mac Dara who was the son of the King of Leinster was into justice as well as religion and even after his death people came to the cross for justice. Under British occupation it was regarded as a cursing stone. Consequently an effort was made three times by three different Archbishops of Tuam to get rid of the cross. The first time it was dropped in the sea at twenty fathoms, the second time at forty fathoms and the third time at sixty fathoms with three shelves in the ocean and each time it was washed up again on the shore of the island and has remained there ever since.

On the face of the cross is a design with four squares to depict the four corners of the world and a little curvature in each which means calling the spirit back from the four corners of the world. On the opposite side the design is circular, meaning Heaven beyond the sky, eternity. The message of the cross is that it is through the centre of the cross, the passion and death of Christ, that Eternity is reached. This is the way to Heaven. All of the sacrificial altars on the island have stone crosses in the centre. These had a strong message that the Lamb had offered himself on the altar so there was no need to sacrifice animals. The Laws of Moses were very strong here and through Christianity were accepted and many customs such as those of St Martin's Eve are still practised.

But the Church and the brand-stone are proof that Christianity came here before St Patrick. So the *seanchaí* religion was the old religion, and the new religion is the Catholic religion. And *seanchas* was passed down through the family. It was passed from one *seanchaí* to another. Now, with television, they're not interested in the *seanchas* anymore. They can't pass it on to them anymore. The children don't have the time. And they're losing a great education. I had *seanchas* when I was fifteen, from the old people, that I wouldn't hardly dare tell my own children until they were at least twenty. And I had some other *seanchas* that I was only told when I was forty. And when I asked why I wasn't told until then, I was told that I was too young to know until then.

A story I tell which is much loved by children is the story of the Garden of Eden. Everything you can think of is growing in this garden, all kinds of fruit and flowers. There are mountains, rivers and lakes there also. There is only one problem. There is a stone wall around the garden, which is too high to climb, not possible to get under and impossible to get through. However, every day that you do a good deed, a stone is removed and you can peep through into the garden. But every day you do something bad, a stone is put back. The moral is to try to continue to do good.

The first priests came here around the 1820s. And at the time we were very short of priests. That first priest came from Mayo and his name was Éamon Ó Máille. And this was the first place he came to after his ordination. He

Hookers at Féile Mhic Dara with Oileán Mhic Dara in the background

started confessions. And he was given a year to get established in the parish. He went out every day visiting people in the parish. But they had been so long without a priest that nobody would listen to him. So when the year was up, he realised that his mission had failed. He was very disappointed. And he was advised that he was better off leaving these people alone.

Now, during his year in the parish the young priest had become friends with a man called Pádraig and his son. Pádraig and his son used to sail to Westport. One night they got caught in a bad storm there and had to stay in a local house. The woman of the house asked them where they were from, and when they told her she said she had a son a priest in that part of the country. She hadn't heard from him since he had gone to live there nearly a year ago. And she was very nice to Pádraig and his son. They went home and told the priest that they had met his mother,

and because she had treated them so well they would be his friends. They told him he could do whatever he wanted. His wish was that he could gather all the people together and hear their confession on his last day with them.

Pádraig was a very powerful and popular man in the parish, so he got everyone to gather outside the priest's house. And the poor priest was inside by the hearth, crying, and he thanked Pádraig for all he had done to help, but said nothing more could be done. So Pádraig went outside and told the first person he saw to go in and tell the priest his sins. But that person was afraid because he didn't know what to say. Pádraig told him what to say and he went in and told the priest what Pádraig had told him to say. And the priest asked who told him to say that and the man told him the truth. And fairly soon the priest was in stitches at what Pádraig was telling the people to say. So that's how 'confession' got started here. Some people would say there were no sins until the priest came to hear confession.

I remember about forty years ago discussing the Wheel of Life with a group of *seanchaí*. According to them, the Wheel of Life consists of seven generations, with each generation spanning twenty to twenty-five years. They were saying that before the Famine morals were low, murder was common and a lot of crimes went unpunished because the British Laws were not being enforced everywhere. With a big population and not enough land many babies were being killed, be it by drowning, by burying the baby alive or by other means. The idea was that the baby should see the light of day and that perhaps if the mother saw the baby she would keep it. They were afraid of abortion as they were terrified of bleeding to death, even though there was a healing prayer which stopped bleeding but very few ever used it.

It was different before the Act of Union when a baby was called a *Tabhartas*, which means a gift from God. If the father was a married man, he had to take the baby into his home and if it was a boy give him his name. This is why you might have children of the same family with the same Christian name. If the baby was a girl, she was called Mary. People knew who the *Tabhartas* were and they were very careful not to marry blood relations.

At the time of the Famine, the rule of the church was that a priest was the witness of a marriage. Therefore, if a woman was taken to a priest against her will, and the man told the priest he was marrying her and she wasn't allowed to speak, the marriage took place anyway and she had to make the best of it. Later the church law changed and a priest, the congregation and two witnesses were necessary so no woman could be forced into marriage. Marriage was arranged always between the two families. And they were bound to that, so no marriages broke up. The 'hand and the word' – *lámh agus focal*. The honour, that was a Celtic tradition, even though they were poor. There was no registration of marriages here until 1942, even though the priest's blessing was around longer than that. Before that they gave the sacrament to one another.

The *seanchaí* believed that low morals, and not the British, brought the Famine on the people because God was angry with them. It took up to the last year of the Famine before a change took place and people again came back to prayer. Very few were going to Mass at the time. After the Famine, the people were very good for three generations but with the fourth generation there was a change and by the fifth generation the Wheel went down again. Fifty years ago if there was a murder, people would talk about it for years and discuss if the murdered would get to Heaven, especially if it was a Protestant because they didn't have Confession. I remember my grandfather coming down on the side of justice for everyone. Now there are murders once a day and we are going the same way. People are not taking the Sacraments. The young people are very good. When it comes to collecting for something they will do it, but they don't bother getting up on Sunday morning for Mass to show what side they are on.

I was told thirty-five years ago and I was the youngest of the *seanchaí* that whatever would happen I would see it and it would come to everyone's door. There was never so much money around and money brings its own trouble. The basic principle of life used to be survival. Now if it doesn't work, they take the easy way out. There is no talk of survival as if there was no other world at all. The *seanchaí* can predict the future based on the way things happened in the past. The last time there was a disaster, it was through poverty. Nobody can save anybody else's soul but their own. I worry about my six children with all the traps that are out there. This life is only a short space, compared to eternity.

Peadar Clancy

Farmer and postman, from Spiddal.
Known locally as Peadairín John.

I went to Spiddal school, where the library is now. That was the Boys' School. The parish priest at the time was Canon Donnelly, and the head teacher was George Flaherty. We went to school until we were fourteen, then we stayed at home. We were kept at home. And often we were kept at home from school when we were going to school, like in the springtime, to cut the seaweed off the stones. We then brought the weed on the donkey, up to the fields, for manure for the potatoes. In the summertime, after school, we had to go to the bog to cut the turf.

And from the first of April we had no shoes on. At that time there were no shoes, just hob-nailed boots. The money was scarce to buy them so from the first of April we went barefooted. The strangers who came here in summertime wore shoes and we used to laugh at them. The boots were made from heavy leather and were bought in Galway, in a shop called Gerald's.

The clothes were made at home. There was a tailor in Ballydonnellan – Joe Conneely's uncle. He was making the clothes for everybody for miles and miles around. He was the only tailor in Spiddal. There were a few tailors in Knock, and there was a tailor in Barna. But the main tailor was the one in Spiddal, and he was kept working six days a week. He had a sewing machine. He had everything.

Old Post Office in Spiddal

And he was very wealthy. He worked by himself. I knew him very well. We used to go in there and he used to measure us for the small trousers we had going to school. There was a small button at the knee. He also made the *báinín* for the old people and a black vest. They wore grey trousers. And no matter how wet the day was you didn't they sold potatoes and cut turf as well. They took the lobsters in baskets on donkeys into Galway. They had to get them in before sunrise, otherwise the lobsters would die. And they covered them with wet weed in the baskets.

No one survived on the sea alone. It was a hell. They bought potatoes in the market every March. They wouldn't sow their own potatoes in the same patch. Every year they had to change it or recycle it. The seed potatoes cost about four pence a stone at that time. Potatoes, fish, butter and buttermilk were the most important foods. There wasn't much meat. A lot of households killed a pig every year for their own bacon. The sow had piglets, and one of them was kept for three months and then sold. And the other piglets, or *banbhs*, were sold at the Fair. They didn't eat beef. No one believed in beef then. They did eat lamb. They killed a lamb every now and again. They had their own chickens and they killed and ate a lot of them. They believed then that there was some cure in the flesh of the chicken. They hadn't many turkeys in those days. In later years they had the black turkeys mostly, the American breed.

There was no such thing as heart attacks. I never heard of anyone who had a heart attack. They made their own bread, buying the flour in Galway or in Spiddal. There was a hundred-weight of flour used up every week in a house. They ate a lot of bread and cooked it in the oven. The oven was on one side of the fire, with heat under it and over it. When the bread was nearly done they took off the lead cover and turned the bread. It was mostly brown bread. We wouldn't see the currant cakes 'til Christmas.

Every house had their own geese and they used to have a goose for Christmas Day – nearly every house.

We used to travel from house to house, visiting. But we weren't allowed to play cards with the older boys. We were too young and the cards had to be played right, with the light of the candle on the table, and a ha'penny. And when the money was involved you couldn't even look at them. The women didn't play cards at all. I saw one old woman smoking a pipe. Nearly all the men smoked the pipe. There were no cigarettes then. And then they came in, and there was one house in the village, with an old lady, and she didn't mind us smoking. She never said a word about it outside. She never told anybody.

I saw dances in the houses in the summertime, when the strangers were going to the Irish College. They might have a dance for them when they were leaving. Before my time they used to have dances in the shed behind the house here. But the parish priest was dead against it. There was shouting from the altar; there was no law and order. Then, when he opened the Irish College, he had a dance hall in it, and they were all allowed to go there.

I worked with my father on the farm until he died. I always lived at home. I was working in a factory. I was one year in England and then I came home. I worked on roads and buildings there. Then, in 1970, I started working with the post. When the postman went on holidays I took his place. Then I took it up altogether from 1980. In 1970 I had my own van and it only took me two hours. But there's a difference now, because you have twenty times as much work. I have five hundred houses now. There wasn't as much mail in the Seventies. In 1970 there was only the ordinary letter. But nowadays you have catalogues and heavy stuff. There might have been the odd parcel from America back then. In the Forties they used to put tea in the parcels and send them over. It was rationed here. During the War it could take up to seven weeks to arrive, because it was dangerous for the Americans with the German submarines and aeroplanes. But they used to send a lot of tea. And the sugar was rationed as well. It was very hard to get sugar. I always drank tea. There was no such thing as coffee. But during the War they started drinking coffee. It was bad coffee then.

The American letters used to come at Christmas and Easter with a few dollars. They'd be watching for them. The few dollars that came made a great Christmas and Easter for them. They put the ordinary dollar in the letter. It was never stolen. And they still come that way today. But there are very few that come now. I suppose that the people here now are just as well-off as they are in America.

I remember the postman when I was growing up. I saw a postman, Mike Mullins from Baile an tSagairt, walking across the fields with the bag on his back. He walked the whole area. He wasn't allowed to have a bicycle, or take a lift. But he wouldn't have a lot to carry, because when you think back he couldn't have any letters only American letters, or a rent letter, or something like that. People weren't writing to one another in those days. He was invited in for a cup of tea, but he didn't go into every house for a cup of tea. He used to leave the letters for a village in one house and the people would come and collect them there. He wasn't allowed to do that, but he did. Some villages were very long, like Baile an tSagairt. And he knew the shortcuts. He used to be attacked by dogs. He had to watch out for them. The postman wasn't well-paid. He might get about ten shillings or a pound a week. That was before the Forties. In the Seventies he got seven pounds a week. Mike Mullins was fond of a pint and he didn't work on the land after delivering the post. He always had a few pints in Spiddal. He's dead now. He was Jimmy Kelly's uncle.

There were telegrams as well. It was usually the man in charge in the Post Office that brought the telegrams around. In the olden days the post came from Galway to Spiddal by horse. The mail had to be brought that way all over Connemara. There were two postmen to each area. They were employed by the Post Office in Galway. They had offices in Dublin. They got their pension then, at a certain age. But the pension then was very little. There was little money coming in to the Post Office at the time. The pension was from two and six to five shillings a week. There was no such thing as Childrens' Allowance or the Widows' Pension. There could be books written about Connolly and the rows that went on in the morning. The Postmen used to have to start at a certain time and finish at a certain time. And sometimes they couldn't keep up with it. When I had the van they didn't care because I wasn't a full-time employee. Monday and Friday were very busy days. On Monday you had all the weekend mail and on Friday you had the dole letters to deliver.

Peait Ó Conghaile, better known locally as Peait Phádraig Tom

then started up the garage. Some people walked barefoot as far as Knocknacarra and then put on their shoes. Others walked barefoot until they got to the market. Máirtín Ó Cadhain mentioned that in one of his books – *An Bóthar go dtí an Ghealchathair* (*The Road to Bright City*).

My parents used to go visiting to their friends and relation on Sundays. Or they used to come and visit them. They used to tell stories, too many stories. They used to tell a lot of stories about fairies and ghosts, or seeing somebody who had died. And they terrified the children. I knew some people that came home drunk, claiming to have seen someone who had died two years before. They used to play cards as well. They were great card players up here. They used to play cards all night, especially in the wintertime. They used to play twenty-fives. There used also be great weddings, country weddings. And further back, between Spiddal and Leitir Móir, they used to have crossroads dances. I remember being back at one in Leitir Móir. They had local musicians playing in the moonlight nights. There was a man from Galway called Stiofánín Rua. He was blind, but he was a great uilleann piper. We had to go into Galway in the side-car and pick him up, and then take him back in the morning. Stiofánín played at a lot of crossroads dances. And if he only got a penny from everyone there he'd be doing great. He also played at weddings and parties and American wakes. They had music and *poitín* at all those parties.

The guards used to come out looking for the *poitín*. They used to walk. They had no other transport. If you

then. People would have nine or ten *banbhs* coming home on the bus on a Saturday evening. CIE bought out all the private companies. CIE bought out the O'Flahertys, who were caught you were fined. Even when times were bad you could be fined six pounds. After that you could be fined twelve pounds if you were caught second time. But not many were caught in those days. They used to be very careful. They used to make the stuff on islands and the guards didn't have any boats then, so they couldn't get to the islands. It was the tradition that every house had a couple of bottles of *poitín*, especially at Christmas time, or for a wake or a wedding or a christening. They used to get seven gallons for a funeral, and seven for a wedding, and more for a christening. They made it from barley. Sometimes they put sugar in it. It was good in those days. You had to malt the barley or wheat. You had to steep it and spread it out on a floor for two weeks. Then you had to kill dry it. Then you crushed it with a grinding stone. A lot of places, especially on the coast made *poitín*. Mostly 'twas made in the places where they didn't have a road. 'Twas their living, and there weren't many of them caught even though the guards were very busy. I suppose that the fine nowadays is up to five hundred pounds. It was a kind of slavery to make *poitín*. None of the youngsters want to do it now. You were up all night and always worried about the guards. It was hard work to make a few bob. Times changed and there are changes now. And you have to go with the times.

The songs that I sang were all Irish and traditional. They were the old songs that were composed or picked up like the Raftery songs. Colm de Bhailís was a famous composer. He lived in Tír an Fhia. He lived in a small place in Leitir Calaidh. He was a tradesman. He composed *Cuairt an tSrutháin Bhuí*. When he came out from Tír an Fhia he used to have to cross by sea. So he could only come out for a few hours and then go home again. And that's why he built the small cabin by the big stone, where he slept. And he composed that song there. In my time there were hardly any English songs in the Gaeltachts. There were songs like *Bean Pháidín and Nancín Bhán* that were composed after the 1920s. Then after many years a lot of these old traditional songs were changed through education. They added to and took from songs. *Peigín Leitir Móir* was composed by a mother putting her baby to bed. The people were intelligent.

I didn't compose any of the songs that I sing. My sister Mary, in Achill, composed some. *Ceol na nOileán* was a good song. I think, myself, that you have to have it in you. It has to be in your mind and blood. A lot of people tell you that you can teach them and learn them. There were good local musicians in Connemara who never had to go to learn the music. Now, it costs a lot for music and dancing. And you don't seem to have, nowadays, the musicians we used to have. The singing has to come, more or less natural. You have to have an explanation in your song and expression in your voice when you're singing. There were people who couldn't read or write who could correct you in your singing if you made a mistake.

There were a lot of love songs, such as *Droighneán Donn*. In that song, he liked the girl, but couldn't talk to her because his parents and her parents mightn't like it.

And they were at a party and she slipped her ring into the glass and he kept it. And he arranged to meet her somewhere else. They ended up together. There was another song about a girl who went to the States and a boy who thought he was her boyfriend. And he composed a song, which was very lonely, and he never saw her again. It was hard in those days. And you had the runaway matches. A lot of people went to the States. And a lot of people married their neighbours and locals, because they were afraid of marrying strangers. Very little marriages broke up. It was in the times. I met my wife in Boluisce. She was staying back in Peter Dan's in Folan's. She came here in 1955. She used to come here on school evenings. And I used to go back to Boluisce and chat and play cards. We used to go to the college. It was good. And we got married in 1959. We moved into my parents' house. My father died in 1962, and my mother died in 1972. It wasn't all sunshine moving in with your in-laws. I'm sorry now to see the day when old people have to move into nursing homes, and that. But at the same time, young and old can never agree. If one of my children wanted to get married I'd never advise them to move into my house. Times have changed too much, and they'll want to do it their way and you might disagree with them.

In Connemara we didn't have much confidence in ourselves because we came from the Gaeltacht. You felt you had to stand back at the end of the queue. In 1937 I worked in Yorkshire, in England. And they had a GAA pitch in a place called New Eltham, and we used to have great days there with matches and that. In 1949 I was asked to go up on stage and sing. That was for traditional singing, and I had a bit of a problem going up, but they pushed me. I got first prize for two Irish songs and second prize for a song in English, which was *John Mitchell.* Then I came home in 1951. In 1954 we had the Open Day here in the Tech, and Hynes wanted to enter me for a competition in the Oireachtas. Again, I had a bit of a problem, with the shyness, entering that as well. But I did and was picked to go to the Oireachtas in Dublin later that year. Joe Heaney from Carna got first prize and I got second. After that I got interested in singing. There was a competition in Newport. It was a really bad day. And I got two first prizes there, for Irish and for English. In those days you didn't have much confidence in yourself that you could compete.

Peait's Wife, Máire

I was born and reared in Camus, about three miles from Ros Muc. Ní Mhaoilchiaráin was my maiden name. I went to the national school in Camus and after that to the Presentation Convent in Tuam. At that time there were scholarships to be had, Gaeltacht Scholarships they called them. I succeeded in getting one of those scholarships. I went to Tuam when I was about thirteen and stayed there for five years.

In Camus when I was growing up we had a lovely quiet way of life. We had boys and girls together in the national school. There was a lady teacher for the lower classes and a man, Pádraig O'Connor, for the higher classes. We walked to school and had to bring money to buy turf for the schoolroom fires. The rooms used to be very cold in the mornings, until the fires lit up. The church was beside the school, and so we were constantly in and out of the church during the day. So you could say that I had two homes when I was going to that school – my own home and the church. We had a lot of knowledge of the church when we were growing up. Every Sunday evening the schoolchildren used to have special prayers in the church. The schoolchildren were responsible for bringing the flowers for the altar in the church. We'd be preparing the altar the night before. There were two Masses, one at nine o'clock and another at eleven. We always went to the earlier Mass because it was more convenient for us. The priest's house was about a mile down the road from the church. And the Berridges had a lodge a little bit up the road. We always called it the Big House.

Peait Ó Conghaile in conversation with Peadar Clancy and his wife Tess

There was Cailleach na hAirde Móire. She wasn't qualified, like the woman from Clifden. It was Cailleach na hAirde Móire that came to the church in Spiddal. And Canon McAlinney ordered her out. She told him to sit down and she said something to him. She used *luibheanna*, herbs, to cure people who were sick and were going to die. And you had to make an offering to the Gods to save somebody. It was paganism.

They say that's what happened at Anach Cuan, when all the people drowned. There was an old lady picking *luibheanna*, and the boat became the offering. They talked about that on Radio na Gaeltachta. She saw the boat and the boat went down. They say that in the song. The boat had a name but the name wasn't mentioned in the song. They're trying to find out the name of the boat now. The parish priest over in Glenamaddy, Fr Michael Goaley, had a relative in that boat. The boat was old and the timber was old. They weren't far from the shore and it didn't sink straight away, but they could have been in a deep pool.

There's very little fish in Boluisce Lake now. Although last year there were a few trout caught there. It has been left for years, neglected. The problem is that the fish aren't spawning in the rivers now. I saw salmon spawning in the Furbo River a few years ago. But when the salmon are spawning they're worth nothing, the flesh is flabby. And if you kill a salmon at that time you're killing millions, because they're spawning.

They used to catch a lot of eels around here in the river. And people from Achill Island used to come down here and catch eels up at the lake. They used to come in October. They stayed in different places, and they used to fish in the other lake as well, Loch an Oileáin. I remember, one time, they caught three boxes – a hundred weight in each. They brought these eels to Castlebar. They got three shilling and sixpence a pound for them, which was good at the time. They probably smoked them and exported them. If you got the right eel they were lovely eating. But there were a lot of *piseogs* about the eel. They used to say that if you put one at the bottom of a barrel it would be on top in the morning. There was a man coming with an eel in his bag and the eel started whistling. So he had to put the bag down behind him and pull it after him. Nearly all the Spiddal salmon spawned in Doire Thoir, and they spawned up there at the bridge as well.

Sean Keady had two boats and he had good customers, from Galway. His best customers were the Emersons and the Gallaghers. The Emersons were Canon McAlinney's crowd. They had the Eglinton Hotel, in Salthill. They used to buy eggs on Sunday. And they used to go out there fishing. But they never brought that fish home. They gave it away. They just enjoyed their day out. Sean rowed the boat up the river and let it come back with the wind. He knew every inch of that river. All along the Boluisce side was better for sea-trout. There was a lot of game-shooting as well. Killanin had the game in Seanadh Gharráin, because that was his preserve. Seanadh Gharráin didn't own that mountain at all until the land was divided. It belonged to some insurance crowd in England before that. But I suppose Killanin bought the shooting rights off those people, whoever they were. It was the Palmers who were landlords in this village. Before that it was the Bunberrys; and the Bunberry's daughter married a Palmer from the Palmer Mills in Galway. They were the landlords here in Leitir Péic and in Leitir Meas, Baile an tSagairt and Leitir Fir. The Palmers had a Distillery in Taylor's Hill. They had a partnership with Pearse. The people from around here used to go in on a Saturday and buy the barrels of stuff, when they were ready with the whiskey, and bring it home to feed the cattle. It was called *triosc*. It was just as good as the rolled oats today.

There were five tenants in this village that owned part of the land by Boluisce Lake. There are five houses in Boluisce and five in Boluisce Uachtar that owned land by the lake. But the good thing is that nobody could take over the lake, because nobody could 'take' the lake. It's the only place in Connemara for free fishing. The Walshes owned the land on the other side of Loch an Oileáin. The Berridges in Maam Cross were the landlords there and the Walshes were herding for them. Eventually, after so many years, when the landlords pulled out the Walshes remained, and they got the land from the Land Commission. The Walshes had been tenants there when the Berridges were there. Tulaig na Sióg belonged to the Mannions. Mannion came from Ros a' Mhíl to Seacomb, and he was herding there for the Costelloes, the wool merchants from Galway. They owned the big place across the road from the Railway Station in Galway. Mannion got half the place after a while.

Na hArd Doiriu was on the other side of Tulaig na Sióg. Father Curran had cattle there. In Doire Thior they didn't have a lot of mountain. They were going back to Fionnán. They were joining Fionnán. All the land in Sheanadh Phéistin was owned by the Land Commission. People were brought in there to settle, like the people that were moved to Meath. Indeed, some of those who settled in Sheanadh Phéistin went to Meath afterwards. But then the Minister of Agriculture decided that it wasn't worth while spending more money in Sheanadh Phéistin. That was when people re-settled in Rathcairn, in County Meath.

Paddy Francis

Baker and grocer. Ran the still flourishing
family business in Spiddal.

My great-great-grandfather came from Menlo outside Galway. And they came into Galway. They had a house opposite Market Street in Galway. Then my grandfather, Patrick, came to Spiddal and he married Margaret Folan. And he set up the business in Spiddal. He started a bakery, around 1850. They were in the horse business in Galway, coaches, livery and that sort. My grandfather had eleven sons and three daughters. Two of them were priests and one was a doctor. And one of them went to America and started a bakery. Another started a bakery in Australia, but he never wrote home.

My business started as a bakery and a small grocery shop. The flour at that time was imported from England. The household flour was called porter flour, but there was a stronger flour for bakeries. The Palmers and the McDonaghs used to mill flour in Galway and we used to get that, and mix it with the English flour, which was stronger. There wasn't any wheat being sown here, until the War came and we had to start sowing ourselves. The flour during the War was called 'black flour'. There was talk about things being scarce, but we had stored up enough white flour to keep us going for three years, because we mixed it with the flour that was coming in. We had to turn that flour once a week,

which was troublesome. We use[d]
Galway from a fellow called Ha[rry]

We had two bakeries. An u[ncle]
my father had the other. We ha[d]
and we had men on the land as well. And [there]
or five staying in the house. It was very hot in the bake[ry]
We had fires going all the time. My mother died when I was eleven-and-a-half years of age. My sister was going to

The October Fair in Spiddal Village

school in Galway. She was staying with an aunt. My aunt owned a bar, the Galway Arms, in Dominick Street, in Galway. But when my mother died my sister had to come home to look after the shop. We had to do a lot of work. In the morning we had to get up and take the cattle out to the land, milk the cows and then go to school. We had a lot of cattle and we kept our own milk. We reared calves and that, and we kept our own pigs and geese. Later on we had turkeys.

Onlookers at Spiddal October Fair

In 1921 we got our first van. Before that we had a horse and cart. We used to go to Leitir Mealláin and Carraroe twice a week to deliver the bread. In 1921 the Black and Tans were around as well. I remember them in Spiddal and them coming out with their berets. They used to go to Barna Wood and fire shots through the wood because they were afraid they'd be ambushed. The trees were a lot thicker in the wood then. So they used to fire to protect themselves. And they used to come to Spiddal and run around the village. We had the coastguards here at the time. They were stationed where the girls' school is now. The coastguards used to be called 'peelers'. Some of them were English and some were Irish. They weren't as bad as the guards. Though, I saw, on one occasion my father being brought out one morning, and the coastguards threatening to shoot him. One of the coastguards owed a bill in the shop, for £30, that was there for a long time. We thought it was because of that.

I remember another time, one of the coastguards climbed up to Leitir Péic and he saw the smoke from a *poitín* still across the mountain. He came down and reported it. Anyway, they got word above that the 'peeler' had reported them. One of the *poitín* makers, Colm Feeney had a hound and when he saw them coming he gave two whistles and the *poitín* makers heard him. Colm was brought down to the barracks. I saw them marching him down the mountain. He was brought to court then. They accused him of notifying the lads by whistling. But he said he was whistling at his hound. That was around 1920.

I remember when the coastguards left after 1920. I heard them going with their furniture and all that. We had the Free State Army at the time and they were to come to Spiddal to the barracks where the coastguards had been. But the Sinn Féiners heard they were coming and burned the barracks. The secondary school is where the Néad was, or the 'soupers'. So the Free State Army came and stayed there for a few years. Then, in the summertime, the teachers used to come and stay in the houses, when they were going to the college to learn Irish. The Protestant Church was down near the pier by Killanins. I don't remember the Protestants being there, but I was very young at the time. I do remember that some of the local lads used to climb up and ring the bell of the Protestant Church on New Year's Eve, to ring in the New Year. And people used to think that it was haunted. The sick house was the hospital. The name *Spidéal* comes from hospital.

We supplied shops with bread. We had contracts with

schools for bread, butter and jam. We were night and day on the job. I had the van. I used to take a hundred and thirty-five dozen bread on the van. We used to do that every day. Then we got electricity and we got an electric oven. When the contracts came up again I applied for double and I got the north side of Connemara as well. I was practically going into Clifden delivering bread. And I was doing the islands as well. I used to go to Roundstone, Camus, Ros Muc, Carna, and down to the Kylemore Road. We used to go twice a week on the north-side and twice on the south-side. And some evenings we went and made a quick extra run. We did six days altogether. We did two days in Galway City as well. We had two vans at the time. Sometimes I only got about an hour's sleep at night. This was in the Sixties and the Seventies.

During the War Years we had rationing. As a matter of fact bread was taken off me, on two occasions, in Carraroe. They were hungry so they took it, but they paid for it, even though they didn't have the rationing cards. I never ran out of bread because I had the flour stored. I did buy flour on the black market and I gave it to people who were hungry. The flour was rationed to four and a half pounds. And the tea was rationed to half a pound. There was a song at the time – 'Bet de Valera and Sean McEntee/ Bet their brown bread and their half-pound of tea.' We had to stick to the rationing. As well as that we had inspectors coming along. I remember, one morning, an inspector came along and went through the books and told me we weren't getting enough tea for the

shop. And we got more tea from Kyles. They calculated how much you should get by the coupons. Another time there was a report sent in that we were giving more tea to the guards and the teachers, And we weren't. And the inspector that came thought I was the guilty one and that I was leaving the customers short. There was a phase at that time when people were writing letters to the inspectors because they were jealous.

I remember when the bridges were knocked down during the War. I saw the Barna Bridge being blown up, and the Furbo Bridge too. And we had to go another way to Galway. There was a bridge near Costelloe that was blown up. And there was Crumin Bridge, near here, that was blown up. We were trying to deliver bread and we couldn't go past. The bridge near Moycullen was blown up. There were a lot of local people involved. They used to come around at night and they used raid the shops. They used to take bags of flour and groceries and clothes. They raided the Post Office then, and I was actually looking at them doing this. And my father told my mother not to cash any Postal Orders, because they had just raided the Post Office. So she didn't.

I remember when Lord Killanin's house was burned. I came home from school at around half three and it was still burning. The Sinn Féiners burned it because they thought the Killanins were English. This was during the Civil War. There was no one there at the time. Local people didn't like it happening, but nobody said anything because you didn't know who was around. There were brothers against brothers. When the Sinn

Féiners burned the Coastguard Station they took the gates and put them somewhere else.

I used to play in Killanin's place as a child. The Dillons were caretakers there. The Roches were there beforehand. Barry's uncle died when we were going to school and we had a great day off for the funeral. We had to march after the coffin. And then we went down marching to the beach. Máirtín Ó Cadhain was drilling us. He was a monitor, and a second cousin of mine. He was very intelligent when it came to Irish. There were three monitors – Eileen Greaney, Jim Dillon and Máirtín Ó Cadhain. An inspector used to come and give them an Exam. That was how Máirtín became a teacher.

In my grandfather's time people were very badly off, so he went over to the priest and told him how poor they were. So they got together and wrote to a committee in Dublin. They got a grant of thirty pounds, which was a lot at that time. And they were able to buy tons of Indian meal with that. That was back in the time of the Famine. I got that information from the priests. It's in the books. After that they wrote again and got fifteen pounds, and later they got more money.

There was only one landlord here and that was Lord Killanin. He was a good landlord. He used to give people work and buy their turf. He had bailiffs along the river. We only delivered bread in the van. My father used to deliver bread to Killanins in the van. We got our first petrol tank in 1925. Before that we used to buy the petrol in tins. We used to buy forty or fifty a week. When the Free State Army was

here they used to take stuff from the shop, and we weren't paid by the Governmnt until years later, because they didn't have the money. The Sinn Féiners never paid us.

My father used to get the *Independent* newspaper on Wednesday and the *Independent* and *Connacht Tribune* on Saturday, when he went into Galway on business. They were the only papers that came into the village and everyone read them. There was an ex-RIC man who used come and read them. And Dr O'Flaherty, who was never fully qualified, used to come for a read too. There was a man from Salathúna who used to come and read them. And on Sunday after Mass, my father used to read the papers, and a crowd would gather round and he would translate the news into Irish and tell them what the papers said. And I remember about all the ambushes in Kerry and Cork and all around there. Dr O'Flaherty used to explain the news to the people in Seanadh Gharráin. There was no radio at the time. They had music and singing and dancing. They were a very musical people. There used to be up to twenty-five *Gaeilgeoirí* staying in the house, even in the thatched houses. And the people themselves used to live in the stables while the strangers were here.

There was another place belonged to the Smiths. They owned the Hughes' land. And they had a thatched house and a lovely glasshouse. They had a big yard, with stables. It was said that Hughes' grandmother bought the lot for a bottle of whiskey. The Smiths were kind of 'big' people, as they say here. The Blakes left their house. The students were staying there. Then they went to Taylor's Hill. It was sold and McCambridge bought it for a thousand pounds. McCambridge wasn't going to live in it, so he took the roof off and sold it. And it was very big and had bathrooms and fine fittings. It had counters as well. There were Blakes living out where the castle is, out where the aerodrome is. The Blakes were all over the place.

I went to college in Galway for two years and did book-keeping and typing and a bit of shorthand. I came home for a weekend. And my first morning home, my father asked me to go down to the van. I did, and I started driving it and that was the end of school.

People weren't going to England at that time. They were going to America. Now, America was very tough and if the girls came home they married the first fellow they got, it didn't matter if he had a hump on his back, because they didn't want to go back to America. I had an aunt in America. She had a three-storey house. Her husband had died. My aunt made *poitín*, or moonshine as they called it there, in the cellar. It was during the time of Prohibition, but the police were on her side and she made a lot of money out of it. She was planning to come home, but my mother died in 1927. Then in 1927 the banks closed in America. My aunt had her money in three different banks. She lost it all. She had a modern distillery in the cellar of her home, with running water and the lot. And the policemen were some of her customers. Well, they were getting it free.

There were sixty-six boys in our school. And there were three times as many girls in the girls' school. There were

Spiddal: the local national school, formerly the Coastguard Station, and the Old Pier (An Sean-Céibh)

always more girls than boys. The girls didn't have a problem getting married. They were freer at that time to do that. But Spiddal was the same as it is now. There might have been more houses. A lot of strangers live here now in Spiddal. We used to have a Fair Day here every month. And the father and the mother would come to the fair. The father would sell the cattle and the mother was the money-minder. He only wanted the price of one or two pints. She'd take the rest home. Then the daughters would come down a few hours later, to meet their boyfriends and have a walk around. And the next day they'd go to the bar and the fathers would be there and the match would be made. And the wedding might happen the following week. And a week later you might see the new bride walking down with a cow and a calf, and that was her dowry. Fair Day was 'match day' at certain fairs of the year.

Lord Killanin (né Michael Morris)

His family have been landlords of Spiddal for several generations. Lived in Dublin after selling Spiddal House, but retained 'St Annins' and the Spiddal connection.

Up to 1660 we were only in Galway City. We were one of the fourteen tribes of Galway. We were in Galway since the 1400s. My father was killed commanding the Irish Guards in the First World War. He was only forty-one years of age. My great-grandmother died of cholera. That time the road ended at Spiddal, there was no bridge. The bridge was only built late in the last century. After that the track wandered off to Inveran, where John Ford came from. He always said his family had everything, because the only thing to eat was salmon and lobster. The parish priest in Moycullen told me that the only reason the Protestant Mission didn't work was that the people were not starving, from Costelloe back to Spiddal, because they had plenty of fish. There were twenty-four Protestant churches between Kilkerrin and Leenane. The house we live in was once a Protestant church. The 'Bird's Nest' used to be where the secondary school is now.

We married into the family here. My grandfather married a Catherine Mhic Giolla Phádraig of Aran, in the 1680s or '90s. She was a niece of Roderick O'Flaherty. The property belonged then to James Fitzpatrick of Aran. The property was only a few acres. I was told, once, that I

One of the carvings on Spiddal House by Michael Shorthall of Loughrea, depicting local sports

would never get shot for my property. My grandfather bought quite a lot of land as well. The original property in Spiddal was a little block of a Georgian house. Then, in 1910, my uncle built an enormous house, designed by Professor Scott. Scott also designed the Catholic Church in Spiddal. The Spiddal house was Romanesque. It was the last house in Ireland to be burned during the Civil War. It was burned by the Irregulars, the same night they burned the Orphanage, the barracks and the Coastguard Station. I inherited that house in 1927. I got my trustees to rebuild it. I added on to it after the Civil War. Then I found it too big for a house and I had to earn my living. That's why I sold it. And I've regretted that ever since.

My family, the Morrisses, were the only Catholics, other than Edward Martin. Most of the Ballinahinch Martins were Protestants. The Martins of Ross were sheer Protestants. But there were a few Catholics. Lady Fingal was Catholic. She was born in Moycullen, where my great-great uncle was parish priest. There's a wall plaque that commemorates him in Moycullen church. His name was Rev Monsignor Blake. He's buried in the old medieval church in Knock. Bishop Brown told me that he was a very grand Monsignor.

Even though my uncle didn't speak Irish himself, he was responsible, with several others, for opening the Irish College in Spiddal. It was well before Canon Donnelly's time. There was a Canon McAlinney in Spiddal then, a very liberal man. He volunteered for service as a Chaplain to the Boers during the South African War. My grandfather found that his knowledge of Irish was a tremendous asset to him on his travels abroad. He spoke only Irish and nobody understood him. Consequently, everyone helped him. For myself, I regret tremendously, emotionally, that I didn't have Irish. And now the language is dying. The language disappeared with the Clifden railway line.

Spiddal village was never an Irish speaking village, because of the various cults there. There was the RIC there. And my good uncle was always trying to fill the

church. He was very ecumenical in that respect. His mother was Church of Ireland, as my wife is. And the next generation is mostly of mixed marriages too. And in Maud's book it is revealed that my uncle used to go to church in a side-car, while his wife went to church in a carriage, and they couldn't both be wrong.

My great-grandmother was a Blake. She was neither a Blake of Furbo, nor of Tully. That Monsignor Blake, the parish priest of Moycullen, was her brother. The family names, the Morrises of Ballinaboy, for instance, were Catholic Morrises. They have the same crest, but not necessarily the same coat of arms, although we happen to use the same coat of arms. Because a grant of arms is a personal grant, whereas anyone of the same name can use the same crest. That's why I often feel like charging a fee for the Morris crest.

My children learned Irish. They all started their education at the national school in Spiddal. The reason I went to school in England was that my father was killed in action in the First World War. He was a Nationalist. They had just formed the Irish Guards, after the South African War, and he was a regular soldier. They wanted an Irish Catholic Nationalist to come into the Irish Guards, as apparently all of the Irish Guards officers were Protestant and all their ranks Papist. So he was given about twenty years promotion. He was only forty-one when he was killed, which was very young for a Lieutenant Colonel before the last War. I didn't have any brothers or sisters. My mother was Church of England and, originally, I think, a Methodist. She came over from Australia and met my father at the Galway Races. She came over at the invitation of Colonel Pierce Joyce of Mervue Park. Joyce took her all the way to Aran on the *Dun Aengus*, and proposed to her. She turned him down. They had the longest journey back that any couple ever had. Then, before the Races, she was staying with the Wilson Lynches in Galway, and that was where she met my father. And I too, met my wife at the Galway Races. So you could say that 'the races' is a great boost to tourism in the area.

After my father was killed, my mother, eventually, married an Englishman. Now, my father would have been of 'The Oratory' of Cardinal Newman's time, which was the equivalent of 'Castle Catholics'. Indeed, because of that direct link with Newman, I still go, when resident in Dublin, to University Church.

In Spiddal we had a very good gardener, called Dillon – James Dillon's grandson. He lives in Bothúna now, and his son, Mick Dillon, is my doctor, a GP working locally. There was another gardener, Pat, whose mother was our washer-woman. She supervised an enormous laundry behind the garage.

Another thing I remember is that there was a car, one of the first in Galway, and certainly the first in Spiddal. It was an 'open' car. You were able to drop the hood down. There are photographs of it in some magazines of that time. And the Royal Irish Automobile Club have records of it. I can remember the Eliot's car as the IM 50. The Head Bailiff for the estate was Lydon, from Bothúna. Lizzie and Pat Lydon looked after the rivers.

The Headmaster of my preparatory school in England was a terrible snob. The first time he called me by my Christian name he put his hand on my shoulder and said, 'Michael, your mother never told me you were going to be a Lord.' But I've always been fairly democratic and easy-going. If my children care to take it up then the title will pass on. The reason my grandfather was made a peer was because he was a Judge, and also the Chief Justice of Ireland, and a Lord of Penal Law. And in those days, the Irish Peers, who were very few, had to sit in the House of Lords. I've sat in the House of Lords. I spoke there around 1991 or 1992, when I got the Irish Government three million pounds, because I was appointed by Sean McBride and Jack Costelloe to be a trustee of land and housing near the Claddagh in Galway City. They were built for Irish volunteers in the First World War. They were being sold, and big money was being made. So I got some of the money given to the Irish Government, to be spent on apolitical projects.

Some of my relations were Civil Servants and were in the Army in India. In the Second World War I was a journalist. I happened to be in Downing Street when Churchill came in waving a piece of paper – 'Peace in Our Time'. I was then with an old Socialist friend of mine, the journalist Hannan Swaffer, who also happened to be a traitor. So I joined the Territorial Army and served during the Second World War, for no particular reason other than that I was anti-Hitler. Swaffer was a great character with long hair and a big, black hat.

I also got to know Denis Johnson very well, and John Heuston. And Tyrone Power was staying as a guest at my house in Spiddal, before he died. He was involved in Four Provinces Films with me. John Ford told me that if he ever heard I'd spoken to John Heuston he'd never speak to me again. John Heuston I knew quite well. His children and mine are great friends. Ricky used to come and stay at Spiddal, occasionally. However, I never dared tell John Ford.

Before the war there was no boat tied up at Spiddal Pier apart from my own. I had a converted lifeboat there at one time. And after that I had a succession of little boats. I used to fish lobsters. I can remember when Spiddal Pier was very active, with the sailing boats plying between Galway and the Aran Islands. They used often put in for the night at Spiddal. The run from Ros a' Mhíl to the Aran Islands was very busy. They took turf over and animals and fish back.

The Killanin Coat of Arms over the front door of Spiddal House

The Berridges were English brewers and lived in Scríb Lodge. They had another home at Ballinahinch. The present Mrs Berridge, the first one to live there, is a first cousin of mine. She lives in Cork now. Her late husband was a very famous cruising yachtsman. Another thing I vividly remember was coming over to bury my uncle in 1927. We travelled by rail from Dublin, and on arrival at Galway Station the coffin was put onto a hearse. And all the drivers had white 'weepers' on them – big sashes.

The Berridges bought the Martin Estate through the Encumbered Estate Court. They leased it to Radji Singy, the Indian cricketer. They called him 'the Connemara Black'. Old Mrs Berridge was American. She was very rich. Eventually they went to live in Scríb. The night of Mr Berridge's funeral I stayed in Scríb and caught my first trout there. The younger generation were Dick, Robert and Jimmy. One is a doctor and two are in the British Army. I think the Brigadier is in Waterford now. They would go hopping mad if you said they were English. But they are. I have two cousins, older than myself, living in Cork. They should remember the Spiddal area. They would certainly remember Mrs Routledge's meringues. Edward Martin was a tremendous friend of my uncle. He was all against signposts. He used to say, 'Why do you want signposts? Everyone knows where to go!' My uncle was on the County Coucil and believed in signposts to show people the way.

I can remember Spiddal on a Fair Day when the most you could get to drink was a bottle of champagne. Every pub had champagne. I can remember drinking more champagne in Spiddal than anywhere else. When you'd made your bargain, or your deal at the fair, you drank champagne. The other popular drinks were porter and bottled Bass. That was until the Thirties, when Sir Grattan Bass made some anti-Irish remark and it was boycotted. You had your Bass with a dash of raspberry cordial in it. The champagne was five bob a bottle, which was dear at the time. I can remember a time when a glass of champagne was eight pence. Deals were sealed with a bottle of champagne in Tim Folan's pub. I used to go to the fair, socially, and to enjoy a few jars.

You couldn't get a meal in Spiddal then. There was no Bridge House Hotel or no Crúiscín. There was no butcher in the village, but there was a very good bakery owned by the Francis family. We always saw school treats as patronising, but we used to have races on the lawn. All that is banished now. I was horrified the other day when I saw a gate at the bridge. And when my uncle built the big lodge he changed the entrance to the driveway from the village. And now the old back lodge has deteriorated.

Coming to Spiddal from Galway, Lord Westmeath's house was on the left. When I was a baby the Westmeaths had it as a summer-house; as was Spiddal House, until my uncle rebuilt it as a proper home. I don't remember Furbo House or Tully. I remember the two old Misses Lynch of Bearna, and I remember my uncle associating with the Burkes of Moycullen. Daisy Burke was a Catholic and she became Lady Fingal. Further down, near Tullokeeaun, there was a house called 'Danesfield'. That's in ruins now. It was the Parochial House, built by Monsignor Blake. And Dr Michael told me that the Monsignor had all the local people there building it. And one day he asked the people, 'Why are you all working with one hand in your pocket?' And they answered, 'That hand is observing the Sabbath.'

I also remember a story from the time they were making *The Quiet Man*. Ward Bond was playing the priest in it. One day a local said to him, 'Mr Bond, you are playing the priest?' And he said, 'Yes, I am.' She said to him, 'You have your hand in your pocket, and no priest would ever put his hand in his pocket.' At that, John Ford came over and said, 'No, they only have their hands in other people's pockets!' They filmed around Cong. It would have been Spiddal, but they had no hotel in Spiddal, and there was a good hotel in Cong.

My aunt Rose, who got lupus as a child, used to visit Mrs Palmer in Baile an tSagairt. I knew Rose quite well. She used to come down to Spiddal on holidays. The garage was done-up specially for her. She had a wonderful, full-time nurse. Because of the lupus she could only talk with her hands. She wore a veil and could only make strange noises that I couldn't understand. If you go down to the sea, west of Spiddal, you can see the foundations of a bathing cabin that my uncle had built for her. It was washed away by the sea. It was always very cold to go bathing there, anyway. I spent my childhood on the beach at Spiddal, with my bucket and spade.

Lady Killanin
(née Sheila Dunlop)

Her father was Parson of Oughterard. Born there, but spent much of her earlier childhood travelling between Ireland, England and India.

We married in 1945. I knew Spiddal, having been over a few times before I met my husband. We went there for our honeymoon, which was very pleasant. Before the children started arriving we did the usual things one does in the country. We did a lot of gardening. The garden had been neglected, hadn't had a great deal done to it for a while. We had this wonderful old gardener, Pat, who had only one tooth left in his head. He was absolutely devoted to the place. And anyone we ever got to help him was, according to Pat, 'no good at all', because they wouldn't work with him all hours of day and night. His surname was Thornton. My husband used to hunt at that time, so I used to follow him around in the car, quite a bit, which was a nice day out. I didn't have much to do in the house, because we had a certain amount of help.

Then, when the children arrived, it was rather different. But we still entertained quite a bit. You see, we had a lot of friends who used to come over from England, as we were much better off here for food, and other things, after the War. And when all the family arrived we used to have great fun exploring and picnicing around Connemara. I knew Connemara very well, because I'd

St Annins, belonging to the Morris family, was built as a Protestant church by the Rev James Mecreedy in 1853

spent a lot of my childhood there. My parents lived in India, but used to come back every two years or so, and we would divide that time between England and Connemara. Between India, England and Ireland, I sometimes don't quite know exactly *where* I was brought up. My father was a chaplain with the Indian Ecclesiastical Establishment. I always felt I belonged to the West more than to anywhere else. Unfortunately, I didn't speak the language, because all my schooling had been in England.

I know the Lord's Prayer in Irish, and that's about all.

But then most people spoke English in Spiddal. Up in the mountains the people spoke Irish only. We used to go up there with Mick Dillon, our 'keeper man' and he'd translate. We had a big garden and used to grow all the vegetables for the house. I remember someone telling me that there were children in Spiddal who had never in their lives seen a banana or a tomato, until they came back on the market after the War. We got our fish from the fishermen sometimes. Though there was very little fishing from Spiddal or Galway city then; just a little lobster fishing, that's all. I used to go to Galway once or twice a week and do a big 'shop', because I didn't have a freezer, just then, after the War. We had good salmon in the summer when the netting went on. We did our ordinary shopping in Folans, which is now Francis'. We had central heating, fuelled by turf. And we had a man who seemed to spend most of his time just throwing turf and sticks into the big boiler. We didn't have any turf bog on the estate, so we had to buy our turf. We had no electricity when we first married. We just had those dreadful paraffin lamps. And then we got very sophisticated and put up generators. We had a little fridge which was run on paraffin, but it always went wrong when we had parties. We used to have two or three parties a month. We sometimes travelled up to sixty miles to our friends' houses for parties. The only restaurants I can remember, from those days, in Galway city, are Lydons and the Great Southern Hotel. We bought our clothes in Morans quite often and in Dublin quite a lot.

I remember Connemara quite well, because my father was the Parson of Oughterard. So I knew all around better than my husband did, because he didn't spend as much time in Connemara as I did. But people have changed a lot since then and a lot of it is due to television. People were a lot poorer. But strange things, like plastic, coloured buckets, you wouldn't have seen years ago. And peoples' lifestyles have changed a lot. I remember when boys wore red, flannel petticoats. They didn't wear trousers, for practical reasons.

There were slated houses around then, but there were also thatched cottages. The countryside has been ruined, except east and west of Spiddal. The houses are awful to look at, but they are probably better than the damp, cold cottages.

We didn't have really big parties. Just about ten or twelve people at them. We had a big dining-room table and that came apart in three pieces. When we moved, to Dublin, we brought two pieces and gave the other piece to one of the children. The table is reputed to have been made from a huge piece of wood washed up on the beach here. It was too big for us to keep.

When we first married we had a large staff here, not very well-trained, but pleasant and very willing. They were all local, which was nice. One of the reasons we decided to sell was that, during our holidays here, I spent most of the time cleaning-up. I still have dreams about Spiddal House, even though we've left it. And in my dream we've gone back, and we have American visitors coming. In the dream too, the house is always untidy, and it's absolutely horrendous, and they're doing terrible things to the outside of it.

Pat Sally Folan

The last weaver in Leitir Móir.

I built this house. I was born in 1912 and brought up about two hundred yards from here. I bought a bit of land and built this house. There are a lot of Folans in this area. This part of the island is called Poll a' Mhuirinn. This is part of Leitir Móir. I don't remember a time when these islands were separate, when you had to go by boat to the mainland. These islands have always been linked up to each other in my time. This is called Garumna Island. And Béal an Daingin is on the other side. Then there's Casla and An Trá Bháin. My father worked there the time the bridge was built. There was no road there at that time. When the high tide came up you couldn't go unless you went by boat. You had to wait until the tide was out to cross on foot. The bridges were built in the late 1800s.

My father was a weaver during his lifetime. And my two uncles were weavers all their lives. Weaving ran in families at that time. I remember a lot of people coming to the house. They came from Leitir Móir and Leitir Mealláin and from around here. It was a very sociable household. My father's name was Michael and my grandfather's name was Eamonn His father wasn't a weaver. I heard how my grandfather got into the weaving. A man from Mayo came here and he was a weaver, and he taught him. There was another weaver in the Aran Islands that was related to us. The Aran Islands had lovely flannels. They had the dyes there. They had a lovely blue colour. When my father started weaving it was only sixpence a yard. That was at the beginning of the century. There were eight of us in the family. I have two brothers in England. The rest stayed in Ireland. I have a sister who is in America, in Washington DC. She went a long time ago. She went very young. She's married to a man named Hunt and they have no family. There was about the same amount from here that went to America and to England.

The old loom in the Heritage Centre came from Tuairín in Carraroe. It's the only one left. There were three or four weavers in Carraroe. Paddy Beatty had an old loom himself from 1934. They had no special wood for making the loom. A bit of pine would do. I made one from Scotch fir. There was no other wood to be got then, because it was 1940. You needed oak for a few pieces. You didn't need special wood for the spinning wheels, except for the wheel itself. There are two hundred threads on each leaf and there are four leaves.

Every house here used to have sheep. And they used to send the wool to Galway to make cloth. They used to buy their own clothes in the shops, sometimes. I did a bit of weaving myself, out there in the Comharchumann. But the thread I got there was worth nothing. The loom was too heavy for the thread they're making now. When I was growing up it was a heavy thread. We were making a fine, grey flannel then. They called it warped and wacked. I learned the weaving from my father. We had the loom made in Donegal. I made one myself after we got that. But we had to get one first because we didn't know how to make it.

Pat Sally Folan at his home in Leitir Móir

My grandfather's loom was different to this. With the hand, they used to wig. They used to throw the shuttle with the hand. But this one hadn't the same ways as the old one. This one was bigger. The shuttle was going on to the end of the sleigh with wheels on. We used to make sixteen yards a day. It took from eight o'clock until six o'clock. It was very concentrated work. It was an awkward trade. Everything had to be right. I worked in a special room in the house. It needed ten-feet by fourteen-feet to go around. The people brought the wool into Galway by boat. The woollen mills in Galway was called Lydon's Mills and they made very good thread. There was a man here in the village, Martin Walshe, who had a boat with three sails, a hooker. He brought most of the wool in. And there was another man called Cloherty who had his own smaller boat.

Droichead an Chuigéil

Then the thread came back to us from Galway and we set it up to make the flannel. There were eight hundred eyes on the needles. And there's another thing that they call the reed. Well, we had to get the thread into the needles first and then into the reed. We had to double the thread into the reed, then we tied it up and started weaving. We got the needles from Donegal, from a factory in Kilcar. They came to Maam Cross by rail. It was a long way to go to pick them up, from here to Casla and on to Maam Cross. We used to go on horse and cart.

Everybody used to bring their thread to me and I charged them to weave it, per yard. Then they took it to a tailor. There were three tailors on this island. There was Ralph Horan and Eamonn Loughlin and another, but I can't remember his name. They're all dead now. We weaved according to the colour of the thread. They dyed the thread with things that grew in the fields. They dyed thread with sweet meadow. We used to make flannel for blankets, and we had a herringbone pattern, and even a shamrock pattern. The weaving was cheap at the time. We charged two shillings a yard. The patterned one was two pounds for twenty yards. But then, everyone was poor at the time. That was in 1933, '34 and '35. I was thirty-five when I started to weave and I didn't like the job very much. There's a different way to make a herringbone pattern. I only spent five years weaving. I was the last weaver around here. When I stopped the weaving they did nothing in the world around here. They just sold the wool.

At that time they used to make their drawers from the wool, with the white flannel. And they used the grey flannel for trousers. You see there were dark sheep around here as well. So the dark and the white threads mixed together made the grey. The grey flannel was for their trousers, jackets and vests, and that flannel was very warm. And if you were out in the rain you wouldn't feel the wet, because the flannel was so warm. In the summer they used to go in their drawers and their shirts. The shirt was made from flannel as well. They were grand people at that time.

I didn't weave for wedding clothes, because they didn't need anything special for weddings at that time. They just had ordinary clothes. The woman might get a new blouse in Galway. The skirts were made by the local tailor. They went to America wearing that flannel and people used to ask them in America where they got the flannel. Some of them used to dye the suit brown and make it dark. They used plants that grew in the fields to dye the suit. They used berries to make the flannel red. I didn't dye the wool. The women used to do that. Some used to dye the wool, others would wait until the flannel was made.

After that I went to England in 1937. It was no good. You got three pounds ten shillings a week and you had to pay for your digs out of that. So I came back and was weaving again. But I had a second trade – building houses. That was good. I used to build good houses, with stone and concrete. But I went over again, this time to Scotland, and I only stayed three months. It was no again. I was in Scotland in 1940. I went over again, since then, to my kids, on holiday. I have two boys and two girls in England. I have one in Australia, one in California and three here. That's nine altogether.

The old temple here was built in 1849. The walls are all that's left now. They say that the temple in the Aran Islands was built overnight. They also say that other temples, like the one here, were built overnight. But I don't believe them. St Finian and his monks built it. And the people here didn't feed them. They were afraid if they did they wouldn't have enough to eat themselves. St Finian got the oats from France and he got a grindstone to grind the grain. The people used to throw the monks' tools into the sea as well. The monks came over by boat from France. The temple is over eleven hundred years old.

There were good storytellers around here. There was Wiliam Berry over in Leitir Meallán. And my uncle, Pat Folan, was good. They gathered then and people used to tell stories. My uncle was very good at telling stories. At the time we didn't listen, we didn't care. If we knew that this carry-on was going to happen we'd have listened. The stories that we heard went away back. It might have been our grandfathers that told them.

When I socialised we played cards, twenty-fives and thirties. You put a penny in. Money was scarce at the time. We went to different houses to play cards. Now they go into one another very seldom. They're looking at television and it isn't worth your while to go visiting. Life is better now in one way. But in another way, it isn't. Nowadays, there's plenty to eat but too much to drink. There was no going to the pub then, except on St MacDara's Day, St Stephen's Day, and days like that, when the old people might have a pint. And we had a Fair Day, once a month in Derrynea. They used to walk from here to Spiddal Fair and back again. Lorries come now and pick up the cattle, so they don't need to go to the fair. They go to the mart now.

Máirtín Nee

A gillie for the Berridges who owned the Scríb fishery and was an expert on Connemara ponies.

The Nees came from Ballinahinch way, up from Kylemore, as far as I know. There were people moving at that time. They used to go somewhere and do a bit of tillage. And then, after a while, they used to move again. That was around the sixteenth or seventeenth century. It took them years to settle down. Even during the time of the Land Commission there was a lot of land in Connemara that wasn't being used, and you could get it for a very small sum and go and live on it. My grandfather had a lot of land. He had land in Ros Muc as well. He decided that he didn't want all the land and gave a lot of it up. And that was the time of the Congested Board. And before that it was the Ashbourne Act that was running the country. Then the Congested Board came in and then the Land Commission. We still have the Land Commission. Anthony Mannion's mother and my father were cousins.

I don't remember Pádraig Pearse, but I have a few stories about him from the old people. When Pearse first came down here he bought the lake from Grealish for five pounds and he got the cottage built. And it was the two Nées who built it, from Turlach, Máirtín Labhráis and Micheál Mhichil Phaidín. Micheál was married to my aunt. Pádraig Pearse kept very much to himself, and he didn't go into houses. Mannions owned the Post Office, where

The Connemara Pony Show in Clifden, every August since 1947. (First) Lorna Murphy on Tulira Blackthorn and (second) Emma McCluskey on Ashfield Country Flight

O'Malleys is now. Pearse went in there for a stamp and Mannion refused him, because he knew that Pearse was an IRA man at that time, and he was on the other side. But Pearse didn't make any trouble. And he could have, if he had reported him to the IRA. An uncle of mine was a boy at the time and he was going to school in Gort Mór. He came into school one day and found Pearse there, talking to one of the teachers, Connery. Colm Ó Gaora was a teacher there too. He used to teach night school. He wrote the book *Mise*. He was great friends with Pádraig Pearse.

We had three boys and three girls in my family. We were reared out there at the hatchery – Scríb Hatchery. I had no place of my own and I bought this when I got married. I got a grant from the Gaeltacht to build the house. This house went up, roughly, on twelve hundred pounds. I met my wife in England. She was Irish. She's from down the road, in the village. She died ten years ago from cancer. She used to work for the Berridges. She used to cook for them. She also worked for Mongan in Carna. He was a TD. They had a hotel there. There used to be a lot of anglers staying there at that time. I went to the old school. I worked in England for about seven or eight years, and made money, and came home and bought this place. A few people did that. But in my young days, there weren't many people from here going to England at all. But then, when one or two went over, they started following one another over. Some of them got good jobs there.

I used to go to the Carna Show from Cnoc an Daimh, back where I was born. I used to walk a pony to the show. At the time it was confined to Connemara only, but the field in Carna was too small. They moved it to Clifden in 1947. For three years before that it was held in Recess, Roundstone and Oughterard. After a few years the Clifden Show became an open show and people started coming from Meath, Cork, Wexford, Kildare, Wicklow, Carlow and Dublin. They have shows in Carraroe and Oughterard too. I was judging at the Carraroe Show last year. I used to come over from England sometimes to go to the Clifden Show. The best is picked not so much on the breeding, but on how well-fed they are. They have to be shiny and shown to be well-fed. A good Connemara pony will fetch top price anywhere. A good Connemara pony has to have a fair bit of ground, a very straight back, a good hindquarter, a good riding shoulder and good legs. They're smaller that an ordinary horse, and they have to

have a good bone. The height of the average Connemara pony is between thirteen and fourteen hands. But there aren't many left now. A lot of them have gone out of the country. One man paid a £1,000 for a foal. Another paid £1,400 . But they're all for showing now. They don't work them any more, not even in saddle.

After coming back from England I got involved in breeding Connemara ponies. We had three mares out in Cnoc an Daimh and we used to breed them. My grandfather had three stallions and he used to breed them too. Mark Geoghegan was the best man in Connemara to handle a pony. There was a stallion called Cannonball and he used to ride him at the races. Miss Berridge had three ponies in Scríb. And she bought another from the Griffins in Wicklow. Then she started breeding. And she got into the Connemara Society and she sold a lot of

*Teaspeáinteas Chois Fharraige, An Spidéal
with Esther Feeney leading the first horse*

Máirtín Nee at his home overlooking the Screebe Fishery

ponies. And she used to name her ponies after her fishing flies. Kingsmill was one, and there was Connemara Black, Thunder and Lightening, Watson's Fancy, Bibio, Black and Silver and Peltam Peckham.

I always had work with the Berridges when they came from England. I spent forty years or so working on the Fishery for them. I retired at sixty-five, about ten years ago. I get an English pension as well. I had insurance stamps in England because I worked there. I worked in the building trade for about two years. I also worked on the railroad for a few years. Then I went to work with a firm building a by-pass. They were an Irish firm, McGregors. They were a good firm. We built six miles of by-pass round the town. They had eighteen bridges on the by-pass. I left and came back home before that was finished.

Presentation by Laragh Standún to winner John McLoughlin at the Teaspeáinteas Chois Fharraige

I remember the railway going to Clifden. My grandfather used to buy food for the cattle in Galway city, and that came out, by train, to Maam Cross and we used to collect it there. We went with a donkey and cart. But the railway closed down when the lorries started. The lorries had taken over, originally, from the hookers. But it was hard on the hookers. If the weather was bad in Galway they'd have to dock there for three or four days. Then they'd have to come back to Ros Muc and unload and load again to leave again.

I spent about forty years, if not more, on the fishery with the Berridge family. I worked for Mr Berridge. There were five in the family. Three boys and two girls. A fellow from Kildare had the contract to build two extra rooms onto it, and they came down to live there in 1927, before it was rightly finished. The eldest son was a Lieutenant Colonel in the British Army. The second son was a doctor. They are both dead now. The youngest, Jimmy, is down in Woodford. He was a Brigadier in the Army, and had twenty-one years' service. He had around two hundred dairy cows. He was married to a Belgian girl. The Colonel was married to one of the Killanins, a relative of Lord Killanin. He moved back and bought a place in Cashel. He was a boat-builder. He built yachts. His wife did the designs and he used build them. And they were very good boats. Then Miss Berridge, Laura Berridge, had the Connemara ponies in Scríb. But she left and went to live in Dublin and then in Wicklow. The second girl, Nancy Berridge, married a Jennings in England. The Jenning's boy, Nancy's son, still comes to fish there. And Jimmy Berridge, his uncle, also comes to fish occasionally. I

The October Fair at Maam Cross

remember going fishing with Jimmy, and after an hour we had over fifty trout in the boat. And that was a lot of fish. But they never sold the fish. They used them themselves and they gave them away. They were a great family to work with.

When Lord Dudley took it over he had the Inbhear Fishery as well. Lord Dudley was very rich and Connemara was very poor at the time. Anyone who came to him got ten shillings. That was a lot. They could go shopping.

Lady Dudley was drowned in Scríb. There was a harbour and she went bathing and whatever happened to her nobody knows. All her money went into the Nursing Homes at the time. That was a lot of money. That's how the nursing improved. She would have been around fifty when she died. They had a son and three daughters. My father knew the son, but he didn't like him. There was Lady Mormard and Lady Anner. I fished with Lady Mormard. She was getting on in years at that time. In the summer there was always another family with them, the Delgettys from Kildare. They used to buy flannel from my mother. At the end of the summer Lord Dudley would go back to live in England, and the Delgettys would return to Kildare. It was a funny thing that Lord and Lady Dudley never spent a night in Scríb Lodge. They always went back to sleep in Inver Lodge. Lord Dudley used to carry on with Nancy Delgetty. I know that. There was something wrong, whatever it was. Another thing I heard was that Lady Dudley ordered him up to the other side of the woods. I also heard that she ordered the men working in the harbour to leave while she went swimming. So I don't know what she was up to. Maybe she wanted to do herself in.

Joe Pheadair Lee

A farmer and fisherman from three miles outside Carna.

I come from Carna. There's not much Irish left there now. In 1922, after the Troubles, they brought in a Bill to revive the Irish. Well, I can't see much of a revival in the Irish. I know that there is no Irish now in Cloch na Rón. There is no Irish out in Carna, or in the small villages going in the direction of Clifden. There are *Gaeilgeoirí* here learning Irish and a lot of them are very good. There's a woman working here. She's a nurse. And she comes from somewhere on the coast of Mexico. She came to England to train to be a nurse. There she met and married one of the Lydons and now she's working here. Her Irish is as good as anyone else here in Áras Mhic Dara. And there's another woman, by the name of Mary Bergin. She's a foreigner (from Dublin) too. She married in Spiddal. She learned Irish and she learned the old Irish songs. Then, she went up to the Oireachtas and won the third prize there.

There's an old saying about the people of Galway and the people of Clare and the potatoes. It goes, 'The Connacht man would have his potatoes dug, cleaned, boiled and eaten, before the Clare man would even sow his new potatoes.' I met up a lot with people from Munster during my lifetime. The Irish speakers I like best would be those from the Déise in Waterford, and those from Tourmakeady in Mayo. I don't like the Kerry Irish, or the Donegal Irish. People left Connemara years ago at thirteen or fourteen. And they went off to America and England. At the time they didn't have two words of English. The ones that went to the convent school weren't too bad. My own mother was very good with the English. She had some schooling in English and was able to speak it and read the papers.

They had good stories long ago. They used to talk about fishing and working on the land. They used to talk about cutting weed and sowing potatoes. There was a man who used to come to our house, Cóilín Mór. And he used to tell stories. The stories were really about life as it was happening, and the past.

I heard that this woman had children, and she used to get milk from another woman. But they got the plague. And when she went to the other woman she wouldn't let her in. So she went to the Holy Well on the way back and water from the well cured them. There's definitely a cure in that well – Roisín na Mainiach. You have to go around it nine times. We used to go down there every Sunday and clean it up and put flowers there. And years ago, on the day the people went to the Holy Well, my mother would make currant bread. And a lot of them used to come in for tea and currant bread on their way back. It was a big day. It was just like a feast day. And when the people used to come in the house my mother would sing *sean-nós*, and my Dad would put on the gramophone. And they would have sets. I remember too, when the people from Máinis were coming back late from the bog, they used to have a big feed in our house with spuds and fish. They used to have to wait for low-tide to bring the donkeys back to the island. Then my Dad would put the gramophone on again, and he'd put back the clock. So when they went down to the strand there would have been a big tide and they'd have to come back to the house again.

The last person to leave the island of Finís was Cóilín Toimín Choilmín. He was a great storyteller. He's dead now. He stayed for a while and they gave him a house on the mainland. The Council got them land on the mainland and they paid rent to the Council. They bought the land. We used to go to Finís, because my mother's people came from there. Máinis has a bridge. It used to be an island. I remember, there was this woman who was expecting a baby. She was out on the bog. And she had no house to go to. And she went to the strand and had the baby, by herself. And she wrapped the baby up and brought it home. A lot of women, in those times, had to bring their babies into the world by themselves.

I lived three miles from Carna. I used to be fishing

Joe Pheadair Lee

lobsters and scallops, and working on the land, sowing potatoes. I used to go to the odd *céilí*. There used always be a dance at Christmas time and St Patrick's Day. And they used to have a dance at the American wakes, when they were going to America. My family, my brothers and sisters died young. None of them emigrated. They were just young children when they died. The only one left was me.

The American wakes were very nice. We used to sing songs. And the weddings were very nice. In my time the bride and groom wore ordinary clothes. They were wearing the *báinín* here for a while, but that's gone out now. The women wore shawls and petticoats and two or three rows of velvet. The velvet wasn't expensive. You'd get a shawl for five pounds at that time. They made beautiful shawls. 'The hand shall gather around the lad that wears the *báinín bán*.' That's what they used to say.

There was a procession on the Feast of Corpus Christi. They had the first one that went from the church to the convent in Carna. And they had seven-a-side that day.

*Tobar Muire, The Holy Well, at Roisín Na Mainiach, Carna,
where Our Lady appeared during the Famine to a poor woman,
pointing out the well which was running with milk*

There were people from Oughterard and Carna, Cois Fharraige, and Galway city. Carna won the competition. They had very good footballers at that time. I was only thirteen or fourteen years of age then. But I remember it well. It was 1929. There was an altar in Carna. And then they went to St Joseph's Field, and from there to the convent. It was a long walk. We then had to walk from the convent to the village to get our bicycles to go home. We were young at that time, so it was all right.

We were a bit afraid of the priests. Peadar Madden was the parish priest for a while. And there was another priest, Fr Martin. He was a very rough fellow. He was terrible. He was a curate in Carna. He was going up the road one day in his car, and there was a man there, working on the road. A woman from Glinsk came along and started talking to the man. When Fr Martin came on them in his car he got out and gave the man a few clouts. He was terrible like that. He used to stop the dances. He used to go into the houses and break up the parties. And he used to wait for the men outside and kick them. He was changed then from Carna. He broke Máirtín John's melodeon, and Sally Goan reported him to the Archbishop. And he went to Annascaul. She wrote the poem, 'Na Beanna Beola'. She was very brave to report the priest to the Archbishop.

They had the stations in the house when I was young. And they had a party, sometimes, afterwards. There was a lot of *poitín* around at that time. It was very good compared to what you'd get now. The kind they have now is very bad stuff. They had the *poitín* for the wakes. They did the *caoineadh* at the wakes. I don't know about the banging on the coffins, but there were five women that used to go around and they cried like a song. Years ago they used to make the coffins themselves. They used to keep the wood that was left over from the coffin in a special place. They had a lot of superstitions then. They used to start sowing potatoes early on a Friday. They used to have a *Tine Chnámh* on St John's Night. And they used to put a sod of turf in with the potatoes. I don't know why, but they used to do it. They used to dance around the fire and say the Rosary around the fire.

Margaret O'Connor

Native of Doire an Locháin, Spiddal.
Mother of thirteen children.

I come from Doire an Locháin, near Furbo. I am here now for over sixty years. I am eighty years old. I'm in pretty good health.

We always had a lot of work to do. When we came home from school we would be out in the fields, working, or on the bog gathering turf, or digging or sowing potatoes. And in summer we'd be saving the hay, and bringing the tea and brown bread to the bog, to the men working there. It used to be like a picnic. And every evening the women would carry home, on their backs, enough turf for the fire. Every Saturday they would go to the market in Galway, with a cart-load of turf and eggs and butter. You sold a pound of butter for only ten pence. I was about twelve when I first started going to Galway with them. Most of our groceries, sugar and tea and that were bought in Galway. You could get them in the shops in Spiddal, but they were dearer there. Even though we didn't have much money we were very happy. We had our own turf, and eggs and butter, and vegetables for ourselves and to sell in the Galway market. And we used to go door-to-door in Galway selling the chickens. You got three shillings and sixpence or four shillings for a chicken.

When we got the wool from the sheep we took it to Lydon's Mills in Galway. We made a lot of our own clothes, but some things we bought in Galway. We always bought boots there. We made shawls and dresses, skirts and socks ourselves.

I went to school in Furbo. There's nothing there now. We had to bring a couple of sods of turf every morning to school. And if you forgot to bring the turf one day you had to bring extra sods the following day. We had a break at twelve o'clock and we finished at three. We walked the two miles to school. We didn't seem to have as much rain then as we do now. And we had very little snow. I was the eldest girl in our family and so I stayed at school until I was fourteen. I didn't go to secondary school. The eldest girl, always stayed at home to look after the parents. And if the parents had to go to Galway to sell turf the eldest was at home to look after the other children. There were seven in our family – three girls and four boys.

My mother never went to hospital to have the babies. She had them all at home. The midwife or a local woman always came in. There was no nurse there in those days. It was hard on women then, depending on a local woman who was a sort of midwife. There was no bathroom or toilet in the houses either. A lot of children died of convulsions in those days. The children would start screaming when they were a few weeks old and then just die. The doctors had no cure then.

My mother did everything in the house. She boiled the potatoes and cooked all the food and baked the bread. We never bought bread but made all our own, every day. We baked it on a turf fire. We put the oven-pot down on the red-hot fire and covered it with a heavy cover. There aren't many people making their own bread nowadays.

We ate bread, potatoes and fish mostly. And we would have meat and cabbage on Sundays. We never had to buy any food. In summertime we used to catch fish in the sea and they were lovely. We used to catch mackerel and salmon, and the salmon was very good. We made a churn on Friday nights to have the butter ready for the Galway market on Saturday morning. And there were also customers in Galway for the buttermilk.

We were pleased with our life then. We had *céilís* in the college in Spiddal. And we'd have a *céilí* at Christmas in someone's house.

Margaret O'Connor in her home in Leitir Meas

The men would bring whiskey and *poitín*, and the women would bring sugar, tea, milk and cakes. That was lovely. They'd be telling stories in the houses and playing cards. My father had a lot of stories – old stories. There would be great singing and dancing the old Irish dances.

The landlords were all gone in my time. But I heard stories about them. I knew Lord Killanin and his son. They used to come here regularly for the game shooting. Lord Killanin was the first man around here to have a motor car. I remember, long ago, going to school and seeing the Black and Tans with their guns in the big lorries. They'd be hunting someone special and when they found him they would kill him. I remember the Black and Tans down in Furbo, and then the soldiers coming past and my mother giving them something to eat. The Black and Tans were bad. They'd take the cart with turf from you and you going into Galway. The IRA were there too. There were a lot of young lads in the IRA and they would be on the run from the Black and Tans, sleeping out at night. And I remember what happened to Fr Griffin. The Black and Tans came in the night and took people from their houses and made prisoners of them.

There wasn't a big lot of people in the IRA around here. I never saw Pádraig Pearse but I heard a lot about him. I visited his cottage in Ros Muc.

The chapel in Furbo is beautiful. When I was young there was over a hundred people going to Mass there. We were in the parish of Spiddal, but we always went to Mass in Furbo. I remember the stations and the priest asking the children questions, and asking the parents how old the children were. After the stations there would be a meal for the priest. Then, when the priest was gone the people would all have tea, and bread and butter, and they used to make porter cake too. There was no *poitín* at the stations.

It was a made-match between my husband and myself. He came to our house with another man. And if the parents were satisfied with him then you had to be satisfied too. Then the father of the girl had to go and see the place where his daughter was going to live. Then the daughter got her dowry of money, cattle or goats. We had pigs also. That's the kind of arrangement there was.

On my wedding day I wore a blue suit and a blouse and shawl. The wedding party would be in the girl's house during the day, and that night in the man's house, 'til morning. There would be *poitín*, bread and tea and cake. And if the man's house was far away there would be side-cars to take everybody there. There would be fifty or sixty people at the wedding. There would be the two families and friends from the two villages. My husband had a brother and a sister living in Boluisce.

A butter churn

We used to go to the market in Galway. That was a distance of over five miles from Spiddal. We went to confession once a month, on Saturday night. And we had to go to first Mass to get Holy Communion, because they never gave Holy Communion at the second Mass. It was difficult, but we were happy. We were very healthy in those times. We had no doctor. But the midwife came when my children were due. Dr O'Beirn's mother was the midwife in my time. The neighbours always came in to visit the mother and new baby. They always gave two shillings or half a crown to the new baby. There was a cradle for the baby. There were no prams or cots there then. There was no talk of going to the dentist in those days. I had thirteen children. I had seven boys and six girls. I wasn't yet twenty when I got married. Most people got married at about that age then. And I was only married a week when I got a letter from my first cousin asking me to come to America. Of course I couldn't go, as I had just been married. There weren't that many people going to America at that time.

I remember I had a white dress for First Communion. It was bought in Galway. And it wasn't too dear then. And for Confirmation as well, there would be a white dress, and a veil and gloves, and a little handbag. There was no question of a party in those days. You went home and had some tea and went out working in the fields after that.

Bairbre Mhic Dhonncha

A retired teacher who taught on Inis Bearcháin (Inis Barra). Great local knowledge of the Ros a' Mhíl (Rossaveal) area.

My father died when I was seven. I barely remember him. I had one brother. He was older than I was. And then my sister Cáit was older than I was too. There were seven of us, and my mother slept with the seven of us. And the baby was six months. And she died very young. I remember her dying and the wake. But I didn't understand it. I remember going to school afterwards.

At that time there was no dole. You had to work for anything you wanted. And I don't know how my mother did it, but she got us on. She was a great housekeeper. And at that time they ate everything and the sea was there. We had some geese, hens and ducks. We had plenty of eggs. And we had two cows. So we had plenty of milk. My older sister was about fifteen. I still speak Irish.

All things considered, we were fine. I never, ever remember us being hungry. My mother always managed to have everything for us. She was always sewing and stitching and knitting. She also did crochet work. My sisters were always helping her. We had sheep and plenty of wool, so we made our own yarn. And out of that my mother used to work with a single thread and crochet some beautiful things for people. She could do anything with her hands. She never had any kind of machine. There was no money but the money from my mother's work

The Martello Tower in Ros a' Mhíl, one of a chain of coastal fortresses built between 1811-1814 against possible French invasion

coming in to the house then. There was no dole and, after my father died, no widow's pension. She had to work and work very hard. With the two eldest, my brother and sister she used to set potatoes and vegetables.

My father used to have a big sailing boat. He took turf

and things to the Aran Islands and to Galway. And coming back he would bring home flour and groceries and things for the local shops. So he did well and always had some money. He fell into a hole in Galway one night and after that was never the same. He sold the boat to an uncle of his and decided to find himself a job. He got a job from Canon McAlinney, painting the church and the schools in the parish. And the Canon said that he was able to give a lovely finish to the things he was painting. He gave a lot of help to Canon McAlinney in putting the new stations of the cross in Spiddal church.

I was fairly clever going to school at that time. They had just begun to give out scholarships. The school wanted me to do the exam, but there was an age limit of fifteen and I was just over that at the time. However, I went to the St Louis Convent in Monaghan. I did well there and I loved my time in Monaghan. Then I got a job teaching Irish and I went to school at the same time. Eventually I got a job teaching in Headford. I was there for six years. I married while I was there, but to a boy from home. He was from Ros a' Mhíl and was teaching in Ballina at the time.

There were lots of *piseogs* too in my time. When a child was being christened they would get a blade of grass and burn it, and place it under the child saying, 'May an angel of God be your companion.' I saw that being done. They believed in the banshee. I had a sister called Ann. And she was nineteen when she died. She got TB. But she was a lovely singer. She was one of the first persons who got the All-Ireland for singing. She was very musical. She's dead over fifty years now. The night before she died my husband's brother and others were visiting. And when they came over they had some kind of *céilí* down on the other side of Tully, near Ros a' Mhíl. And when they were coming back they heard a crying around our house. And they went in to their mother and found out that Ann was dead. And my two sisters went outside when the wake was on, and they heard a ferocious, lonely scream in the sky. That was about three in the morning. And the scream was going towards where my sister was being buried. We all loved her. She was very innocent and she knew that she was dying. She used to bring the accordion to bed and play it. She made people laugh. She was the only one of our family that died of TB, although there were a lot of people dying of TB at that time. She got pleurisy. And she was such an airy person. She was sick but she went to the Races in Galway. It was a wet day and she got soaked in the rain. She was so full of the joys of spring. Then she was sent to hospital, and they found it was dry pleurisy, but she wouldn't stay. She came home and went to a dance and got wet again. Then shortly after that she got TB and died. They didn't isolate many around here with the TB. There was a sanatorium in Merlin Park, in Galway, where they isolated a lot of people.

There was a monastery near the church, down a side-road. There were a good few monks there when I was young. It was a beautiful place. And I used to go there every morning and sometimes they would let me in. And then I started doing the forty stations. Which was doing

209

*Old headquarters of The Black and Tans
and Coastguards in Ros a' Mhíl*

the stations for forty nights. And I kept on dreaming about this. It was the first dream I'd had since my sister died. I dreamt that I was in St Peter's Church in Athlone.

When I was in Headford we used to do plays in the school and we won the All-Ireland. My husband Pat taught in the school beside us here (in Carna), and I used to do sub. I love plays. We brought a crowd from Carna to Spiddal to see our play. When we arrived there were a hundred and one children in the school. But they had to close it later because the numbers had dropped to about thirty. My husband was quite well known in the area. They called him Pat Mór. He was in a programme on television called *Bring Down the Lamp*. In the programme it was called Pat Mór's Pub. And for years, people would come around here looking for this pub. Sure, the 'pub' was right here in this house. He used to go to Dublin every weekend to rehearse. He was a good man. He was very quiet. We did singing and dancing and storytelling on *Bring Down the Lamp*.

Christmas night was lovely in Connemara years ago. They never closed the door, so that the baby Jesus could come in, and they had candles lit by the window. At that time they used to make lots of cakes at Christmas. And even if they couldn't afford candles they used thick blades with white wick. And they poured over a small drop of paraffin. Every child had an oyster or barnacle shell. And we were always waiting for Santa Claus. We had currant bread for him, and candy sticks – *maidí mílse*. My mother would make them. And I was always praying that Santa Claus would give me a pair of buckled shoes. We had plenty of money when my father was alive.

My mother was great, though, when my father died. She looked after the farm and she was always knitting. She wore a little black shawl and a red petticoat. It was beautiful. When I started teaching I got her a shawl. It was ten pounds. That was about two or three month's pay at the time. She was delighted with the shawl. It was handmade and it was beautiful on her. She had dark curly hair. We didn't have a lot for Christmas, but we loved it. And we were never hungry. You could have a different menu every day. On Sundays we had duck or chicken. And we had fish the rest of the week. We had *diúilicíní* and mussles. My mother used to make a lovely dish with it, with vegetables. We used to go back to Cill Chiaráin, and you'd have a bucket of shellfish. It could be cockles or mussels. My brother used to fish from the rock and he used to get a lot of fish. You could have one kind of fish one day, and another kind the next. The pier was small but there were lots of sailing boats.

Tom Mac Diarmada

Well-known storyteller, from the parish of Knock. Attended the Oireachtais several times.

I was born and reared in this place. But I spent nearly forty years working in Dublin. I worked in Dunsink Observatory. That was about nine miles outside the city. The Observatory was there for all things relating to the solar system, the weather and all that. I was employed as caretaker there and we had a lovely lodge to live in right beside where I worked. I was married when I came to work in Dunsink. Married to a Connemara girl from the islands, near Tír an Fhia. She's getting the Old Age Pension now for a couple of years. We have four children, three girls and a boy. Our son is working in Amsterdam, and sometimes he's in Germany and London. The youngest girl Anne is married to a Sri Lankan, in London, and they have two sons. We had a nice easy life in Dublin and I made a lot of friends at Dunsink. I made a lot of friends among the *Gaeilgeoirí* from the settlement in Ráth Chairn, not very far away in County Meath. They had all been resettled from various parts of Connemara. We would get together at weekends and have a lot of fun and high jinks.

In Connemara, growing up, life was hard. It was a kind of slavery. My brothers and myself would often go out fishing for lobsters at three and four o'clock in the morning, during the summer months. I was fishing like that from the time I was about twelve years old, until I was well over twenty and went to work in Dunsink. We used to sell our lobsters to a big trawler that came across from Clare. An Englishman owned it. He had a large concrete pond constructed in such a way that the tide could flood in and out of it. He stored the lobsters in this until he shipped them off to France and other places.

My father before me was a fisherman. But he was young when he died. Only fifty. And he had a hand in his own death. It was on 15th June, 1917 during the First World War. My father had a great love of the sea and was very well-experienced in its ways. He went out to fish, that March day, with my mother's brother. They saw out beyond them what looked like a buoy. They took it into the boat. It was a mine, and they never realised that. When they landed it on the beach ten other men gathered round to see it. By the time they realised what they had and began to run it was too late. The mine exploded and killed nine of them. My father was killed, but my uncle wasn't. We had a young mare and a foal at the time, and before he left that morning my father had said to my mother, 'I'll let the mare and foal out into the field before I go fishing. I'll be back before long.' But he never came back. He was only gone a short time when he was killed by the mine.

After my father died life was very hard. My father had worked hard all his life and had made a good living, but there was no money saved when he died. We hadn't a red penny. My eldest sister, Máire, had gone to America just one week before he was killed. In those days it took at least

Tom Mac Diarmada near his home in Inveran

two weeks to make the crossing. The first news she got when she landed in the States was that her father was dead. I had three sisters go to America. Two of them are still alive there. Máire is dead nearly thirty years now. From the start they always sent some money. It wasn't very much, because pay was small for them then in the States. They always sent money at Christmas and at Easter. I remember, one year they sent us thirty pounds, which was a lot of money then. They were great.

I don't remember their going away, but I do remember something of my father. I was about seven when he was killed. I think I can remember some things that happened when I was about two and a half. But my mother laughs at that. She says no child remembers anything before three or three and a half. Still, I'm sure I can remember little things from that very early age. Maybe that's the reason I have such an interest in storytelling. And also, we always had a *tine seanchais* in our house. It was always open to visitors in the evenings and we had songs and stories and dancing. That was before my father's death. After that my mother was so heart-broken that there was no music or singing, just the storytelling.

We fished for lobster then. You got seven shillings for a dozen lobsters. You always gave thirteen to the dozen when you sold them. We never ate the lobsters ourselves. They were always for selling. There were plenty of lobsters then, but hardly any there now. There was no contamination in the sea in those days. Nothing like there is now. When we caught fish, not the shellfish, we always salted some of it away in barrels and it would last us through the winter to the next spring.

We might sell some cattle or some goats, but we could never take any of the money we got for those. That money had to be put aside to pay the rent and rates. There wasn't much drinking in the pub in those days. My cousin had a pub – Tigh Gabha. He would get a barrel of porter in February. He only sold drink on local Fair Days and on Feast Days, like St Patrick's Day. There would be a fair about every three weeks in that area. After deals had been done at the fair the buyers and sellers would go to the pub for a drink. And they wouldn't have another pint 'til the next Fair Day or the next Feast Day. Women didn't usually go into the pub at all. My mother was an exception. After my father died she had to go to the fairs herself, and she would always go for one pint after the fair. She always went into a quiet little room called 'The Snug'. I never saw a young girl in the pub, in my time, nor a young girl with a cigarette in her mouth.

The day of a christening was a big day. We had no midwife or doctor, and babies were never born in hospital in those days. Sometimes a nurse would come if she thought it was going to be a difficult birth for the woman. But if there wasn't any danger then there would be no need of the nurse. My mother assisted at the birth of every child that was born in our area when I was growing up. She was regarded as being as good as any midwife. She had great knowledge and experience. People would come calling for my mother from ten miles away. Mary

Tom was her name. She called me Tom, after her own father. I heard stories from her of the poor people who were expecting a baby and had no money. But she never took money.

One night a man came knocking on our window and woke my mother. She was needed by a young woman giving birth to her second child. We had to set off to Tigh Larry with the man. From whatever the man said to her my mother thought this birth might be complicated, so she asked him to send for the doctor too. But the doctor wasn't at home and couldn't be found. Then, a second doctor, from Carraroe, was gone to a woman in labour far from Carraroe. So my mother had to do everything herself. She soon found that this wasn't just a second child. The poor woman was having triplets. The first two were born dead, but the third was alive and well. Before we left that house the woman was out of her bed and going about her housework.

The blacksmith worked close to the pub, The Poitín Stil. He had a workshop there. He tried to have nothing to do, like most people, with the Blakes. The Morrisses are

Part of the ruin of Cashel House, residence of the Blakes in Inveran beside what is now the airport

the Killanins. Killanin is the Barony. The Killanins are much more sociable than the Blakes. They were always very well thought of by the local people. Unlike the Blakes who were disliked greatly by everybody. The Blakes were a bad lot. They were Protestant. Their old house is gone now and the airport is built very near where it was. Parts of the old walls are still standing, and there is also the Rector's house. The Protestant Rector lived there up to 1920. Now, I don't know an awful lot about the Blakes, but I do remember one of them, Ned Blake. He was a very big man. He had people working for him for no pay. As his tenants they were at his beck and call. There were other Blake families in Carna, Ros Muc and Cill Chiaráin. They were all related. They were also in Monivea and Corrandulla. They came from England originally and after service to the Crown in various wars they were given lands in Ireland. They quickly became notorious as landlords. If they saw a fine specimen of a cow or horse with one of their tenants they immediately came and took it, without any payment. It was the same when they saw a particularly pretty young girl. They took her into their service and broke her. They fathered children all over the countryside. So many that no one could keep count of them. They'd been here since the time of the plantations in 1631. They were at the Battle of Kinsale. The infamous Ned Blake was married seven times. In the end their luck ran out and they disappeared.

I hated school, because the teachers were so bad and they were constantly beating the children. I didn't like that. I remember being very frightened when I saw one of the teachers beating a boy with a stick. I started crying and screaming. We had four teachers in the school. In my time the boys and girls were separated in the classroom. The girls were at the east end of the school and there were partitions between the two. Even outside, between the boys' toilets and the girls' toilets, there was a big fence. The boys and girls weren't allowed to mix at all. It was very difficult. There were more girls than boys in the school in those days. At that time we had no buses or cars and we went to school in our bare feet, even in the frost and snow.

The Clan McDermott are there a long time. Still, I could never find a single shop in Galway with the name McDermott on it. I could only trace the one McDermott in Galway, and that was a surgeon in the hospital, called Harold McDermott. He was from Roscommon. He lived in Lord Killanin's house for a while. I never heard of another McDermott, except ourselves, in Carraroe, Leitir Móir, Carna, or even as far west as Clifden. There was the McDermott Mór branch of the clan and the McDermott Roe branch. The McDermott Roes came into Roscommon, Mayo, Leitrim, Sligo and Donegal after the Battle of the Yellow Ford. My mother's name was Ó Cualáin.

Dónall Ó Conchúin

Poet, folklorist and businessman. His father, a Garda in Spiddal, appeared with Michael McLiammoir in the first play in the Galway Taibhdearc – Diarmiad agus Gráinne.

An tOileáinín Beannaithe (the Blessed Little Island) is situated at the mouth of the stream, beside the lakes where they come out at Casla Bay. Now there are not many people living on the little island itself, but there are many stories told, and poems written, about the cures that happened to the people who visited the Blessed Island and prayed there. The people of the Gaeltacht have always had a great love and respect for the Blessed Island and the places associated with the saints.

We have a deep insight into this special meaning through an event which happened here over 100 years ago, when a ganger failed to force workers to remove stones off the island to repair a holey pathway. One must bear in mind that neither stones, sand, lorries nor diggers were easy to get at that time. But since the wee holy island was beside the roadway and had an abundance of rocks, the ganger saw that as a simple solution. However, the local workers would not interfere with the island's rocks; obviously, the ganger was not a local. The ganger reported the problem to the parish priest. Both of them asked the men to dig up the rocks, but to no avail. Now the island is as it was, and will be, on account of the stand taken by the workmen.

Certainly one can draw a comparison between this little

Dónall Ó Conchúin at his home in Carraroe

island and our own country. The strangers are coming and want to use the resources to suit themselves. The islands have a lot in common, in terms of a faith perspective and the fight for civil rights. At long last our island is free, apart from Northern Ireland. Were it not for the faith of these workmen and their respect for customs and rituals, this Holy Island, this special place, would be unheard of now. If others had the same spirit, we would have a greater knowledge of our heritage, which is gradually slipping away.

There is a little strand between the Lake of the Mill and

the Pier of the Stream. Because the stream was not deep, at the point where there now is a bridge, it was easy enough for people to cross over. A thief used to come occasionally and steal a sheep from the inhabitants of Baile an Chillín (the village of the small church, or grave), and carry it over the stream on his shoulders. It was in the daytime that this used to occur, and so nobody noticed. But one fine day he met a small lady at the crossing and she asked him to help her across, after he had brought the sheep across. He was carrying her across when, suddenly, she began to beat him with a stick. She left him for dead. Now, even though the thief was dead, the villagers of Baile an Chillín weren't all that overjoyed – particularly as it was a woman who had stopped the thieving. They spoke a lot about the number of

Mass celebrated at Teampall Bharr An Doire in Carraroe on Lá Féile Mhic Dara, 16th July

sheep that were still left on the island, rather than dwelling on the number stolen. It is certain that this thief had come from the east – some say from the region of Gráinne Ní Mháille, but it was very difficult to ascertain who this small lady was. It seems likely that she was from Baile an Chillín, since she was so anxious to get rid of the thief. It is possible that she did the deed of her own volition and this would explain why the locals did not rejoice. The thief in question must have been a big strong man, when you consider that he killed the sheep on the spot and carried the dead body across the ford. The question has often been asked – why did the old lady ask the thief to

help her across? It seems likely that this incident took place about 1870, because there were no sheep on the commonage after that time, and the first bridge was built in 1880. A lot of famous people visited the place between 1886 and 1890. The 16th of July is the date of Lá Fhéile Mhic Dara. We remember it, as it was in the Forties and Fifties, on account of a boat that arrived in Sruthán Pier to shelter from a storm. Now, this boat was on its way to Oileán Mhic Dara, with sweets and small cakes, but sold them all on the banks at Sruthán. The following year a cabin to sell things was erected in the town further back, at Doire Fhatharta crossroads. Year on year, after that, more stalls and cabins and games appeared on the spot for Lá Fhéile Mhic Dara.

By the 1900s, great crowds of pilgrims were coming every year on Macdara's Day. Old and middle-aged mostly, they were all coming to do the pilgrimage at the Saint's Lake beside Cnoc an Phobail. The youth would all be hanging around the cabins and the stalls near where *Tigh Táilliúra* pub is now. Crowds came from Ros Muc, Spiddal, Oughterard, and from the islands. The side-cars were parked on the side of the road, from Tobar na Croise, and down Bothár Cillín at the top of the road. Before they began praying around the lake, they took seven small stones in their hands, and as they went around, they threw one into the water, to keep count. Because of the rough state of the roadway a drop of *poitín* was always welcome at the end of the pilgrim's walk around the lake.

The Battle of Carraroe happened in 1880, in the months of January and June. Whilst these may have been just minor events during the Land Wars, they showed that when the public fought for their rights, the might of the landlords, police and army were not able to overcome them. Michael Davitt recognised, while he was beginning the Land Wars, that the people of Connemara were very supportive of each other. He was one of the main speakers in Carraroe during a massive rally there. The area was very, very poor at that time. Although there were 2,000 acres there, only about 110 acres were tilled. It is reported that there existed, in the whole area, only 4 horses, 15 donkeys, 120 cows, 52 sheep and 14 pigs. There were high rents to be paid to the local landlords, Kirwan and Lambert. There were separate dues on the land, houses and stables. Some households had to pay between £5 and £10, which was a lot of money at the time. There were many ways of providing for the rent dues; such as the sale of *poitín* and money from abroad – mainly from the USA. When the son of a tenant married the rent was raised, from £5 to £10.

If the tenants had a bad year, and were unable to pay rent, the landlord served a summons, which had to be served on a special day. The bailiffs and the police accompanied the man who was serving the summons, but the people of Carraroe were prepared to thwart the people of the law. All the roadways were cut up, with people going every which way. Men and women were working hand in hand; they had huge fires, with pots and saucepans of boiling water, ready for use in the event of an attack. 'Quay House' on Bóthar Buí was the first on the list and that's where the racket started. The summonses were taken and torn up. Then when the police came to the rescue, a saucepan of boiling water was thrown in the face of an officer. The police charged with their bayonets, but the locals stood firm, and won the day. They sent the lawmen back to their barracks. This was in the first week of January 1880. It took a couple of days for the lawmen to arrange reinforcements; meantime they were confined to barracks, with no food. When the reinforcements did arrive it was too late to serve the summons. The lawmen had to leave town. This victory has been compared to Lexington, in the USA, where the English were confronted, for the first time, in 1775.

In June 1880, the steamer *City of the Tribes* left Galway, with 200 police and soldiers aboard, and sailed into Casla Bay. Summonses were to be served, and the people were told they would be evicted if rents were not paid. But there was no trouble. Seven summonses were served, and in the case of one, it was put under the door as there was nobody there. At this very time there was a debate in the House of Commons about introducing a new Bill – the Peace Preservation Act 1885, or else amend it. Among those who spoke were Lord Oranmore Brown, and Tottenham from Leitrim. Foster, who was the new Secretary General, stated that there was a need for the Police and Army in the Carraroe affair, as he called it. But the Bill did not succeed and England had the same problem all over Ireland with rent collection. Due to the events in Carraroe in 1880, this sounded the death knell of the Landlord system.

Nicholas O'Fegan

A native of Barna. Worked for CIÉ and the County Council.

We've been here for over 100 years. My mother's name is Concannon. My grandfather is buried in the graveyard down there. He's buried there over a hundred years. It's the little cemetery over there by the pier, the original cemetery in Barna. It's filled up now, so people go to Rahoon, but there is still some space down there. It's neglected, like a lot of other graveyards round the country.

My grand-uncle was the same name as myself – Nicholas O'Fegan. He died in 1929, and was parish priest of Castlebar. He was around sixty, and was a great preacher, either in Irish or in English. It was he who spoke at the internment of Fr Griffin's remains in Loughrea Cathedral, and it's worth your while to have a look there at Fr Griffin's grave, as it's a masterpiece. There is also a monument to Fr Griffin here in Barna. It was rebuilt. There was a ceremony up there just last Sunday.

I knew Fr Griffin when I was a child. He was very well-liked. The sad thing was, that when he was killed, the person who asked him to come out of the house seemed to have a fluent knowledge of Irish. The man who was in charge of the Black and Tans here at the time resigned afterwards, disgusted by the whole procedure. They were oftener drunk than sober – the Black and Tans. I don't remember that much, but I do remember the night he was taken. My uncle was beaten up that night – my uncle,

Fr Griffin's monument in Barna

Paddy Concannon – a farmer. He was left for dead, outside the gate of Eagle Lodge. Eagle Lodge is a hundred yards over the road. It's a building on the left. There's a new house beside it now. Dr. Callaghan owns it now. There was a Protestant lady living there in my time, called Mrs Benningham. She always took the kids out for a tour in the summertime, the boys and the girls on separate occasions. She was a Protestant, but she was very kind. Nobody took any notice of Protestants at the time.

There was a Protestant church about half a mile out the road, towards Spiddal. There was a 'soup kitchen' then, near Colm O'Byrne's house, and it became a Protestant church afterwards. They tried to convert the people to the Protestant religion years ago, but I wouldn't think that they succeeded much. Some called it 'The Mission House', others called it 'Teach na Jumpers'. Mick Waller lived there and took charge of the place, and had the church ready within the house, and had it ready for service on Sundays. There was always something fashionable for harvest time – the Harvest Festival. It was a special ceremony where all the crops were displayed. It was a big celebration for the Protestants, though there weren't many of them – only five or six. The Clarke family were Protestant, and Mrs Murren, and Mrs Benningham and her maid, Mary Owen. And that was it.

Eagle Lodge was a large dwelling house. Jacksons lived in it, Delaneys were living there, after Mrs Benningham, and then Conor O'Malley, the surgeon, was living in it. That's where the O'Malley family were reared. Then Ann O'Malley married Simon John Kelly, and they were living there, until they built a new house and sold the old one. O'Malleys were very well-known. He was a surgeon and his wife, Sal, was a doctor, and she lectured in the college – the Regional. One of their daughters married a Captain Ringrose.

About Barna House. I remember the Lynches. There were two sisters, Esther and Bridie. Esther was a nun in Clarinbridge, and she was brought home to look after the sister. They got on well in the community. Kept very much to themselves. They were very old when I knew them. They had a huge garden. They were reasonably good landlords, though they weren't landlords here. The landlords here were Campbell and Stratheden, as far as Liberty Stream. And

Barna House, which was the former home of the Lynch Family

then the Blakes were landlords out as far as Spiddal. There were Lynches too. They were landlords from Eagle Lodge to Knocknacarragh. They had a huge estate, but it didn't go as far as the village, only as far as Eagle Lodge.

Barna House was about a mile over the road, where the caravan park is. The old house was knocked. The Lynchs weren't natives of Barna, but married into the O'Halloran's estate. Apparently the Lynches had plenty of money and the O'Hallorans had the land, but were short of cash. One of the Lynchs married one of the O'Hallorans. That's how they got over there. The remains of the house was there where that new estate is going up. The golf course was over at Cappagh Road. Shanballyduff was the name of the golf course. It extended from there to the Ballymoneen Road, where the new church is. The Club House was knocked.

I grew up around there, but I never played golf there. Very few played it. It was only a nine-hole course. It was very hard to acquire land here at that time. They moved to the O'Hara estate in Salthill, and built an eighteen-hole course. The locals were delighted because the land was divided amongst the farmers. My father got three acres. They had to be tenants of the Lynchs. It was Dr Michael O'Malley who started that golf course. He lived in the Lynch house after the Lynchs left. The two sisters were last in the Lynch line. The Land Commission took over most

The Old Cemetery in Barna

of the estate after the ladies died, except a few acres around the house and the cliff at Silver Strand, and Dr O'Malley bought that, and the tenants got the most of the land.

The pier was an important pier in my young days. Nimmo built that pier. He was a Scottish engineer. He also built Nimmo's Pier in Galway, and the pier at Roundstone. And he made the road to Clifden. In making that road he avoided most of the hills, because it was all horse transport at that time. The boats weren't there in my time. They had finished then. Lynchs had a pier down there – a wooden pier – before Nimmo built a pier. They had a boat down there, but they never did a lot of fishing. It was mostly used for pleasure trips. They hadn't a car, but they had a coach and four. They had fine stables beside the house. Eventually, they bought a car.

There were some of the Lynchs in the Boer War. One of them became friendly with a black family, and gave them his name and address when the War ended. Lo and behold, didn't one of the black family arrive over here and live in Lynch's house for years. A very likeable character – he could dance a jig with a glass of water balanced on his head, and he wouldn't spill it. He had a fluent knowledge of Irish before he died. He was very friendly with my father and very popular with the ladies.

My father was working on our farm. We didn't sell any turf. *Nineteen Acres* was a book written by John Healy. He was a Press Correspondent and he gave a true description of life in Ireland the time he wrote it. I got a scholarship to Mountbellew Agricultural College, and I spent twelve months there. There were five scholarships then to the Royal Albert Agricultural College. I tried that, but couldn't finish it. After that I was then a bus conductor for GSR. That was the Great Southern Railway, before it became CIÉ. They also owned the Great Southern Hotels in Ireland.

I went to England for a while during the War. You had the feeling that the bombs weren't going to fall on you, somehow. I wasn't nervous. It didn't cost me a thought. I came home when the War ended and worked in the County Council, as caretaker for the waterworks in Barna. I stayed at that job until I retired.

They used to sell a lot of fish in Galway. I used to go into Galway every Saturday with my mother, on the donkey and cart. She used to sell eggs and butter. All the people were fluent Irish speakers. Some hadn't a word of English. When my father went to school, he told me, they were flogged if they didn't have English. They'd put one child up on another child's back and flog them. He was fined five shillings for having the name in Irish on the cart, and not in English. You were supposed to have your name on the cart at that time, in English, and that still stands. I had both languages. Joyce was teaching my father.

He was taken off and shot and never found, because

he was a British spy. A spy for the Black and Tans. His mare was intercepted at Dublin Castle and he was taken out that night and that was the last that was seen of him. He was a schoolteacher at Barna National School, over where the ball alley is now. He's buried somewhere about three miles from here. Someone will be cutting turf someday, and if he cuts deep enough he'll find Joyce's remains. It was after that Fr Griffin was shot as a reprisal.

They'd have to go to Spiddal or Galway for animal fairs. There weren't any around here. There was a pig fair here, for a few years, about forty years ago, but it didn't last for long. People used to come every week to Galway to buy pigs. It used to be at the Claddagh, at Fair Hill. 'Twas to the fair at Fair Hill that the boatload of people from Annaghdown were going when their boat sank and there were nineteen people drowned. A sheep put a foot through the bottom of the boat.

Professor Dillon was a Professor in UCG and he lived here. That's his daughter that wrote *Across the Bitter Sea*, and a son of his, Michael Dillon, was the well-known Agricultural Correspondent. He had another daughter married here.

Chevasse – Lord Claude Chevasse – also lived here for a long time. He also had Ross Castle. He was a fluent Irish speaker, even though he was of English extraction. He'd go into the shops and ask for a box of matches, in Irish, and if they weren't Irish-manufactured, he wouldn't buy them.

The Bishop of Rochester lived in Ross House, beside the castle. He used to wear kilts. No matter where there might be a *poitín* still, he'd locate it. And when he'd be coming home he'd be half-drunk and getting caught in the briars, and his legs would be all cut. One of my uncles used to wear a kilt also.

The houses down by the pier were all lived in by fishermen and farmers. They were all burned down by the Tans. The Coastguard Station was down where the restaurant is now, and there were quite a few of the RIC people living down there too.

Glossary

báinín: woven, woollen cloth

beater: man employed to rouse game

buaile: summer pasture

blas: accent, or fluency

cailleach: wise woman, fortune-teller

caoineadh: mourning music and song, at wakes

caonach: moss on the rocks

currach: traditional rowing boat, with light, wooden frame covered with tarred canvas

cosáinín: carrageen moss

craic: fun.

deoch: a drink

fíodóir: weaver

gaeilgeoir: student of Irish language in the *Gaelteacht*

Gaeltacht: An Irish-speaking district

ginnie: a jennet

gurnard: a fish, also called gurnet

kelp: a type of seaweed

naíonáin: playschool

potters/sappers: people responsible for dividing the shoreline among farmers

poitín: illegally made alcoholic drink

piseog: superstition

píobairín: diminutive of píobaire, meaning piper

púcán: small boat, with sails

ráiméis: rubbish, in the verbal sense

scoil cois claí: hedge school with a travelling teacher, one or two days a week

scioból: shed used for school

séipéal: church, chapel

síbín: illegal pub

seanchaí: traditional storyteller

strainséirí: visitors, or strangers in an area

táilliúir: tailor

tick or **ling:** giving credit

tine chnámh: St John's bonfire night